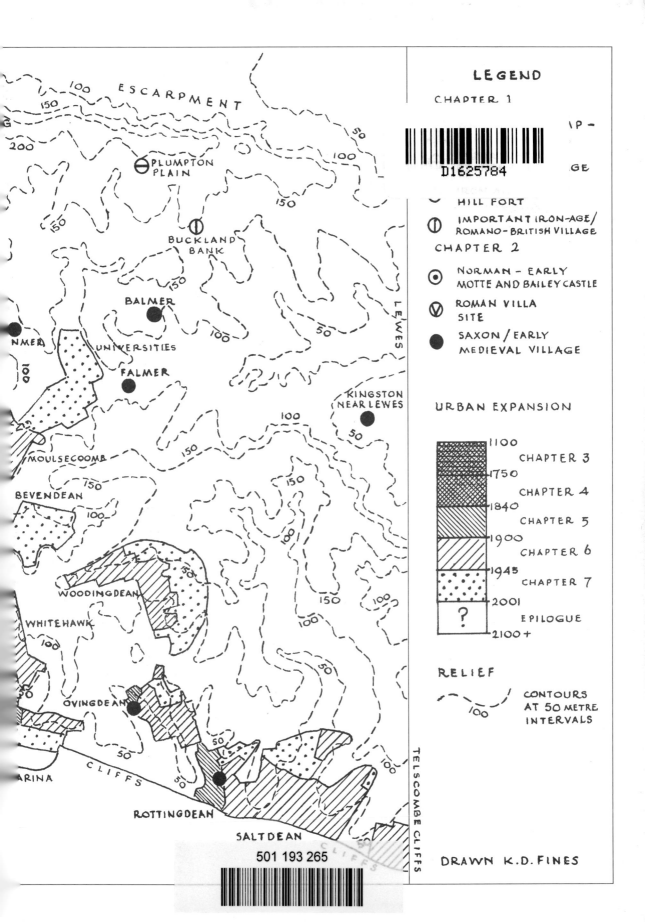

A History of

BRIGHTON and HOVE

EAR _911

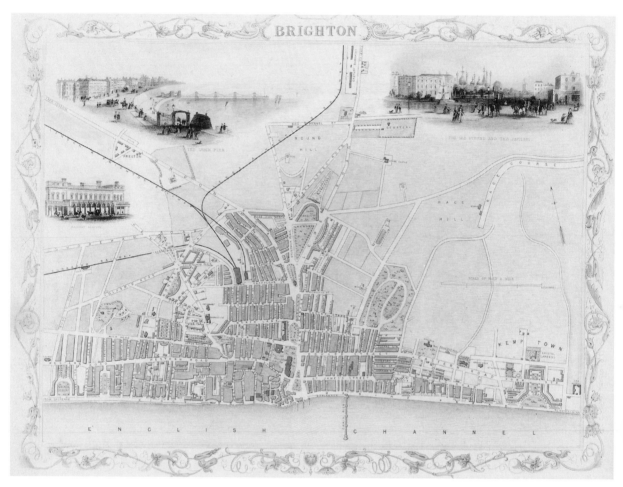

Plan of Brighton (with Brunswick Town in the parish of Hove at the western end) by John Tallis, c.1855-65.

A History of
BRIGHTON & HOVE

Stone-Age Whitehawk to Millennium City

Ken Fines

Phillimore

2002

Published by
PHILLIMORE & CO. LTD
Shopwyke Manor Barn, Chichester, West Sussex

ISBN 1 86077 231 5

Printed and bound in Great Britain by
BOOKCRAFT LTD
Midsomer Norton, Bath

Dedicated to my late, beloved wife Betty (née Tizzard), with whom I shared 62 years of this history. Also to our family, without whose support in bereavement I could not have progressed this book: in particular, our daughters Susan Barnbrook and Julie Smith; grandchildren Ellen and Daniel Smith; our honorary son Niall Clarke; and our brothers and sisters Bob and Daphne Fines, Grace and Ian Cassam, and Frank and Gladys Tizzard.

Contents

List of Illustrations

Frontispiece: Brighton and Brunswick Town, *c*.1855-65

Acknowledgements

Firstly, I would like to pay tribute to the writers, journalists, archaeologists, artists and photographers who have recorded the unfolding history of Brighton and Hove, in the great majority of cases without the benefit of modern technology. Without their treasure house of knowledge it would not have been possible to chronicle the evolution of our city through more than five millennia.

Then I must acknowledge the invaluable work of the archivists, curators and librarians who have custody of this treasure house and helpfully make its contents available for research: in particular, I wish to thank Jessica Rutherford, Head of Libraries and Museums and Director of the Royal Pavilion, and the staff (past and present) of the excellent libraries and museums of Brighton and Hove; also of the County Archives at Lewes. In the bibliography I have tried to record most of the relevant documents that I have read or consulted over very many years, so that readers may, hopefully, pursue an interest in local history in greater detail.

Heartfelt thanks are due to all my friends and colleagues in the Brighton Urban Structure Plan Team (1970-4) and the Brighton Planning Department (1974-83), and to all the councillors, officers and voluntary bodies with whom we worked in the cause of conserving the heritage of Greater Brighton, not only for its own sake but also in the promotion of prosperity. I would like to give a special mention to Michael Ray, former Director of Planning (later Chief Executive) of Hove, Selma Montford, Secretary of the Brighton Society, and John Saunders, former Deputy Librarian of East Sussex, who, in particular, were ardent supporters of the cause of North Laine.

In writing my book I have been able to pick the brains of many experts, including Superintendent Derek Oakensen of Sussex Police, Bob Halliwell of East Sussex County Fire Brigade, John Layhe of Sussex Ambulance NHS Trust, Richard Clark former director of Brighton Buses, David Dunstall of the Shoreham Airport Collection, John Daley of Brighton Marina, and Councillor Andy Durr of Sussex University and Brighton Fishing Museum. Many other people have readily responded to my telephone requests for information concerning businesses, schools and public institutions. I would like to give a special thankyou to John Patching of Patching and Son, builders, a firm established in Brighthelmston in 1774, even before George, Prince of Wales first visited the embryonic resort.

Serendipity even came to my aid when I telephoned Brighton General Hospital for some information and was put through to Sue Trimingham, whom it so happened I knew 20 years ago when she was working for *The Evening Argus* (now *The Argus*) with her husband

Adam Trimingham. Sue not only sent me a history of the hospital and the former workhouse, but also told Adam about my book. As a result, he has kindly contributed the Foreword. I am most grateful to both of them; also to *The Argus* generally for keeping me abreast of local history as it unfolds.

Lastly, I must thank my computer gurus, Bob Rimmington and my old friend Roy Metcalfe, without whose timely help I might well have lost the text before it saw the light of day. At least those historians of yore did not face such hazards of modern technology!

Foreword

by Adam Trimingham
the 'Sage of Sussex' of *The Argus*

As a planning officer, Ken Fines was the right man, and in the right place at the right time. He arrived in Brighton as planning officer just as the mania for demolishing historic buildings and putting roads before homes was waning.

His greatest achievement was one which many people, including me, derided at the time and that was to make the down-at-heel North Laine district of Brighton into a conservation area. He had realised the area was ripe for revival after the threat of an elevated road through the middle of it had gone and he found the way to achieve it. Now North Laine (and he chose the name because of its historical associations) is a thriving part of Brighton and a tourist attraction in its own right to rival the Lanes.

I always thought that Ken Fines had earned his place in history. I had no idea he would write a history about the place. But here it is, covering thousands of years in just one modest volume. There have been separate histories and encyclopaedias of both Brighton and Hove over the years, many of them still worth reading today. But no one until now has thought of a combined history of two proud towns which now form a city by the sea.

Ken Fines has accomplished this feat using his considerable knowledge but always retaining both a sense of proportion and a sense of humour. He is as interested in the navvies who built the railways as he is in the famous men and women who made Brighton fashionable. That gives this book humanity and also makes it a rattling good read.

Preface

Few cities have as fascinating a history as Brighton and Hove, the 'City-by-the-Sea', a regional centre and an international resort. On 1 April 1997 the two towns were amalgamated as a unitary authority after over a century of stand-off and confrontation. Then, in 2001, to mark the millennium the Queen awarded the twin towns city status.

My grandfather, Norris Fines, came from Leicester in the 1860s to find work as a bootmaker in the expanding town of Hove where many of the new residents were 'well-heeled'. He married a Brighton girl, Mary Ann Povey, whose maternal grandparents, Francis and Mary Fowler, lived in Hove in the early 19th century when it was still an isolated fishing village clustered around what is now Hove Street. They are buried in land once part of the graveyard behind the old parish church of St Andrew. Alas, their mortal remains are now destined to lie beneath a proposed superstore.

My father, also Norris (but known as Bob), was born in 1895. The recently published 1901 census shows that he was one of a family of 11 living in a 'two-up, two-down' terraced house in Shirley Street, Hove, which was also used as the bootmaker's workshop. Bob, who became an electrician on Brighton's Palace Pier, married Alice Kathleen Jacques (or Jakes), a young nursemaid working in Brighton's fashionable Regency Square. Alice's own mother, Ellen, had already died of the dreaded consumption, and her father, James, was in the equally dreaded workhouse. I was born in 1923 and my brother Bob in 1931 when the family were still living in Shirley Street.

Notwithstanding our humble antecedents, I discovered after years of genealogical research that the Fines (Fiennes) family had roots in Sussex that extended back to the Norman invasion. In fact, one line led back to William de Warenne and his wife, the saintly Gundrada. William was made Lord of the Rape of Lewes and among his territorial possessions was the Saxon village of Bristelmestune! Domesday Book tells us that this village—which was to become Brighton—had a rental value of 4,000 herrings! It is perhaps not surprising that with an ancestry that encompasses the social spectrum I have long been enthralled by the history of our city.

In 1939, long before I embarked upon my research, I started work as a junior clerk in Alfred Waterhouse's splendid Victorian town hall in Church Road, Hove (sadly destroyed by fire in 1966). Hove was sometimes referred to as the 'posh end of Brighton': it had rather a snobbish image and the Borough Council used to disassociate the town from its raffish neighbour. I remember being sent on a clandestine mission during one confrontation to count Brighton buses in the Old Steine, the heart of enemy territory. Nevertheless, the two towns had much in common—including a team in the Football League named Brighton and Hove Albion!

Eventually I became Assistant County Planning Officer in East Sussex, which at the time included the Municipal Borough of Hove and the Urban District of Portslade, then Director of the Greater Brighton Structure Plan (1970-4), and finally (1974-83) Borough Planning Officer of 'Big Brother Brighton' itself. I enjoyed an excellent relationship with my opposite number in Hove, Michael Ray. We shared the same belief in the importance of conserving our heritage of townscape and landscape and the identity of the villages and neighbourhoods that, historically, have merged to form one conurbation. Michael and I established a good relationship with the amenity and other societies that represent the interests of our communities. Their officers and members give generously of their time on a voluntary basis; none more so than Selma Montford, a lady of many roles, who founded the Brighton Society some thirty years ago and has remained their secretary and a champion of Brighton's heritage ever since. It was, in fact, Selma who encouraged me to write this book.

I have tried to make it entertaining, sometimes even amusing, reflecting the romance of local history and the 'visitable past'. It is written from the perspective of an ardent native who happens to be a town planner, being structured into chapters by the historical phases of development, most of which ended with crisis and stagnation. I have tried to highlight the factors that brought decline and those that in turn brought renaissance: often charismatic personalities, local initiatives, innovative forms of transport and fortuitous events. I do not apologise for starting with the prehistoric folk who first settled in this area: their legacy of earthworks and burial mounds on the Downs are a part of the heritage that we must conserve, and some of their trackways underlie our transportation infrastructure to this day. Nor do I regret finally having a peek into an uncertain future.

I hope that the book will appeal to everyone—whether or not they are citizens of Brighton and Hove—who is interested in local history, transportation or town planning. Hopefully, more may be encouraged to forsake their cars and explore our city and its downland hinterland on foot in search of the historical treasure that lies all around. Such activity has given me endless enjoyment and I still come upon new links with the past, and even sense intuitively that something of the spirit has been captured in ancient walls and earthworks; that time is illusory and that communication across the ages is possible.

One

The Prehistoric 'Brightonians'

Neolithic Settlement

The first 'Brightonians' were a people of Mediterranean stock: not tourists, conference delegates or language students, but Neolithic immigrants who may even have had cannibalistic tendencies! Unlike the aboriginal hunter-gatherers of the Palaeolithic and Mesolithic eras they were settlers rather than nomads. On Whitehawk Hill, on the narrow ridge just to the north of the actual summit, they built a great causewayed camp, typical of the Neolithic or New Stone Age. Modern radio carbon dating indicates that it was probably built during the early Neolithic period in the fourth millennium B.C. (4000-3000 B.C.). This is earlier than previously thought, although it may not have been in continuous occupation. It comprised four roughly concentric earthworks in an oval formation covering some 12 acres, the greatest dimension from north to south being about 900 ft. The earthworks were interrupted in several places by causeways providing access for the inhabitants and their animals. Many present-day Brightonians who use Manor Hill Road to cross the open ridge between the Whitehawk Estate and the Elm Grove area may not realise that they are passing through one of the oldest settlement sites in Britain. The ditches are silted up and the ramparts eroded, so that the earthworks are hard to trace amidst the rough grass and scrub. Even the 'pulling up' ground of Brighton Racecourse penetrates this scheduled ancient monument.

Archaeological research has shown that the inhabitants of Whitehawk Camp not only domesticated animals but also practised some primitive cultivation on the hillsides. They had brought the manufacture of tools and weapons from flint and other hard stones to a fine

1 *The author's impression of Whitehawk Camp, 3500 B.C., and the view to the west across the site of the future Millennium City. The broad estuary of the River Adur can be seen, and in the far distance the Isle of Wight. In the centre of the downland range beyond the Adur is Cissbury Hill, where the best flints were mined. The mouth of the Wellesbourne can be seen in the foreground.*

art and also had knowledge of basic crafts such as pottery and weaving. From the summit of Whitehawk Hill, at a height of about 400 ft., the settlers would have commanded a panoramic view to the west across the downland ridges and valleys that in ages to come would be the site of Brighton, the 'Queen of Watering Places', and its sister town of Hove. Beyond, some 12 miles away, they would have been able to see Cissbury Hill where some of the best flint was mined. On a clear day they would glimpse the hump of St Boniface Down on the Isle of Wight, some 40 miles away. Of course, we know not what names, if any, the settlers gave these landmarks, nor if they had any appreciation of a landscape that is held in such esteem today.

In Neolithic times the climate was warmer and wetter and much of the chalk downs would have been covered in scrub or light forest. Springs high in the valleys fed streams that reached the sea a mile or so to the south of the present shoreline. One of the largest was the Wellesbourne in the valley immediately to the west of Whitehawk Hill, which now brings the London Road into Brighton. It may even have had a significant tidal estuary. It now runs underground, although in the torrential rains of 1960 and 2000 it came to the surface, flowing relentlessly across Mill Road and flooding houses in Patcham. Hove, too, had its main stream, the Westbourne, which flowed down the Goldstone Valley, veering westward as it reached the coastal plain to flow into the sea at Aldrington. The main river valleys of the Adur and Ouse further to the west and east were in those ancient times wide inlets of the sea as far as present-day Bramber and Lewes respectively, so that the block of downland in between, bounded on the north by the steep escarpment, was somewhat isolated.

The prehistoric settlers were skilled mariners. Most of the Neolithic immigrants would have sailed from the Mediterranean, braving the turbulent waters of the Western Approaches to make an initial landfall in the West of England and Ireland. Boat building is one of the most ancient of crafts, again developing from intelligent adaptation. It is known that the Ancient Egyptians built ships apparently constructed of planks, propelled by oars and sails, but it is unlikely that the Neolithic immigrants would have had such an advanced technology. In 1972 the Norwegian explorer Thor Heyerdahl tested a theory that the Ancient Egyptians could have sailed to the Americas in a papyrus boat. He successfully sailed such a vessel, *Ra 2*, from Africa to Barbados. It is more likely that the people of the New Stone Age reached the British Isles by such means and reed boats might once have been a familiar sight in the broad estuaries of the Adur and Ouse—and even in the mouth of Brighton's own Wellesbourne.

The Great Bronze-Age Revolution

In the second millennium B.C. the Bronze Age, accompanied by a colder and drier climate, gradually superseded the New Stone Age. More continental immigrants arrived, generally known today as the 'Beaker Folk' from their characteristic flat-bottomed, decorated storage jars and cremation urns. They were altogether more sophisticated, and bracelets of gold and silver have even been unearthed on the Downs at Patcham. They knew how to combine copper and tin with other additives to produce bronze, from which they fashioned more advanced tools and weapons, although flint continued in use at least until the second half of the millennium.

The people of the Bronze Age settled and farmed extensively on the dip-slopes of the Downs, rather than on the hilltops, although there is evidence that Whitehawk Camp was again occupied during this period. One of the most important village sites is on Plumpton Plain north of Falmer, but a very interesting hut site was excavated only recently at Coldean in advance of the construction of the Brighton by-pass. There, stake and postholes indicated a round hut that would have had walls of wattle and a thatched roof, and evidence was found of a double wall, similar to a modern cavity wall, on the side facing the prevailing wind!

Bronze-Age people were responsible for most of the mystical stone and wood circles on the chalk of southern England known as *henges*. A henge site was discovered at Mile Oak, Portslade in another rescue dig in advance of the construction of the by-pass; the indications were that the henge itself was of wood and not stone. The most numerous of the Bronze-Age remains are the round barrows or burial mounds. There are many on the ridges and spurs of the Downs north of Brighton and Hove, but one of the largest and most famous, about 12 ft. in height and 86 ft. in diameter, was situated on the coastal plain at Hove. It was the focus of a traditional Good Friday celebration until it was removed in 1856/7 prior to the construction of Palmeira Avenue. About 9 ft. below the surface was found the remains of an oak coffin with decayed bone fragments and a number of grave goods, the most important being a beautiful red amber cup.

Prehistoric man managed to transport quite heavy loads, such as flints, pottery clay, timber, agricultural produce and, later, iron ore from the depths of the Wealden forest. The wheel was not known in Britain, however, until the late Bronze Age. It may well have developed from the use of a type of sledge on log rollers to transport henge stones: by intelligent adaptation solid slices of log would be attached rigidly to an axle on a crude cart drawn by oxen. Later, wheels revolving on a fixed axle by means of hub naves were in use. A further advance brought lighter wheels with spokes and, during the succeeding Iron Age, horses were commonly used to haul carts and chariots. It is interesting to surmise how prehistoric man might have carried heavy loads before the development of the wheel during what has been called 'the Great Bronze-Age Revolution'. Clues to such puzzles can sometimes be obtained by studying the methods of so-called primitive societies. For example, North American Indians not only transported loads in back-packs but used a *travois* drawn by dog or horse: this consisted of two poles attached at one end to a harness with the other ends trailing on the ground, the load being carried on a frame between the poles.

Iron-Age Settlement

In the first millennium B.C. there was a gradual infiltration of Celtic immigrants from across the Channel. They knew how to smelt and forge iron, and thus produce more advanced tools and weapons. The Celts practised arable farming on a much wider scale than hitherto, and Celtic fields separated by banks or *lynchets* are still a common feature of the dip-slopes of the Downs, as on the slopes of Tegdown Hill north of Patcham. The Celts had a tribal

2 *The Iron-Age village, Butser Hill, was recreated at the foot of the highest hill on the South Downs.*

organisation and built forts on prominent hilltops, particularly for refuge in time of conflict. The earthworks of such forts, which were once surmounted by wooden palisades, are still a feature of heights forming an arc around the city, particularly Hollingbury Hill, Ditchling Beacon, Wolstonbury, Devil's Dyke and Thundersbarrow Hill.

In the first century B.C. there was a further immigration of cultured people of Celtic/German stock generally known as the Belgae. They had an aptitude for government and organised the native tribal society into kingdoms. There were some thirty Iron-Age settlements between the Rivers Adur and Ouse, and when the Romans invaded in A.D. 43 under Claudius the Downs from Brighton westwards were part of a Belgic kingdom under Cogidumnus, who founded Chichester as his capital. His subjects were nothing like the woad-painted, uncouth Ancient Britons of folklore; their costumes and jewellery would have pleased any of today's ethnic dressers!

In the course of three millennia the prehistoric settlers of the Brighton and Hove area established a network of trackways serving the villages, hillforts and field systems. Some are still in use as footpaths and bridleways, in particular the downland ridgeways and the hollow-ways that descend the steep northern escarpment to the Weald below. Some of the modern roads out of Brighton, such as Dyke Road and Ditchling Road, undoubtedly follow these ancient trackways. Access tracks through the Celtic fields can still be traced by double-lynchets, a good example being on Round Hill at Hangleton.

In the late Iron Age wooden ships would have been common along the Sussex coast. There was a shipbuilding industry at Chichester and an extensive trade with the eastern Mediterranean from the Manhood Peninsula, furs and skins being exported in exchange for fabrics and precious metals. Dugout canoes, specimens of which have been found preserved in river beds, including one at South Stoke in West Sussex, were probably still used locally for river transport.

Two

Roman, Saxon and Norman Invaders

Roman Settlement

In A.D. 43 the Romans invaded Britain, which for 350 years was a province of the Roman Empire. King Cogidumnus of the Regni became an ally of his new masters and his domain was extended to include the whole of present-day Sussex, the inhabited parts of which were then virtually a peninsula between the sea and the dense Wealden Forest known as Anderida. Chichester (Noviomagus) remained the capital and was the nearest Roman town of any size to the Brighton and Hove area. However, there is reason to believe that a small port was located at the mouth of the Wellesbourne, the remains of which are today buried in the seabed somewhere south of the Palace Pier. A local diver, Ken Dawes, has actually seen what looks like foundations in the vicinity, although he was unaware of the port at the time.

The more wealthy Romans, and even citizens of Romano-British stock, were able to enjoy an affluent lifestyle in country villas of brick, stone and tile complete with baths and under-floor heating. Fine examples can be seen at Fishbourne and Bignor in West Sussex, but sites are known locally at Southwick, Portslade, West Blatchington (Hove) and south of Preston Park, Brighton. There are also local Romano-British village sites where agriculture and various crafts were practised in comparatively peaceful conditions. Perhaps the best known is at Buckland Bank, Falmer, located in a remote downland valley in the far north-east of the parish. These villages still comprised huts mainly of wattle and daub, but at Buckland Bank there is also evidence of a round *circus* or meeting place.

The Romans were renowned highway engineers. They established a hierarchy of roads throughout England (Britannia) and beyond, the primary routes being mainly military roads connecting London (Londinium) with the major towns and fortifications. For example, Stane Street connected the capital with Chichester (Noviomagus). The secondary and minor routes were mainly for trade. Although the Romans believed that the shortest distance between two points was a straight line, their surveyors were quite prepared to respect the lie of the land in hill country, such as the South Downs, and to make use of the ancient trackways where appropriate. The main constructional feature was a cambered embankment or *agger* up to 35 ft. in width, sometimes bordered by drainage diches. This was as often as not covered in one or more layers of road metal, such as flint, gravel or other local stone. Iron slag was commonly used in Sussex. In some minor roads the agger was dispensed with where the surface was firm and well drained.

A secondary road, known as the London-Brighton Way (sometimes the London-Portslade Way), connected London with the Brighton and Hove area by way of Croydon, Godstone, Felbridge, Haywards Heath, Burgess Hill, Hassocks and Clayton. From Clayton a number of ancient trackways across the Downs were used, one of which followed the wind gap to Patcham, passing the villa at Preston to the supposed port at the mouth of the Wellesbourne.

There were two branches over the Downs from Clayton to Portslade. The first skirted the escarpment of Wolstonbury Hill and Newtimber Hill westwards and then entered the steep valley of the Devil's Dyke, climbing the south side by a terrace way, which is still used as a bridlepath. It then swung southwards following the ancient trackway known as Port's Road over Round Hill to Hangleton, from where it veered to the south-west, passing the sites of the present St Helen's Church and Hangleton Manor to cross East Hill into what is now Old Portslade village. From there it continued on to Southwick.

The second branch turned to the south-west at Pyecombe, crossing the Downs by way of Varncombe Hill to Skeleton Hovel on Round Hill where it intersected the first branch. It then carried on over Benfield Hill into Portslade. At one time it was thought that the legendary Roman *Portus Adurni* was located near Portslade, but this is now believed to have been at Portchester. In fact, the River Adur was only given this name in 1622 because of this mistaken belief; previously it had been named after various settlements along its bank.

A Roman coastal road has also been identified connecting with the above branch and following the line of the present Old Shoreham Road into what is now Brighton. Somewhere near Preston Circus it would have formed a crossroads with the London-Brighton Way, bridging the Wellesbourne and its tributary in the Lewes Road Valley just above the tidal limit. Elm Grove marks its eastern continuation over the Downs to follow the ridge of Newmarket Hill and Kingston Hill to Lewes, where it connected with another road from London. There was yet another branch running northwards across the Winterbourne Valley from Newmarket Hill, serving the Romano-British villages at Buckland Bank and other places on the Falmer Downs.

At the height of the 'Pax Romana', say in the second century, two-wheeled carts and larger four-wheeled wagons drawn by oxen or horses would have been a common sight at the Preston Circus crossroads, carrying everything from corn to road stone, from wine in amphorae to silverware and glassware imported from the continent for the wealthy villa dwellers. In those days there were no specialised commercial vehicles and the ubiquitous wagon would undoubtedly have been used also as a primitive omnibus, hearse and removal van. Horse riders, foot-sloggers and pack horses would have shared the roadway, perhaps on occasion giving way to a *centuria* of soldiers headed by its centurion resplendent in a horse-drawn chariot.

The sailing ships visiting Brighton's supposed port or harbour would have been built of planks of pine or cedar caulked with flax and with bows of oak clamped in copper. Sometimes a fast galley propelled by oars as well as a square sail might be seen bringing passengers or even mail.

During the third century, raids by barbarians were experienced along the coast, so that life became more unsettled. Wooden forts had to be built, so it is possible that the Wellesbourne harbour was fortified. Subsequently, with threats along the continental frontiers of the Roman Empire, legions had to be withdrawn. At the beginning of the fifth century the colony of Britannia and its Romano-British inhabitants were abandoned.

Saxon Settlement and the Norman Conquest

Raids probably continued throughout the fifth century, but it is known from the *Anglo-Saxon Chronicles* that in A.D. 477 Ella the Saxon and his three sons landed with their forces from three ships on the Manhood Peninsula south of Chichester. By A.D. 490 they had seized control of the coastal area as far east as the 'City of Andred' (Pevensey). Thus, Sussex derived its name from the 'Land of the South Saxons'. The Romano-British inhabitants were routed and many survivors fled into the Wealden forest, which the Saxons now called Andredswald. A native of 'Hefful' (Heathfield) in the High Weald says that when she was a girl at the beginning of the 20th century descendants of the Romano-British could still be distinguished by the shape of their heads!

The Saxons preferred the lowlands to the hills and in the course of time they established villages along the spring-line at the foot of the escarpment of the Downs, along the coastal plain and in the neighbouring downland valleys. They used heavier two-yoke, oxen-drawn ploughs capable of tackling clay soils, working the fields around the villages on a communal basis.

Little is known about Saxon life in Sussex during the earlier centuries. The Roman roads fell into disrepair and the Downs and coastal plain were even more isolated from the other kingdoms of Saxon England. However, in A.D. 681 St Wilfrid landed on the Manhood Peninsula and converted the hitherto barbaric Saxons to Christianity. Churches of wood were built, but later these were replaced by buildings of local stone. During the ninth century the Christian Saxons had to endure the same insecurity as their Romano-British predecessors, this time at the hands of the Vikings. There is no direct evidence of incursions in what is now the Brighton and Hove area, although there were raids elsewhere in Sussex.

By the time the Normans invaded, Saxon England was well organised into counties, the boundaries of which remained little changed until the local government reorganisation of 1974. In turn, Sussex, in particular, was divided into *hundreds*, each including one or more villages, and into ecclesiastical parishes. Thus, there was an element of autocratic local government and priestly authority in existence.

In 1066 William the Conqueror, Duke of Normandy, landed at Pevensey, defeated the 'upstart' King Harold at the Battle of Hastings, and marched on London to claim the throne, which the Saxon King Edward the Confessor had bequeathed to his Norman kinsmen. The story is depicted in the famous Bayeux Tapestry, and from this we have knowledge of the high-prowed ships under sail and oar which transported the Norman soldiers and their horses. Twenty years after the conquest King William I undertook

3 *The Bayeux Tapestry depicting the Battle of Hastings. William the Conqueror raises his helmet to show he is alive, and the Count of Boulogne (Eustace II) points at him in order to rally the Norman army.*

a detailed inventory of his realm: Domesday Book of 1086. It is from this remarkable survey that we know about the legacy of the Saxon villages in the Brighton and Hove area. William had already divided Sussex into six north-south divisions known as *rapes*, which were granted to loyal followers. Each rape was based on a fortified stronghold and a port. Our study area was in the Rape of Lewes, which was granted to the author's Norman ancestor William de Warenne, whose wife, Gundrada, has been regarded in Sussex as something of a saint.

Below is a list of the hundreds and their settlements that largely made up the Brighton and Hove area. The landowner is William de Warenne, except where otherwise stated:

> **Welesmere Hundred** (Whalesbourne or Wellesbourne)
> Bristelmestune (Brighton—divided into three manors)
> Rotingedene (Rottingdean)
> Hovingdene (Ovingdean)

Presetune Hundred (Preston)
Piceham (Patcham)
Presetune (Preston)

Eldretune Hundred (Aldrington)
Eldretune (Aldrington)
Porteslage (Portslade)
Hangetone (Hangleton)
Esmerewic (Benfield)

Falemere Hundred (Falmer)
Falemere (Falmer)
Burgemere (Balmer)
Bevedene (Bevendean)
Stamere (Stanmer—land of the Archbishop)
Molstan (Moulstone—probably a farmstead but now only the name of a valley)

It will be seen that the villages which eventually merged as development took place to become Brighton and Hove were established by the Saxons. A notable exception is Hove itself, which if it existed at all was not worthy of note, although Henry C. Porter in his engaging *History of Hove* (1897) stated that Hove 'figured in the career of the South Coast from the period when Britain was peopled by the family of Japheth, the youngest son of Noah'!

The village of Bristelmestune, which was to enjoy various spellings until it officially became Brighton some 800 years later, was located on a small plateau above the west bank of the Wellesbourne. The square called The Knab at the junction of Brighton Place and Market Street identifies the centre of the Saxon settlement of timber and thatch, although it is doubtful if the population exceeded one hundred. The name of the village is thought to have been derived from that of Brighthelm, a Saxon bishop. There may have been a wooden church, now under the sea. The old parish church of St Nicholas on Church Hill (now Dyke Road) is of a later date, although it may have been erected on the site of an earlier place of worship.

The mouth of the Wellesbourne was nearer to the present coastline than in earlier times and a harbour serving the village may have been located on the site of the present Pool Valley. Fishing was obviously an important activity, as Domesday Book records that a 'tribute' of 4,000 herrings had to be paid to the landowner or his sub-tenant. It is said that St Wilfrid had been responsible for introducing the Saxons to fishing. In addition to the nearby fields cultivated in common, there would have been sheep pasture on the Downs where once there were Celtic cornfields. At Patcham 10 shepherds were recorded.

By the time of the Domesday survey all the Saxon landowners had been replaced by Norman sub-tenants owing allegiance to the overall landowner. A rigid feudal manorial system was imposed whereby every villein, bordar, serf and slave knew his place in the pecking order. But at least they were not banished to the depths of the Wealden forest.

Carts and wagons, pack horses and horsemen would still have been seen at the Preston Circus crossroads, but traffic and trade were probably less sophisticated than in Roman times. The main linkage would have been with Lewes, where the Lord of the Rape had built his fortress. William the Conqueror established his capital at Winchester, so it is likely that the ancient trackway along the ridge of the Downs, now followed by the South Downs Way, was an important trade route. It was along this trackway on Edburton Hill north of Portslade that the Normans built an early timber motte-and-bailey castle at the boundary between the rapes of Lewes and Bramber. Many of the other ancient trackways and Roman roads would have continued in use.

Three

The Old Town of Brighthelmston

Medieval Settlement and Street Pattern

The transition from the Saxon village of Bristelmestune to the small medieval town of Brighthelmston was a gradual one and probably paralled the slow integration of the Saxon and Norman peoples. A small chapel and priory dedicated to St Bartholomew was built in the 12th century on a site now commemorated by the street known as Bartholomews by Brighton Town Hall. The old parish church on Church Hill high above the old town was not built until the early 14th century, although the site may have been of ancient religious significance. It was dedicated to St Nicholas, Bishop of Myra in southern Turkey (died A.D. 342), who was patron saint of mariners and fishermen (and of children, pawnbrokers—and Russia!). Its embattled tower served as both a landmark for mariners and as a lookout. There is a legend that a descendant of William de Warenne came from Lewes Castle to keep a vigil from the tower when his son was due to return from a crusade, but to his horror he saw the ship sink as it sailed up the channel and a ghost ship is said to make its appearance from time to time off Brighton.

Brighthelmston perhaps came of age in the 14th century when Edward II granted a market charter and fair. However, until the 18th century the town remained confined to the area between East Street, West Street, North Street and the sea and was not as important as the county town of Lewes or the shipbuilding port of Shoreham. The economy of Brighthelmston was based on fishing and farming. The fishing community lived mainly in the 'Lower Town' between the sea and the low cliff; the farming and trading communities occupied the 'Upper Town'. It is considered that a village becomes a town when a surplus of produce enables the community to support a range of trades: locally these would probably have included carpenters, wheelwrights, cartwrights, carters, saddlers, tinkers, millwrights, blacksmiths and market traders.

Surprisingly, the basic pattern of the Upper Town still remains in the narrow lanes and 'twittens' (footpaths), which today are a famous tourist attraction. Here small houses with low ceilings were huddled together for protection from the storms which ravaged the coast. Until the 17th century these were mainly timber-framed with an infilling of wattle and daub or tarred cobblestones, often using material found on the beach, including old ships' timbers. The upper floors of many of the houses would have 'oversailed' the narrow lanes, adding to the sense of enclosure.

4 *One of the narrow lanes in the old town of Brighton is Meeting House Lane. The Lanes are now a national centre for the antiques trade, but were once a warren of cottages occupied by fisherfolk and labourers.*

To the west, north and east of the Old Town were the open fields or *laines*, which were farmed on a communal basis. These were served by tracks called *leakways*, some of which are followed by modern streets. Beyond was sheep down, much more extensive than in Saxon times. Wool was perhaps the most important export of medieval England, certainly of the South Downs. All the outlying villages would have prospered from this trade, although one must spare a thought for hapless Hangleton. The medieval village north of the surviving church of St Helen's seems to have succumbed to the Black Death in the 14th century and was abandoned. Hangleton Manor on the ancient Port's Road to the south of the church was not built until about 1540, possibly on the site of the former Saxon village. It is now a popular hostelry and is believed to be the oldest inhabited secular building in Sussex.

The increase in the number of tradesmen in the Old Town would inevitably have led to a considerable growth in the number of carts, wagons, pack horses and equestrians, so that at times the narrow lanes must have been congested. External traffic would mainly have been to and from Lewes and Shoreham. The ancient trackway later followed by the Roman road across the Downs to Lewes became known as Juggs Road, being the main route followed by the women known by that name, who carried fish to market, usually on foot. The Old Shoreham Road, also a former Roman road, was the main route to Shoreham, this being reached by way of Church Hill, although a lesser track probably followed a southern route passing the churches at Aldrington, Southwick and Kingston Buci.

Fishermen, Smugglers and French Raiders

The old Saxon harbour at the mouth of the Wellesbourne gradually silted up and, although the stream still flowed, the valley now occupied by the Old Steine would probably have become a stony salt marsh. The fishing boats were, therefore, kept on the beach exposed to the elements. In time a special type of local vessel called a hog-boat or *hoggie* was developed. This was broad in the beam so that it could not easily be capsized; and with a shallow draught could more readily be hauled either manually or by horses onto the beach. Another characteristic feature were *lee-boards*, triangular boards hung on the sides to counteract a tendency to be blown to windward. These hog-boats had a unique spitsail rig on one or two masts, a cabin or cuddy, and a hold for the catch. There can be little doubt that the development of this innovative form of maritime transport secured the survival of Brighthelmston as a fishing town.

During the wars with the French there were a number of raids on this part of the Sussex coast. In 1377, during the Hundred Years War, a French navy, having been repulsed at Winchelsea and Hastings, landed a raiding party at the fishing village of Rottingdean. The Frenchmen put the humble cottages to the torch, and when some of the villagers sought sanctuary in St Margaret's Church the raiders fired that as well. It is said that because of the poverty-stricken state of the village the church was not fully restored for 500 years.

Brighthelmston itself was attacked in 1514 and again in 1545. On the first occasion the entire town—but not the church—was torched. The second, lesser, raid came after a French navy had launched the unsuccessful attack on the Isle of Wight and Portsmouth that resulted in the capsizing of the *Mary Rose*, the flagship of Henry VIII. A well-known drawing in the British Museum purports to show the attack on Brighthelmston of 1545, but is now thought to be a representation of the earlier one. Houses on fire in the upper and lower towns are clearly depicted. Some 13 warships are shown offshore, while a number of raiding *galeyes* are beached. An interesting feature of the drawing is the area of open land known as the Hempshares depicted within the Old Town limits. This is where hemp for rope and twine was grown. According to Prof. Edmund W. Gilbert (see Bibliography) in

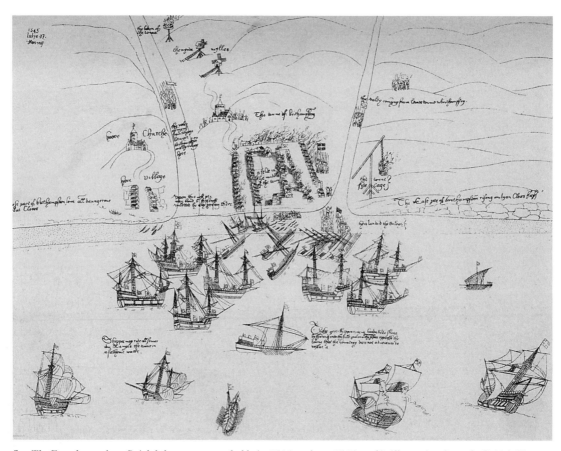

5   *The French attack on Brighthelmston was probably in 1514 and not 1545 as this illustration from the British Museum states. The old fishermen's dwellings and boats beneath the low cliff can be seen. Raiding 'galleys' are beached and the town has been torched.*

1579 there were 10,000 fishing nets, 400 mariners and 'fourscore' fishing boats. The fishing village of Hove also is shown, a single line of buildings in what is now Hove Street. As a result of the French raids no medieval buildings survive within the Old Town, with the possible exception of some old cobbled walls. Many of the buildings were rebuilt of brick, flint and cobbles in later years.

The inhabitants of Brighthelmston and the neighbouring villages, and also Shoreham, were not altogether innocent victims of French violence: smuggling, piracy, privateering and 'wrecking' are writ large in the annals of the Sussex coast and may even have been as important an economic activity as fishing. Many a boat from these shores smuggled in wine, brandy and French lace and smuggled out wool in return. Rottingdean was said to be a village of smugglers in the 17th and 18th centuries, and at one time even the vicar was an accomplice! Privateering was legalised piracy and various ships built and berthed at Shoreham were licensed as privateers to attack or seize French and Spanish merchantmen; in the

1620s some well-known residents of West Blatchington (now part of Hove), Captain Richard Gyffard, Tuppyn Scrace and William Scrace, were granted licences for the Shoreham-based ships *Peter* (believed to have been a prize ship from Dunkirk) and *Fortune*. Wrecking, involving the looting of ships stranded or deliberately lured onto rocks, was always a popular pastime!

In 1651 an historic maritime event put Brighthelmston briefly in the limelight. Charles II, escaping from defeat at the Battle of Worcester, came on horseback over the Downs to the town. He stayed overnight at the *George Inn*, believed to have been in West Street, and the next day boarded the coal-brig *Surprise* in Shoreham harbour. The captain, Nicholas Tattersall, set sail for Normandy and thus saved the King, apparently in the nick of time as soldiers arrived seeking a 'tall black man'. After the Restoration in 1660 Tattersall was rewarded and his ship, renamed *Royal Escape*, taken into the King's navy. Tattersall's monument can be seen in the churchyard of St Nicholas, proclaiming that he 'preserved the Church, the Crowne [*sic*] and Nation'.

6 *Brighthelmston boats fishing for mackerel, from an etching of 1847.*

7 *Ruined Block House near the bottom of East Street, c.1750. The old town suffered heavy damage from storms in the early 18th century.*

The Brink of Extinction

After the French raids the townsfolk were obliged not only to rebuild the town, but also to erect defences at considerable expense and establish a battery of guns on the seafront (the oval of grass in front of the *Grand Hotel* now marks the site). The fishing industry prospered for a time during the 17th century, thanks to the development of the hog-boat, but then early in the 18th century catastrophic storms lashed Brighthelmston, inundating what was left of the Lower Town. In a few years the population declined from about 3,000 to 1,500. By 1750 there was a fear of total destruction.

Four

Royal Patronage and the Brighton Road

Is there a Doctor in the House?

In the mid-18th century Brighthelmston was little more than a strip of buildings along the shore, the outlying villages being hidden in the folds of the Downs. The increase in population through five millennia had been negligible. The coastal area remained isolated by the great Weald beyond the Downs, even though the dense forests had been depleted to provide timber for shipbuilding and other industries. In 1749 Horace Walpole, man of letters, wrote to a friend about an 'expedition' to Arundel near the coast: 'if you love good roads, conveniences, good inns, plenty of postilions and horses, be so kind as never to go in to Sussex'. In 1752 he ventured into the county again on a visit to Herstmonceux Castle and wrote to another friend: 'the roads grew bad beyond all badness, the night beyond all darkness, our guide frightened beyond all frightfulness'. From the evidence of his published letters Walpole never dared to visit the coast in between—nor did the intrepid Celia Fiennes, who had ridden side-saddle the length and breadth of England a few years before!

However, in the mid-18th century Britain was on the threshold of unimaginable change with the coming of the Industrial Revolution. It was not to affect Brighthelmston until the 19th century and in the meantime the ailing town badly needed a doctor. As sometimes happens, salvation came when it was least expected, for in 1750 a Lewes doctor, Richard Russell, published a book in Latin entitled *De Tabe Glandulari Sive De Usa Aquae Marinae In Morbis Glandularum Dissertatio*. An unauthorised edition was published in 1752 called *Dissertation on the Use of Sea Water in the Diseases of the Glands*. The original choice of language had obviously been designed to attract the interest of the learned classes.

Dr Russell not only advocated sea bathing, which was not unknown as a cure, but also imbibing the stuff! Because of the popularity of his treatments the good doctor built 'Russell House' where the *Albion Hotel* now stands in the Old Steine, so that he was able to accommodate patients close to the sea. Many wealthy people braved the perils of the heavy Wealden clay to visit Brighthelmston, which in time became known—amongst other epithets—as 'Doctor Brighton'.

The townsfolk were delighted by a new-found prosperity. Some became lodging-house keepers, others 'bathers' and 'dippers', whose job was to dunk the male and female patients respectively in the briny. Later in the 18th century an ingenious form of transport (believed to have originated in Scarborough) made its appearance on the town's beaches:

the 'bathing machine' was a hut on four large iron wheels hauled by a horse. It would transport a disrobed patient into the water, where he or she would descend a flight of steps into the arms of the appropriate attendant, of whom 'Smoaker' Miles and Martha Gunn were to become famous local examples.

Other medical practitioners came to eulogise upon the advantages of Brighthelmston, notably Drs Relhan and Awsiter. In 1769 the latter, recognising that not all invalids relished bathing in a cold and windy sea, built hot and cold sea-water baths on the western side of Pool Valley. A long groyne with a pump house was constructed on the beach opposite. He also concocted his own gentle remedial cocktails by mixing sea-water with milk!

Although Hove was still a small fishing village about one-and-a-half miles west of the Old Town, the parish itself managed to get in on the act quite early when in 1754 a letter from a physician was published in London stating:

> There is near the town of Brighthelmstone in Sussex, a Spring of Living Water ... The person in whose Ground this Spring is has given me the strongest assurances that, for several Years last past, those Ewes of his Flock that have drank the Water of this Spring have never failed bringing two Lambs ... I would advise your Nobility and Gentry to make Use of these Waters, and not lose their Time and be disappointed in their Expectations by going to Tunbridge, Scarborough or elsewhere.

This chalybeate, which still manages to flow, became known as St Ann's Well.

Prinny and his Marine Pavilion

In August 1762 the 'great guns of the platform' were fired and a ball held for the nobility and gentry by Samuel Shergold, the proprietor of the *Castle Inn* (which gave its name to Castle Square). The occasion was the birth of a son to King George III, who was to gain an heir but before long lose his American colonies. Little did the company know that baby George was to become the Royal Patron of the 'Queen of Watering Places'.

In 1779, following the death of Dr Russell, the King's brother, Henry Frederick, Duke of Cumberland, visited Brighthelmston and rented Russell House. The Duke was something of a reprobate and became leader of the local gambling fraternity. He and his friends were largely instrumental in establishing Brighton Racecourse on the ideal turf of Whitehawk Down, undoubtedly ignorant of the significance of the ancient earthworks. The first races were held in August 1783. In the following month George, the young Prince of Wales, paid his first visit to his uncle at Brighthelmston and expressed his delight with the town. On subsequent visits 'Prinny' took a great interest in the races and all things equestrian. In July 1784 he actually rode on horseback from Brighthelmston to London and back in one day, so eager was he to return to the seaside with its amorous attractions.

In December 1785 the Prince quietly married the beautiful Maria Fitzherbert, who had been twice widowed. As she was a member of an old Roman Catholic family it was a morganatic marriage, unacceptable to the King. In the following year the Prince took a lease of a house on the Steine just to the north of the *Castle Inn* and installed Maria in another house nearby, apparently not wishing to be seen living under the same roof as his bride. In the following year the Prince commissioned Henry Holland, a well-known architect and

8 *The Dome, the Prince of Wales' Riding House and Stables, was built 1804-8 to the design of William Porden and was even larger than the Prince's Marine Pavilion.*

9 *The east front of the Royal Pavilion facing the Old Steine.*

10 *The north gateway of the Royal Pavilion was built in honour of King William IV.*

11 *The south entrance to the Royal Pavilion. The Pavilion became a hospital for wounded Indian soldiers during the First World War and in commemoration a new gateway was built after the war. It is said that some who recovered consciousness and saw the fabulous Oriental interior thought they were in heaven.*

12 *The Banqueting Room at the Royal Pavilion.*

a partner of the famous landscape designer 'Capability' Brown, to rebuild his house in a simple classical style. It is said that more than 150 workmen were employed to complete the new 'Marine Pavilion' in just three months.

In 1794 the Prince announced that he had broken off his relationship with Maria and the next year he married the eligible Princess Caroline of Brunswick. This was to prove disastrous, and he continued an amorous liaison with Maria—and others—at Brighthelmston. At the turn of the century the Prince and Maria affected a public reconciliation and he once again had ambitions for the reconstruction of his seaside residence, this time in a fantastic Indo-Chinese style, undoubtedly influenced by William Daniel's *Views of Oriental Scenery*, but work was to extend over many years with bewildering changes of architect and design. Initially much internal work was carried out, but in 1805 the separate Royal Stables were built in the Oriental style with a magnificent glass dome to the design of William Porden. This building, now the Dome Concert Hall, reflected the Prince's enduring involvement with the horse as a means of transport and sport for himself and his fashionable friends.

In 1811 the Prince of Wales became Prince Regent, when his father was pronounced insane, and in 1820 he became King George IV, reigning until his death in 1830. During the period 1815-22 the famous Regency architect John Nash transformed the Marine Pavilion into the fabulous Oriental extravaganza with its 'onion' domes and minarets that is now the Royal Pavilion, the jewel in the crown of the city and one of the most visited palaces or stately homes in Britain.

Social and Political Life

Even before the arrival of the Prince of Wales in 1783 the nobility and gentry could enjoy the good life in Brighthelmston, which centred upon rival assembly rooms at the two principal inns, the *Castle* and the *Old Ship*. The *Castle* on the north side of what is now Castle Square was erected in 1755. In 1766 its adjoining assembly rooms were built for the proprietor Samuel Shergold to the designs of the architect John Crunden, who had worked for the well-known builder Henry Holland, father of the architect of the same name who later built the Prince's first classical Pavilion. The main facilities were the ballroom and card room. Crunden had been influenced by the architect Robert Adam, and his ballroom reflected the latter's graceful interpretation of the neo-classical style. It was to become one of the most remarkable buildings in the town. In 1822 it was purchased by King George IV and converted into the Royal Chapel, and when the Town Commissioners acquired the Royal Pavilion Estate in 1850 the Church of England claimed the consecrated building. It was demolished carefully and re-erected two years later in Montpelier Place as St Stephen's Church. It closed in 1939 and later became an institute for the deaf and dumb. Today it is the First Base Day Centre for the homeless and inadequately housed and a success story for the Brighton Housing Trust and its Director, Jenny Backwell. The remarkable thing is that behind the rather plain exterior of the listed building much of that graceful neo-classical ballroom has been beautifully preserved.

In 1775 John Hicks, landlord of the *Old Ship*, where balls had been held for some years, commissioned the London architect Robert Golden to design assembly rooms, including a ballroom and card room, similar to those at the *Castle*. There had been intense rivalry between Hicks and Shergold and this was eventually resolved by the appointment of a Master of Ceremonies to oversee the programme of events at the two establishments. The first to hold the office was Captain William Wade, whose great-uncle was Field Marshal Wade, Commander-in-Chief of His Majesty's Forces. The new MC previously held a similar office at Bath and for a while officiated at both towns, until he became unpopular at Bath and moved to Brighthelmston in 1770. By all accounts, Wade had great influence on the social life of the town and even acted as a sort of dating agency. He died in 1808, but his successor, William Firth, lacked Wade's charisma, and Hicks, in particular, would have nothing to do with him.

As Brighthelmston expanded, new assembly rooms were deemed to be necessary to serve the western part of the town. Accordingly, in 1825 the architect Amon Henry Wilds built the Royal Newburgh Assembly Rooms at the corner of Cannon Place and St Margaret's Place. The building still stands, but in more recent times it has been converted in connection with the redevelopment of the area for the exhibition halls at the rear of the *Metropole Hotel*. However, the building and its fine classical portico with acanthus leaf capitals and pediment have been carefully preserved.

Circulating libraries became centres of daytime social life—and gossip. The first was erected on the east side of the Steine by a Mr Baker in 1760. Books could be purchased, borrowed or read, and also there was a billiard room popular with the ladies! Later a rotunda was added where a small band could play. At first the library closed in October, when the fashionable visitors departed, but the next proprietor, Mr Thomas, kept it open all the year. In 1767 another library was opened on the south side of the Steine, followed by one more near the first. Small shops were established in the vicinity of the libraries, selling fashionable goods—including tea—some of which were known to have been smuggled! Some goods were even secured by gambling on the throw of dice in a 'rattle trap' (not unlike the amusement centres that have opened in shopping centres in recent years). By 1787 Wade was even asserting his authority over the libraries, threatening prosecution if there was fighting—or cricket! The grassed area of the Steine was a location for that popular outdoor activity—promenading, otherwise taking the

13 *'Captain' William Wade, Master of Ceremonies, c.1780, was MC at Bath before moving to Brighthelmston.*

air while parading one's finery, although the Steine was still used by the fisherfolk for spreading their nets, and promenaders complained about tripping over them.

In 1793 pleasure gardens known as the Brighthelmston Promenade Grove were opened on what is now the western lawn of the Royal Pavilion. This amenity was only a small version of the famous Vauxhall Pleasure Gardens opened in 1660, but offered attractions such as firework displays, concerts, illuminations and donkey racing. The Prince attended with his entourage, and in 1802 decided to buy the Promenade Grove to add to his growing estate. He allowed the gardens to remain open for another year with the rent being donated to the poor. At the time the main road from London passed immediately in front of the western front of the Pavilion, not only separating the Palace from the pleasure gardens but preventing total privacy. The Prince, therefore, ordered the construction of New Road to

14 *Brill's (lately Lamprell's) Baths were built at the foot of East Street in 1821, when fashionable visitors were tiring of sea-bathing. It was called 'The Bunion' as it stuck out leaving only a narrow gap along the seafront, a hazard for pedestrians and equestrians in heavy seas. Charles Brill was Lamprell's nephew.*

15 *An advertisement showing the interior of Brill's Baths. They were completely rebuilt in a Venetian Gothic style between East Street and Pool Valley and the old baths were demolished in the 1860s. It is said that Princess Mary of Teck, later Queen Mary, had her first swimming lessons there! The most remarkable of several baths in the town was the 'Vapour and Shampooing (Massage) Bath'. It was built in 1786 on the site of the present Queen's Hotel by the Indian Sake Deen Mahomed, who was appointed 'Shampooing Surgeon to His Majesty King George IV'.*

the west of the gardens, thus creating for himself a small enclosed picturesque garden laid out by Lapidge and Hooper, pupils of 'Capability' Brown. New Road was actually constructed by soldiers under the command of William Porden, the architect appointed to design the Royal Riding Stables.

In 1806 a small Theatre Royal in Duke Street in the Old Town was closed and replaced in the following year by a theatre in New Road. This in turn was refurbished and reopened as the Theatre Royal on 23 July 1814 under the patronage of the Prince Regent and the management of an actor, Thomas Trotter, with a performance of the comedy *Honey Moon*. The Prince Regent had his own box by the stage divided from the box adjoining by golden lattice-work. For the nobility and gentry this was clearly 'the place to be'. The present, much-respected Theatre Royal in New Road with its façade of red brick and terracotta dates from major reconstructions of the earlier building in 1866 and 1894.

The grassed area known as The Level north of St Peter's Church has long been a place of public resort. In Regency times it extended further northwards to include the land since occupied by Park Crescent and its communal garden, but was then the Prince's Cricket Ground. Formal festivities, which were not confined to 'the Company', were held on the southern part to celebrate the Prince's birthdays and other important events. These

16 *'Beauties of Brighton', a satire by George Cruickshank, 1826.*

17 *A cricket match being played north of St Peter's Church, probably Ireland's Cricket Ground, c.1825.*

included sports and ox roasting. One momentous celebration was held in August 1814 to mark the overthrow of Napoleon. Beef and plum puddings were served to 7,000 people and a whole range of activities organised, such as dancing, 'foot-racing', blind-man's buff, stoolball and 'kiss-in-the-ring'.

When the Prince became King in 1820 he gave up cricket and his land on The Level. The lord of the manor duly made a grant of the land to the town for the purposes of recreation. A road was constructed across the centre (now Union Road), and in 1822 James Ireland, a wool draper and undertaker, bought 10 acres north of the road and, in the following year, opened Ireland's Gardens and Cricket Ground there. (The odd connection between Ireland's trades may be due to the fact that burial 'in wool' was at one time encouraged in order to protect the wool industry.) In 1806 he had bought the drapery business of Daniel and William Constable in North Street which eventually became the well-known department store of Hannington and Son on the corner of East Street, which has only recently closed. Between the pleasure garden and the cricket ground Ireland built a spacious assembly room with reading and refreshment rooms on the ground floor and a promenade room above. Inside the entrance to the garden were a grotto, aviary and a ladies' bowling green, while to the north a bridge crossed a lake to a Gothic Tower and a maze.

On one occasion the town crier announced that Constable would 'fly' across Ireland's gardens from the top of the assembly room. This he did by gliding down a wire attached to a pulley, suitably attired and wearing a pair of wings! Apparently, the crowds were none too pleased with his deception. However, a real flight took place in 1824 when a balloon ascent from the gardens was arranged. But despite all these attractions, Ireland's enterprise was not as successful as he had hoped, and soon afterwards the gardens became neglected. In 1829 Park Crescent, designed in the Regency style by Amon Henry Wilds, was built on the site of the gardens and the more successful cricket ground. The intrepid William Constable later brought the new science of photography to the town in the form of the daguerreotype and opened a studio, known as the Blue Room, in Marine Parade in 1841.

There was one thing that Brighthelmston lacked as a fashionable resort and that was a health-giving mineral water spring like the one that attracted visitors to the spa town of Tunbridge Wells. The small chalybeate spring of St Ann's Well in Hove was considered to be rather too far out of town. A German, Dr Struve, had the solution—an artificial spa. He had already provided one in Dresden and in 1825 opened his successful German Spa at the southern end of a private park, which was later to become the publicly owned Queen's Park. This spa, which was built by the firm of Cooper and Lyon for about £2,500, was a delightful classical pavilion with a portico comprising six Grecian columns. Inside were a series of round-headed alcoves each containing a tap labelled with the name of a particular foreign spa, the waters of which could be imbibed therefrom. Out of sight, various minerals were added to water, which at least was pure and *local*, being drawn from an artesian well dug deep into the chalk of Brighthelmston. After obtaining the patronage of King George IV, Dr Struve named his popular facility the Royal German Spa; after all, the King was a member of the House of Hanover through his great-grandfather King George I. Dr Struve dubbed himself a Knight of the Saxon Order of Civil Merit and Fidelity and even sold his waters in bottles in London and elsewhere!

The spa even increased in popularity during the reign of William IV and actually continued well into the reign of Queen Victoria. It ceased to operate in 1866, but continued to function until 1960 as a mineral water manufactory under the well-known name of Hooper Struve Ltd. The building deteriorated, but the portico has been preserved as a listed building at the southern end of Queen's Park. It is interesting to note that this beautiful landscaped park with its lake even has its own artificial stream and cataract!

Another amazing—but less successful—facility was built in the 1830s on a site later occupied by Palmeira Square in Hove, near the great Bronze-Age burial mound. This was a vast iron and glass dome, larger even than that of St Peter's in Rome, called the Antheum. It was planned by a well-known local botanist, Henry Phillips, as a giant conservatory for exotic plants (not unlike the modern Eden Project in Cornwall). The first stages of the building were supervised by the architect Amon Henry Wilds, but he withdrew when it was proposed that a central iron column should be excluded from the design. Just before it was opened, the contractor removed the scaffolding without permission and the structure collapsed in a tangle of iron and glass. Phillips was so shocked that he went blind, but fortunately nobody was killed. The ruins remained on the site for some years afterwards, but were undoubtedly still a local attraction. In 1833 Wilds built for his own occupation the charming little Western Pavilion in the Oriental style that still stands in Western Terrace, just off the south side of Western Road.

Sporting events that almost all people today regard as objectionable even raised complaint in some quarters at the time, such as bull-baiting at the villages of Hove, Rottingdean and Preston, which went on until about 1810. The last public advertisement for cock fighting appeared about the same time, but the 'sport' almost certainly continued in private for many years. In 1780 the Duke of Cumberland, brother of King George III, released a stag in the Steine. It was pursued with hounds as far as Rottingdean where, rather than be torn to pieces, the stricken beast leapt over the cliff.

Whitehawk Down provided a fine location for a racecourse (as well as a Neolithic settlement), and it was the Duke of Cumberland who organised the first public racing there in 1783, the year of the Prince's first visit to the town. Prinny attended these races for the first time the following year. However, occasional private races had been held on the Down for some years. In 1770, a race took place between the horses of Samuel Shergold of the *Castle* and Dr Kipping, an expert swordsman who had once humiliated an army officer in a duel in West Street. In 1788 a small stand was erected on the two-mile hairpin course. Today Brighton Racecourse with its fine modern grandstand is one of the best known in the country. It was featured as the venue of the 1930s race gangs in the 1947 film *Brighton Rock* starring Richard Attenborough as the young gangster 'Pinky'. Northern Racing now runs the course, with the City Council retaining a stake in the trust that owns the land.

The South Downs around Brighthelmston provided an ideal place for horse riding and trips by horse-drawn carriage. One of the most popular destinations was the Devil's Dyke on the main ridge of the Downs some five miles north-west of Brighton, the site of an Iron-Age fort and a Roman road. There are two natural attractions there: the deep combe or gorge, and the breathtaking view from the summit. Legend has it that the 'Poor Man' (as the Devil is politely called locally) dug the gorge to flood the Weald and its churches from the sea. He had to abort his mission when he mistook an old lady's lighted candle for the first glimmer of dawn. The first inn at the Dyke was built about 1817. One of the earliest of its landlords was a fiddler by the name of Tommy King. A print dated about ten years later shows this inn to be little more than a hut with a stable adjoining about 350 yards west of the present hotel on the summit. This print shows Regency folk admiring the view. There is a stylish equestrian, a coach-and-four, an open landau and two one-horse carriages, all of which have undoubtedly journeyed up the rough Dyke Road from Brighthelmston.

Political life was centred on the activities of the Town Commissioners, who were established by Act of Parliament in 1773 to provide sea defences and to pave, light and cleanse the streets, and also two separate, long-established local government bodies: the High Constable, with two Headboroughs, elected by a jury of inhabitants to appoint constables and watchmen, and generally to maintain law and order; and the Churchwardens and Overseers of the Parish, whose main responsibility was to maintain the 'deserving poor' and provide a workhouse for them. The latter body was elected by a meeting of ratepayers of the parish known as the Vestry. A small town hall of sorts, which also included a workhouse and a 'black hole' for offenders, had been built in Bartholomews in the Old Town in 1727. The Vestry sometimes met there, but also in various public houses, including the *Castle* and the *Old Ship*, as did the Town Commissioners.

In about 1800 the workhouse was enlarged on its existing site to provide for 150 inmates, whose life was harsh to say the least: their diet appears to have consisted of beef, peas, oatmeal, bread, cheese and beer, but no sweet food or hot beverages (only the gentry could afford to drink tea or coffee). Under a second Act of Parliament in 1810 a special body of Directors and Guardians of the Poor was established, who until 1825 were appointed by the Town Commissioners, and subsequently by the Vestry. The Directors and Guardians instituted an even harsher regime when they took over the workhouse and made various economies in the relief of poverty. They reduced the number of persons on indoor relief on the basis that the institution should be a 'workhouse and not a playhouse', and insisted that outdoor relief should be restricted to persons prepared to be put to work. They even branded many in the fishing community as idle and drunken persons who declined to put money aside for a rainy day.

In 1818, with the growth of both the town and the incidence of poverty, the Directors and Guardians decided to sell the old workhouse building in Bartholomews to the Town Commissioners and build a larger one elsewhere. A site on Church Hill north of St Nicholas's Church was acquired for £1,800 and a new workhouse in a simple classical idiom built there in 1822 for £10,000. The architect was William Mackie of London and the builder John Cheeseman.

Under the Poor Law Amendment Act of 1834 a National Board of Commissioners was appointed to control the administration of the Poor Law. They could direct the building of workhouses or create unions of parishes under a Board of Guardians for the purpose. Outdoor relief was virtually discontinued and all able-bodied, as well as infirm, paupers were obliged to enter a workhouse if they needed relief. This required considerable investment in new workhouses. The parishes of Hove and Portslade were placed in the Steyning Union and their Board of Guardians provided a workhouse and infirmary at Kingston Buci, Shoreham, which subsequently became the nucleus of Southlands Hospital (Steyning gave its name to the union as it was the largest parish at the time). In the case of Brighthelmston, the Directors and Guardians feared that the parish would be united with other parishes that might not make a fair financial contribution, but this was avoided after they petitioned the new Commissioners that the existing arrangements already met the requirements of the Act. In fact, Brighthelmston was the only parish in East Sussex not to be a part of a union of parishes. However, the Directors and Guardians were sometimes in disrepute because of irregularities in their accounts, and the Vestry even reported that the former were in the habit of consuming, at the expense of the parish, lavish meals with wine, brandy, tea, coffee and cigars in a summerhouse that they had built at the workhouse for the purpose. However, no action was taken: sleaze was ever so!

In 1828 the Town Commissioners decided that they ought to have a town hall worthy of the Royal Resort. Over thirty schemes were considered and that submitted by the architect Thomas Cooper, who had previously designed the seafront *Bedford Hotel*, was chosen. It was built in 1830, the year in which King George IV died. In some respects the rather ponderous classical edifice, which lacked the Regency refinement of the style, was somewhat pretentious for a body such as the Town Commissioners. In particular, it was criticised for the disproportionate space devoted to the grand entrance hall rising to three storeys and the majestic staircase. However, a proposed southern wing was never built. The site in Bartholomews between Market Street and Little East Street had previously been the town's market place and, until a new market hall was built to the west later in the century, market business was carried out in Bartholomews alongside the Town Hall. Cooper's Town Hall has served Brighton well and is still in use, although the main offices of the City Council are now in the former *Princes Hotel* at the bottom of Grand Avenue, Hove.

As Brighthelmston was not one of the ancient boroughs it had no parliamentary representation until the Reform Act of 1832, but the Vestry was most vociferous in its demands for electoral reform both before and after the passing of the Act, and even adopted the People's Charter of the London Working Men's Association, which advocated radical proposals such as manhood suffrage, voting by ballot and the ending of the property qualification for Members of Parliament. They considered that corruption was still ongoing, despite the passing of the Act. There had been a strong radical tradition in the town since the arrival in 1783 of the Prince of Wales, who openly supported the Whig Party, the lineal predecessors of the Liberals. When he supported the Tory Party on becoming Prince Regent in 1811, the town on the whole remained both radical and royalist.

Turnpikes and the Coaching Era

The coach—basically an enclosed four-wheeled vehicle drawn by horses—dates from the middle of the 16th century but public stage-coaches were not widely used until the 18th century. Outside passengers had to cling to the luggage or ride in a basket nicknamed a 'rubble-tumble' towed at the rear, an appalling experience on atrocious roads such as those of the Weald of Sussex. The breakthrough came in the 1760s with the introduction of springs and, then, the first turnpike roads. Previously the only public transport from London to Brighthelmston was the carrier's wagon—and the journey could take two days!

18 *Aerial view of part of Brunswick Town, Hove, showing Adelaide Crescent and Palmeira Square. In the 1930s there was a move to redevelop the area, a threat which led to the formation of the Regency Society. In 1965 it was proposed to demolish the 'Decimus Burton' ramps in the foreground to widen the coast road, but this was averted as a result of public opposition.*

19 *The* Bedford Hotel *in King's Road opened in 1829 and was designed by Thomas Cooper, who also designed the Town Hall. The building was destroyed by fire on 1 April 1964 and rebuilt in a 1960s idiom.*

20 *St Ann's Well, Chalybeate Spa, Hove. This attractive classical Spa Pavilion was demolished in the 1930s. The site is now marked by an imitation well, but a tiny stream—the only one in the city—still flows for a short distance before sinking back into the ground. This part of St Ann's Well Gardens is carefully managed as a conservation area.*

21 *Devil's Dyke, c.1827, with visitors from Brighton and a miscellany of transports.*

Legislation for turnpike roads, under which private trusts could be set up to improve roads and levy tolls, had existed since 1663, but little had been achieved nationally. The name 'turnpike' comes from the 'turns' or toll-bars over the roads. With the growing popularity of Brighthelmston, improved roads became essential. The main routes to London were to the north-east via Falmer, Lewes and Lindfield, and to the north-west via Steyning and Horsham. The latter crossed the Downs from the Old Shoreham Road at Holmbush Farm to New Erringham Farm, where there was at one time a coaching inn, and then reached the Adur Valley by way of the 'Beeding Gorge'.

The escarpment of the Downs to the north of Brighthelmston was still a formidable obstacle to travel on a more direct line to London, although routes following the old trackways were still used. One of these was over Ditchling Beacon, the highest point in East Sussex, which—as now—descended the escarpment by way of what can only be described as a mountain road before continuing through the villages of Ditchling and Lindfield. It is, perhaps, no wonder that Gilbert White in his *Natural History of Selborne* (1788) referred to the South Downs as a 'chain of majestic mountains'.

Reference is made in 1775 to a new turnpike road to London that followed the Wellesbourne Valley through Preston, Patcham and Pyecombe, crossing the escarpment to Clayton and then to the capital via Cuckfield, Crawley and Reigate. This route was later referred to as the 'Appian Way for the high Nobility of England'. In 1810, however, the present route to London was generally established when a short-cut was constructed by a turnpike trust from Pyecombe through Bolney, Warninglid Cross and Handcross, saving about two miles and avoiding the steeper hill at Clayton. It is thought this route had previously been avoided because of the exceptional tenacity of the Weald clay south of

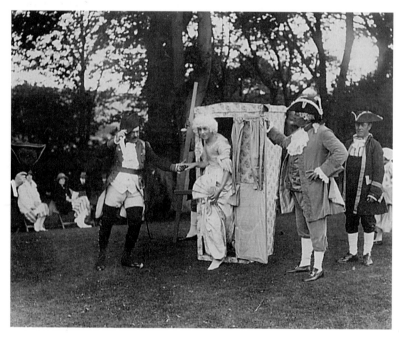

22 *Georgian elegance recreated at a Telscombe village pageant in 1925. The Sedan chair carried by two 'chairmen' derives its name from Sedan in France.*

Bolney. However, such problems would have been largely overcome by the surfacing techniques using layers of stone introduced by Thomas Telford and John McAdam early in the 19th century—reminiscent, perhaps, of those Roman roads 1,500 years earlier! By the time of the Regency the road to Lewes had also been turnpiked, and in 1823 a turnpike road was constructed along the coast from Brighthelmston to New Shoreham (now followed by the A259), which facilitated access to the harbour.

The first stage-coach hung on steel springs was apparently Tubb's 'New Flying Machine', which was advertised in 1762 as leaving the *George Inn*, Hay Market at 6 a.m., three days a week, and reaching *The Ship*, Brighthelmston via Lewes the same day, returning the following day. The single fare all the way was about 16 shillings for inside passengers and half price for those on the outside, 14 lb. of luggage per person being allowed before a surcharge of one penny per pound in weight was charged. Thus a journey to the seaside in those days was a realistic proposition only for the wealthy.

By the beginning of the 19th century some ten coaches were running daily from Brighthelmston to London, these being augmented by night coaches during the summer season. In 1822 about 39 coaches were making the same journey each day; and in addition there were another 23 coaches running from Brighthelmston to other destinations, principally Lewes, Hastings, Tunbridge Wells, Worthing, Portsmouth, Southampton, Oxford and Windsor.

In 1823 William Cobbett, the outspoken author, pamphleteer and reformist politician, wrote of Brighthelmston in his journal:

> It is so situated that a coach, which leaves it early in the morning, reaches London by noon; and, starting to go back in two hours and a half afterwards, reaches Brighton not very late at night. Great parcels of stock-jobbers stay at Brighton with the women and children. They skip backward and forward on the coaches, and actually carry on stock-jobbing in Change Alley, though they reside in Brighton.

Thus are commemorated the town's first London commuters. Bearing in mind the unreliability of the coaches, the stops at roadside inns and the fact that on occasions, according to Cobbett, the passengers had to push the vehicle up Reigate Hill, life for those early 'yuppies' must have been unbearably stressful. However, it says much for the salubriousness of Doctor Brighton! It will be noticed that Cobbett uses the spelling Brighton, which in his days was coming into common usage, although the name of the town had probably long been pronounced as such. In this book the modern spelling will be used in subsequent chapters.

In 1830 six of the principal coaching firms, including the famous Crossweller's, were based around Castle Square, which must have been not unlike a busy railway terminus, thronged as it was by passengers, porters and hustlers touting for business. In the vicinity were a number of well-known coaching inns, of which the *Royal Pavilion Hotel* in Castle Square is still in business.

A study of despatches from Brighthelmston in the national and Sussex newspapers can be quite revealing. The style may be archaic and the headlines minuscule, but it is obvious that interest in the 'Royals' and their entourage was as great then as it is today, and after the lawful marriage of 1795 reference is frequently made to the Princess of Wales! Amongst the gossip can often be found an indication of the type of conveyance in use. Apart from the private coach, of which the Abinger coach in Brighton Museum is a fine example, three types of carriage were especially popular: the post-chaise, an open four-wheeled carriage for two or four passengers and a postillion, drawn by the fast post-horses; the phaeton, an open four-wheeled carriage drawn by one or two horses; and the landau, a carriage with a folding top. Such conveyances were available for hire locally, as well as being privately owned.

All these fine carriages would have contended for road space with the carts and wagons of the local traders. The carter sometimes carried passengers as well as goods. In his excellent book *The Story of Shoreham* (1921) Henry Cheal tells the story of one such carter, John Moorey. In the early 19th century his 'Shoreham Cart' was the only means of conveying goods between Shoreham and Brighthelmston. He left Shoreham each morning at nine o'clock, reaching the *King's Head* in West Street by way of the turnpike road three hours later, returning at three o'clock. John not only served as a carrier, but also dispensed quack remedies, which must have had a ready market in Brighthelmston. Furthermore, he seems to have been something of a soothsayer: on 21 October 1805 as he passed *Bo-peep*, a hostelry under the cliff west of Copperas Gap, Portslade, he is said to have had a vision of Nelson's victorious naval battle that day at Trafalgar. It is possible that Trafalgar Road, Portslade, which leads down to the gap via Church Road, and its *Battle of Trafalgar* public house, commemorate John Moorey's legendary vision.

Post Boys, Mail Coaches—and Highwaymen!

The earliest known record of local post boys—who were controlled by the General Post Office—is an advertisement in the *London Gazette* of 24 May 1686 which announced that post boys on pack horses left for Brighthelmston and other places on Monday nights, returning the next day, postage being paid by the recipients. Some of these boys were only 11 or 12 years of age and robberies were frequent. A story often told is of the robbery of a post boy, John Stephenson, in 1792 on the Old Shoreham Road just to the west of Goldstone Bottom (now in Hove). The villains, James Rook and Edward Howell, were apprehended and sentenced to be hanged and gibbeted at the place where the robbery took place. In time, Rook's mother nightly collected her son's bones and buried them secretly in the churchyard at Old Shoreham where she lived. Until the 1930s Gibbet Barn on a farm of the same name commemorated the tragic event—as does Lord Tennyson's poem *Rizpah*.

As the roads improved and the volume of mail increased, private mail-coaches, with guards armed with blunderbusses, superseded the post boys. The first between London and Brighthelmston ran about the time of the above robbery. However, they were replaced in turn by Royal Mail coaches, which in the 1830s were regularly completing the one-way journey in less than six hours, the record time being 3hr. 40 min. There were two such coaches daily carrying passengers as well as mail on the London to Brighthelmston run and services between the 'royal' towns of Brighthelmston and Windsor and between Brighthelmston and Oxford. With the increasing speed, accidents were common as coaches overturned, resulting in the deaths of both passengers and coachmen. In 1790 the Prince of Wales himself was involved in an accident when his coach overturned.

The Brighton Camps—and a Mutiny

In the aftermath of the French revolution and during the subsequent Napoleonic wars there were extensive military camps between Brighthelmston and Hove, and also reviews and manoeuvres on the Downs, all of which were visited by the local royalty. In addition, large cavalry barracks were built on the Lewes Road outside Brighthelmston in the parish of Preston. A newspaper report in 1795 refers to a consignment of timber for the barracks being landed on the beach. A smaller barracks was built north of the Pavilion between Church Street and North Road, a special feature of which was a hatch in the wall which enabled the soldiers to partake of refreshment from the adjacent *King and Queen* hostelry in Marlborough Place!

Another tragic event occurred at Goldstone Bottom in the spring of 1795, this time connected with the local military. According to a contemporary newspaper report, about 400 men of the Oxfordshire Regiment stationed near Seaford mutinied because of the high price of corn and provisions. They took meat and bread from local shops in Seaford and beer from brewers in Newhaven, and also raided the Tide Mills there, taking away sacks of corn. The insurgents finally threw away their arms after a confrontation with a party of Lancashire Dragoons and the 'Brighton Artillery' despatched by the War Office. About forty were taken prisoner and twenty ringleaders 'secured in the Lewes House of Correction'. The rest were penitent, particularly after the arrival of their colonel, Lord Charles Spencer. Subsequently, in June 1795 the Oxfordshire Regiment was marched from Seaford to Goldstone Bottom (now in Hove) to witness the execution of two of their ringleaders, soldiers Cooke and Parish. To guard against further insurrection some 3,000 cavalry were posted on the rising ground above the valley, followed by the Horse Artillery with their guns 'pointed and match lighted'. It is worth quoting the newspaper report of the event:

> From the disposition of the ground, and from the arrangement of the Troops, a more magnificent and a more awful spectacle was never exhibited in this Country ... After the corporal punishment had been inflicted upon the offenders of less note, Cooke and Parish, the two unfortunate men condemned to die, were brought forward with a very strong escort. They walked along the vale in slow and solemn procession, accompanied by the Clergyman, who had devoted his time so conscientiously to them, from the moment the Sentence had been made known, that they were fully prepared to meet their fate. They approached the fatal spot, not only with resignation, but with the fullest confidence of passing into a happy and eternal state of existence hereafter. They then kneeled down upon their coffins with cool and deliberate firmness; when the one who was to drop the signal, said to his Comrade—'Are you ready?'—Upon the reply being made, he dropped a prayer-book; and the party did their duty at about six yards. One of them not appearing to be entirely dead, was instantly shot through the head ... After this the whole Line was ordered to march round the dead bodies.

Apparently the distraught clergyman did not survive the ordeal and followed Cooke and Parish into the Hereafter.

23 *Goldstone Bottom and the site of the execution of the mutineers Cooke and Parish. Hove Park opened in 1906. This picture shows the 'Goldstone', which was unearthed after being buried by the landowner because of unwanted visitors. This huge sarsen stone is traditionally said to be a 'dolmen' or holy stone of the Druids. Legend has it that it was thrown by the Devil when he was frustrated in his attempt to dig the Devil's Dyke to the sea to flood the Weald. Some say it bears the face of Christ!*

Maritime Brighthelmston and the Chain Pier

Fishing, and smuggling, continued to be important economic activities in Brighthelmston, Hove and Rottingdean. The hog-boat was still the standard fishing vessel into the 19th century, but the two- or three-masted lugger with a running bowsprit and lug-sails (with a gaff but no boom) and usually two or three jibs gradually became more popular as the century progressed. Frequent mention is made in the newspapers of the time of local maritime activity, which includes the following incidents.

1758 A French privateer captured a fishing boat with an old man and a boy aboard and carried them towards France. Later the privateer was attacked by a vessel of six guns and ten men and obliged to sheer off. However, no mention was made in the despatch of the fate of the hapless captives.

1790 A lioness, two hyenas and two ostriches, intended as a present for the King, were exhibited on the deck of an East Indiaman off Brighthelmston. A great number of people went off in boats to view these exotic beasts. The same despatch reports that a fine coach-horse worth 60 guineas was drowned in the sea when a man was swimming him therein!

1790 Two 'Dutchmen' collided in fog killing 16 of the crew, 14 survivors being put ashore at Brighthelmston by a Dover cutter. Later they set off for London assisted with money from a local bank.

1795 A fleet consisting of '150 sail of Transports and Merchantmen, under cover of three large ships of war, sailed by Brighthelmston to the Westward'. The fleet afforded a fine spectacle nearly all day. In the same year a number of refugees landed with horrific tales of Robespierre and a 'rusty' guillotine!

1798 One evening some gentlemen in a pleasure boat witnessed, as did others, an extraordinary moonlight phenomenon:

It had the appearance of a prodigious volcanic mountain, with the lava flowing down its sides into the ocean: it preserved this shape about 10 minutes, and then gradually stretched into an immense and regular formed column of fire, continuing in this state about an equal time; from thence it changed to the most perfect resemblance of a castle, or rather an immense bastion of transparent fire, which remained entire, preserving this most beautiful and astonishing appearance above half an hour.

1803 Three French luggers appeared 'in the offing'. A signal gun was fired from the Brighthelmston battery and an armed brig, the *Dragon*, sailed in pursuit. People from all over the town flocked to the fort, even deserting the churches. With little wind it seemed that the suspected privateers would not be caught, so fishermen and others armed with cutlasses and boarding pikes put to sea in 'row gallies', determined either to capture the privateers or perish in the attempt. However, when they ran alongside the luggers they found them manned by British seamen who were bound for Portsmouth following a naval action off Havre-de-Grace the night before.

After the defeat of Napoleon at Waterloo in 1815 there was a considerable increase in cross-Channel passenger traffic. Sailing packet boats plying between Dieppe and Brighthelmston had to anchor off-shore, passengers being ferried to and from the beach in the vicinity of Ship Street in rowing boats called 'punts'. Luggage, horses and carriages were loaded onto rafts and hauled ashore by horses. So appalling was this situation that in 1818 Lady Mountjoy, an invalid, was taken on board from her coach, which had to be driven into the water, only to be brought back a few weeks later 'a corpse'. The same foreshore was also used to off-load coal brigs and merchantmen. However, as there was only a 200-yard length of road along the seafront, the carts and wagons had to converge on North Street by way of the comparatively narrow Ship Street, Black Lion Street, Little East Street or East Street, adding greatly to traffic congestion in the Old Town.

With no natural harbour, there was a great clamour for a pier to serve the packet boats. In 1821 a prospectus was issued proposing the formation of a joint stock company to construct a pier off the Old Steine (on the site of the much later Palace Pier). However, in the following year a site at the foot of the cliff about 350 yards further to the east was chosen (opposite New Steine) to be approached by a new esplanade along the line of what is now Madeira Drive. Work commenced in January 1823: thus was born the famous Brighthelmston Suspension Pier, commonly known as the Chain Pier.

The engineer, Captain Samuel Brown, was a retired naval officer who had been responsible for improvements in the design of chain cables and suspension chains. His pier was 350 yards in length, the foundations being four clumps of metal-tipped timber piles driven 10 ft. into the chalk sea-bed and rising 14 ft. above high water mark. Above each group of piles was a pyramidal cast-iron tower 25 ft. in height with a central archway. The pier deck was supported by two suspension chains passing over the top of each tower and fastened to huge iron plates embedded 54 ft. in the cliff. The seaward end of the deck formed a larger T-shaped platform paved with Purbeck stone, from which steps led down to embarkation platforms.

Remarkably, this beautiful structure, later to be the subject of paintings by Turner and Constable, was completed in less than one year. It was opened on 23 November 1823 with

24 *The Chain Pier was built in 1823 but was destroyed in a storm in 1896. The engineer was Sir Samuel Brown.*

great ceremony, witnessed by most of the townsfolk. It had been hoped that the pier would be formally opened by King George IV, but for some reason he stayed away. Well-deserved praise was bestowed on Captain Samuel Brown, who some years later was awarded a knighthood.

In May 1824 one of the old sailing packets began to run from the pier, but at the same time the steam packet *Rapid* was introduced, sailing three times a week and taking 9 or 10 hours to reach Dieppe. In the following month the *Union* steam packet was introduced as well, and eventually, because of their unreliability, the sailing packets were discontinued altogether.

The pier soon became popular with promenaders, who had to pay old 'Ratty', the toll-keeper at the entrance to the new esplanade, tuppence for the privilege. Shopping kiosks selling refreshments and souvenirs were provided in the towers and a reading room constructed at the base of the cliff. In July 1824 as many as 3,000 promenaders visited the pier in one day, although many of the local mariners resented the construction of the Chain Pier as it had taken away their trade.

25 *Pier share certificate in the name of Sir Samuel Brown.*

26 *Regency legacy—Brighton seafront in the 1840s. This shows the Royal Albion Rooms, Marine Parade on the cliffs, and the Chain Pier with the entrance to the access road. In the distance is Rottingdean Windmill.*

Phoebe Hessell—the 'Female Warrior' of Brighthelmston

The story of Phoebe Hessell (sometimes spelt *Hassell* or *Hessel*) is remarkable in that she became known and respected by the nobility and gentry of fashionable Brighthelmston, although she was far from being one of their number. The record that follows is based on that of John Ackerson Erredge, who had the privilege of knowing the good lady long before his *History of Brighthelmston* was published posthumously in 1862; it brings to life much of the history of the town covered in this chapter.

Phoebe was born in March 1713 to a respectable family, apparently by the name of Smith, who lived in Stepney, which was then a large rural parish with maritime connections east of the City of London. She told Erredge that at 15, when she was 'a fine lass for her years', she fell in love with a private soldier by the name of Samuel Golding. He was serving with 'Kirke's Lambs' (nickname at the time of the Queen's Own Royal Regiment of Foot), which in 1728 was ordered to the West Indies. Phoebe donned the garb of a man and in this disguise managed to enlist in the Fifth Regiment of Foot under the command of General Pearce, which was also destined for the West Indies, where she served for five years. When her regiment returned to England it was ordered to join the forces under the Duke of Cumberland serving on the continent. Her disguise remarkably still undetected, Phoebe remained with the regiment for at least another 13 years, and on 1 May 1745 fought at the Battle of Fontenoy (now in Belgium) in the War of the Austrian Succession, when the French under Marshal Saxe defeated the forces of the Duke and his allies. Phoebe was to suffer a bayonet wound in the elbow, possibly even from an Irish soldier, as it is said that the Irish Brigade serving with the French were irresistible.

Subsequently both Phoebe's and Samuel Golding's regiments were posted to Gibraltar. There Samuel, in turn, was wounded, presumably when the Spaniards besieged the Colony, and as a result he was repatriated to a hospital in Plymouth. It was time for Phoebe to reveal her true sex. She confided in the 'Lady of General Pearce' who secured her discharge and repatriation to Plymouth, where she was allowed to nurse her lover. When Samuel left hospital, discharged on pension, they at last married, living happily together until he died some twenty years later.

After a short widowhood, Phoebe married William Hessell. Little is known about him, but the parish records of Brighthelmston reveal that in 1792 they were living there in poverty and that at a meeting of the churchwardens and overseers at the *Castle Tavern* on 5 December that year it was 'Ordered that Phoebe wife of William Hassell [*sic*] be paid 3 guineas to get their bed and netts, which they had pledged [i.e. pawned] to pay Dr. Henderson for medicine'. Notwithstanding this quaintly worded minute, William died about that time.

By now Phoebe was about 80, yet it seems that her celebrity status was only just beginning. Assisted by some local residents, she purchased a donkey and cart and sold fish and other commodities, travelling as far afield as the villages west of Brighthelmston, which must have included the small village of Hove. It may have been on one of these journeys early in 1793 that she became involved in the arrest and execution of the 'highwaymen'

Rook and Howell for the robbery of the post boy near Goldstone Bottom. She had visited the *Red Lion* at Old Shoreham when James Rook happened to be there, and became suspicious when he appeared to flaunt a detailed knowledge of the robbery. Phoebe informed the parish constable and the villains were duly apprehended.

The Brighthelmston Vestry Book for 1797 records that at a meeting held at the *Hen and Chickens* in King Street on 20 May the churchwardens and overseers ordered 'That Phoebe Hassell's rent be paid for the present time, and that her weekly allowance be discontinued'. However, early in the 19th century Phoebe was taken into the workhouse, which was then in Bartholomews. In August 1806 she was discharged at her own request at the age of 93. A minute of the Vestry dated 14 August states 'That Phoebe Hassell be allowed a pair of stockings and one change on leaving the poor-house'. She again set up in business, this time selling fruit, bull's eyes, pincushions and other commodities from a pitch at the junction of Marine Parade and Old Steine Street. It is said that in sunny weather she used to sit on a chair with her basket of wares and had a good amount of custom. Erredge says that she wore a brown serge dress, a white apron (always clean), a black cloth cloak with a hood surmounted by a red handkerchief spotted with white, and also 'an antique bonnet over a mob cap'. Her shoes had 'no respect for left or right'. It is perhaps no wonder that Phoebe became a conspicuous figure in the street life of Brighthelmston, especially as, despite her voluminous apparel, she was always ready to reveal the scar of her bayonet wound.

She was a keen supporter of an old Sussex custom on St Thomas's Day, 21 December, when she went 'gooding', visiting wealthy parishioners to gossip about the past, partake of hot elderberry wine and plum cake, and receive 'doles in money or materials to furnish home comforts for Christmas' (the custom was more often known as 'gooden', 'goodening' or 'gooders', and apparently widows had a right to a double dole!) One of Phoebe's calls was to the residence of Robert Ackerson, who was undoubtedly a relative of John Ackerson Erredge as he mentions that it was there that he often heard 'the old female warrior tell of her deeds of arms'. Apparently, Phoebe predicted that Robert's wife would live to a good age; and so she did—to the age of 97 some 50 years later.

On 12 August 1814 a festival was held at the Royal Cricket Ground to commemorate the peace following Napoleon's retirement to the island of Elba. As the oldest inhabitant, at the age of 101, Phoebe was privileged to sit on the left of the vicar, the Rev. Robert Carr, and receive presents of 'silver and one pound notes'. In 1820 Phoebe, although virtually blind, took part in the celebrations on The Level to mark the coronation of King George IV, this time sitting with the Rev. Carr in a carriage and cheerfully joining in the National Anthem. Several ladies, pleased with her respectable character, raised a subscription, each subscriber being presented with Phoebe's likeness and the inscription 'An Industrious Woman living at Brighton, with very slender means of Support, which she can only earn by selling the contents of her basket, for whose assistance this Etching is sold'. In fact, for some years the King, formerly Prince Regent, had allowed Phoebe half-a-guinea a week; apparently she declined his offer of a whole guinea, saying that half that sum was enough to maintain her!

In the following year a Mr Hone saw Phoebe when she was confined to bed, having lost the use of her limbs, as well as most of her sight. He said that he had seen many women of 60 or 70 looking older: 'Her cheeks were round, and seemed firm, though ploughed with many a small wrinkle.' She told him that her masculine voice had helped her keep her secret during her army service, but said, 'For you Sir, a drunken man and a child always tell the truth. But I told my secret to the ground. I dug a hole that would hold a gallon, and whispered it there.' She was obviously proud of the fact that King George IV had called her 'a jolly fellow'.

Phoebe Hessell died on 12 December 1821 at the age of 108 and was buried four days later on the south side of the entrance to the parish church of St Nicholas. The entry in the parish register shows that she was honoured by having the vicar and not the usual curate perform the ceremony. Her place of abode is given as Woburn Place, which was one of the narrow lanes with minuscule dwellings off Carlton Hill where the Milner Flats now stand. She probably occupied just one room. A tombstone was erected by Hyam Lewis, the father of Benjamin Lewis, a silversmith and jeweller of Ship Street. Inscribed on it is an account of her army experience. The stone has been well maintained and can be seen to this day. Appropriately, Phoebe's mortal remains lies near those of another local celebrity, Martha Gunn, who died on 2 May 1815 at the age of 88 after 70 years as a bather in the town. Phoebe is thought to have had nine children, probably all by Samuel Golding, but none reached any age except her eldest son, who became a sailor, although Phoebe had not heard of him for some time prior to her passing. The fate of this son and whether or not Phoebe, through him, has any living descendants are intriguing mysteries waiting to be solved.

Consequential Growth—Brighthelmston becomes Brighton

A large painting by Rex Whistler in the Royal Pavilion depicts a portly 'Prinny' clad only in the blue ribbon of the Garter gently awakening a nymph wearing only a blue girdle bearing the name Brighthelmstone. It is entitled *Allegory: H.R.H. the Prince Regent awakening the Spirit of Brighton* (the fascinating story of this painting is told by Clifford Musgrave in his *Life in Brighton*). 'Prinny' indeed flicked the switch—with the help of Dr Russell—but it was surely the new turnpike roads and the timely development of the sprung coach, that

27 Allegory: H.R.H. The Prince Regent awakening the Spirit of Brighton. *Painted by Rex Whistler in 1944 on the wall of a house in Preston Park Avenue where he was billeted prior to D-Day. He was the first officer of the Welsh Guards to be killed after the Normandy landings, but his fine, richly coloured allegorical painting was carefully removed, restored and is now preserved as one of the Royal Pavilion's treasures.*

rescued the ailing, obscure fishing town in the nick of time, giving it a new lease of life as a seaside resort, thus generating growth and prosperity.

By 1793 the marshy Steine had been laid out as an open space, and the Wellesbourne Stream consigned ignominiously to an underground brick sewer. In the next few years the Steine became a fashionable rendezvous surrounded by new dwellings and lodging-houses in a charming variety of styles and materials, often reflecting the cobbled vernacular of the Old Town. In the early years of the 19th century, however, Brighthelmston saw a number of unified architectural compositions. The earliest was Royal Crescent (1798-1807), set apart on the east side of the town; it reflected a building form characteristic of Bath, but was faced with black mathematical tiles. Then came Bedford Square (1810-18), followed by Regency Square (1818-28), similarly detached on the west side of the town, the latter with characteristic bow windows and verandas.

These unified compositions were soon linked to the Old Town as building development in a variety of Regency styles took place in between. Then came two even more splendid Regency compositions, similarly detached at first but further to the east and west, which in concept were more akin to small select townships. The first, Kemp Town, was started in 1823 by Thomas Read Kemp, lord of the manor of Brighthelmston, and designed by the renowned architectural partnership of Wilds and Busby. It comprised Lewes Crescent and Sussex Square surrounding private landscaped gardens with tunnel access under the coast road (now Marine Parade) leading through green slopes to the sea. Chichester and Arundel Terraces fronting the coast road on either side formed wings that completed the composition. The second (1825-7), again designed by Wilds and Busby, was actually over the border in the parish of Hove, but still some way from the fishing village. It comprised Brunswick Square with Brunswick Terrace forming wings fronting the coast road. As it expanded with additional streets, this development became known as Brunswick Town and even had its own Town Commissioners, town hall (in Brunswick Street West), chapel of ease (St Andrew in Waterloo Street) and market hall. A significant feature of these otherwise spacious Regency masterpieces was the mews, a discreet courtyard or lane where the horses were stabled, the carriages garaged and the grooms and coachmen accommodated.

The names of the architects, Amon Wilds, his son Amon Henry Wilds and Charles Augustus Busby, are virtually synonymous with the Regency development of Brighton and Hove, although their refined classical style characterised the first half of the 19th century and not just the Regency of 1811-20. Busby also had a scholarly interest in astronomy and navigation, and in 1832 built a model steamboat that seems to have caused some consternation among local mariners! Less is known about the builders of the time as it was—and still is— the architect who took most of the credit. The firm of Wilds and Busby were not only architects but also builders in their own right, but probably the most prolific of the builders during the first half of the 19th century was Thomas Cubitt of London, who worked for Kemp and was known to hobnob with royalty.

In 1823 Thomas Read Kemp became a Member of Parliament for Arundel. He obtained an Act of Parliament to build St George's Chapel in St George's Road to serve

28 *Regency legacy—the Steine in the 1840s. Here we see the Pavilion, the Victoria Fountain, with Brighton's symbolic dolphins (designed by Amon Henry Wilds), St Peter's Church and in the distance the windmill on Round Hill.*

29 *Royal Crescent, Brighton.*

fashionable Kemp Town. It was designed in the Regency style by Charles Busby and built in 1824-5 at a cost of £11,000, which Kemp hoped would be recovered by the pew rents! Queen Adelaide, wife of William IV, attended the chapel when in Brighton. In time it became so crowded that a gallery had to be provided and this was actually constructed by Thomas Cubitt in one week! His firm had previously completed Chichester Terrace, part of Kemp Town, to a high standard of workmanship. St George's remains, complete with its gallery, to this day.

When the young Queen Victoria came to the throne in 1837 Brighthelmston had become a fashionable resort which extended along the coast for two and a half miles from Brunswick Town to Kemp Town and inland for one mile from the sea to Ireland's Royal Gardens (where Park Crescent now stands), fronting a splendid boulevard formed by the Old Steine, the North Steine (now the Valley Gardens) and The Level. The Royal Pavilion dominated the southern end and the new church of St Peter the northern end. The latter, which was built in 1824-8 by William Ranger, was the first important work of a young architect, Charles Barry, who later designed the Houses of Parliament, for which he was knighted. As with other churches, the proposed spire was never built. Development also extended north of St Peter's Church along London Road (as far as Preston Circus), and along St James's Street, Edward Street and the eastern part of Western Road.

In about 1829 Charles Barry built a fine Italian villa, which became known as Attree Villa, for Thomas Attree, the son of William Attree, a prominent local solicitor who was both Clerk to the Town Commissioners and Vestry Clerk. This was located to the north of Brighton Park where the Royal German Spa was situated. Attree, who owned the land, later obtained the permission of King William IV to rename his park Queen's Park in honour of Queen Adelaide. Until the park came into the possession of Brighton Council in 1891 one had to pay for admission. Attree had intended that similar villas would be built around the park, but the scheme did not materialise. Regrettably, Attree Villa was demolished in the 1960s, but one of the associated buildings that still remains is the domed-topped tower known as the Pepper-pot, on the east side of Queen's Park Road, which was probably a water tower.

But not all was fashionable, for no resort could survive without its quota of clerks, artisans and labourers. These essential people were housed for the most part in mean, narrow streets, 'rows' and courts leading off the roads up the hillsides to the east and west of the Valley Gardens. Here the rows of small terraced houses were virtually back-to-back, separated merely by the tiniest of backyards. As if to compensate for the squalor, some of them were given romantic names, such as Regent Court, Marine View, Park Place, Paradise Street and Lavender Street.

Many of the so-called 'working classes' came from the depressed parts of Sussex, attracted by the prospect of employment, which could not be sustained throughout the year. Poverty and disease, therefore, were commonplace. The sycophantic newspapers of the day often referred to the charity of the nobility and gentry: for example, as early as 1795 reference was made to the lord of the manor's 'bounty of pea-broth'. But there was, as yet,

30 *Adelaide Crescent, Hove.*

31 *The development of Brunswick Place, Hove by Wilds and Busby, began in the 1830s in the northern part of Brunswick Town. With typical Regency bow fronts and balconies, the houses were subordinate to the overall composition. With the decline in royal patronage it took at least fifteen years to complete.*

no piped water or main drainage, and wells and cesspits were often in close proximity. However, a gas works had been constructed in 1818-19 on the cliff at Black Rock. As this was outside the Brighton boundary in the parish of Rottingdean dues levied on coal could be avoided. The coal was landed on the beach from brigs and taken up through a tunnel to the gas works. The Royal Pavilion and the new Theatre Royal were lit by gas forthwith, followed by some of the main streets. Another significant improvement was the construction of a continuous road along the seafront, which was achieved by extending out over the low cliff between the Hove boundary and the Old Steine, the road being supported by a series of brick arches.

32 *The Pepper-pot in Queen's Park Road. This is not an observatory as is sometimes thought, but a water tower for Thomas Attree's villa and his abortive development around Queen's Park.*

Despite the outward show of prosperity, however, there seems to have been a frisson of uncertainty in the 1830s over the continuation of royal patronage. Three years before his death in 1830 King George IV ceased to visit the town, apparently annoyed by the commoners gawping at him. His brother, who succeeded him as William IV, continued to come to the Pavilion, but he was not in the same league as 'Prinny'. Before long Queen Victoria was to show disdain for the intrusive townsfolk in the same manner as her Uncle George. There may have been little connection, but houses in Kemp Town became hard to let, and work on Adelaide Crescent on the west side of Brunswick Town, which was commenced in 1830, stopped in 1834 after only 10 houses had been built. Perhaps Brighthelmston, with an estimated population (including Brunswick Town) of the order of 45,000, had become too big for its Regency boots, and that another lucky break was required.

Five

Queen Victoria and the Brighton Line

The Coming of Steam

In Brighton's new mid-century crisis its true saviours were to be neither doctors nor Royals but engineers and 'navvies' and the new form of transport they were to create. The steam engine was one of those inventions that came before its time. Ctesibus of Alexandria demonstrated its principal in 150 B.C., when Brighton was still in the Iron Age, but it was not until Thomas Savery's pumping engine of 1698 that there was any practical application. Thomas Newcomen and John Calley followed, in 1705, but its full-scale development must be credited to James Watt from 1765 onwards. As we have seen, Brighton became familiar with its first application of steam power when the steam packet boats arrived at the Chain Pier in 1823.

Rails were first used as tracks for hand and horse-drawn wagons in the 18th century, particularly in the mines; but early in the 19th century Richard Trevithick combined the steam engine and the railway. Improvements followed and George Stephenson began designing locomotives for colliery use. In 1825 the Stockton and Darlington Railway opened for traffic, the first locomotive being Stephenson's *Locomotion*. The first passenger line, the Liverpool and Manchester Railway, followed in 1830 with Stephenson's *Rocket* hauling the first train. Intense competition to construct railways nationwide ensued.

Brighton tried to be in the forefront of the new means of transport. As early as 1825 a town meeting resolved that a railway should be built between Shoreham and Brighton in order to convey coal from the port, thus obviating the necessity for brigs to unload on the beach. In the same year the engineer John Rennie proposed that a railway should be built from London to Bristol via Brighton! However, it was not the steam *train* that was first to arrive in Brighton but the steam *carriage*. According to a contemporary newspaper report, in 1833 a Mr Walter Hancock drove his steam carriage *Infant* from Shalford in Essex to Brighton. The report stated: 'The appearance of the self-propelling vehicle excited much attention in Brighton, being the first that had ever arrived there direct from London. It is understood that the journey, with proper arrangements for fuel and water, can be easily accomplished in five hours, and that without the application of any extra steam pressure'.

By 1835 six companies were vying to construct a railway line from London to Brighton. As with the roads, the escarpment of the Downs presented a formidable obstacle to the most direct route, even more so with the railway's severe limitations on gradients. Routes following the Adur and Ouse valleys to the west and east were, therefore, serious contenders. However, after much argument, on 15 July 1837 Parliament finally agreed to a direct line, and the necessary Bill received the royal assent of Queen Victoria—just 25 days after she came to the throne.

The direct route chosen was one proposed by Sir John Rennie, but not as part of a line to Bristol. Branches from Brighton to Shoreham, Lewes and Newhaven were, however, included. Rennie's line, which has remained little changed, involved much tunnelling and a great viaduct across the Upper Ouse Valley south of Balcombe, the Downs being penetrated by tunnels at Clayton and Patcham. Rennie had originally proposed a terminus just to the north of St Peter's Church, but as this idea received nothing but derision the present site on the hillside to the west was eventually chosen, even though it involved excavation and terracing on a massive scale, as is now evidenced by the man-made cliffs on the approach to Brighton Central station. In the early days an isolated chalk mass known as 'The Mountain' still remained to the east of these cliffs.

33 *Queen Victoria arriving in Brighton under the 'Triumphal Rustic Arch' on 4 October 1837, drawn on stone by W. Walton from a sketch by I. Cordwell. This was the year of her accession to the throne: even the precise time is given, '20 minutes past four'.*

34 *Clayton Tunnel, the gateway through the Downs escarpment, was built between 1840 and 1841. The northern castellated entrance was to reassure travellers of a safe passage!*

The engineer appointed by the new London to Brighton Railway Company to execute Rennie's design was John Urpeth Rastrick. The first section of rail was laid at Hassocks Gate in February 1839; but about the same time a length of track was laid at Portslade for the Shoreham branch, as it was thought necessary to retain the support of Shoreham, which then had two Members of Parliament. David Mocatta, a pupil of Sir John Soane, was appointed architect of the station-house at the Brighton terminus, as well as other stations and buildings on the line. He designed in a classical Italianate style that presaged Royal Osborne House on the Isle of Wight and much of Victorian Hove. In fact, a guidebook stated in 1840 that Mocatta's station-house '... resembles the palace of a prince; while it vies in size and beauty with the town hall'.

But great credit is due to the army of labourers, or 'navvies', who built the railway in record time, a feat that might well be envied today despite modern technology. Records show that over 3,500 men with 570 horses were engaged on building at Brighton station alone. The term navvy was derived from the construction of the canals or 'navigations'. Because of its geography, Brighton had missed out on this earlier form of transportation, but the River Ouse navigation played an important part in the construction of the Brighton railway, as bricks for the spectacular Balcombe Viaduct were transported up-river by canal barges. The 1841 census shows that a large encampment for the workmen was located at Pyecombe, probably in connection with Clayton Tunnel, which is 2,266 yards in length. It is rare to see a record giving the names of the men who did the hard graft.

The Shoreham branch was the first line to be completed, and this was ceremoniously opened on 11 May 1840 before a multitude of spectators at Brighton. During the day 1,750

35 *The Station House at the Brighton Terminus opened in 1840 and was designed by David Mocatta. It still exists today, but is now obscured by the canopy over the forecourt.*

36 *Brighton Station with its fine glass and iron structure was saved from demolition in the early 1970s. It has recently been restored by Railtrack.*

37 *Brighton Station, c.1900.*

passengers were carried on the five-and-a-half mile journey, which took about fifteen minutes, 1,000 free tickets having been issued. Many of the travellers visited the Swiss Gardens at Shoreham, a popular attraction that had been opened two years previously by James Britton Bailey, a shipbuilder, and included an ornamental lake (later with a steamboat), sports facilities, a large ballroom and a refreshment room for 1,000 people. Similar pleasure gardens accessed by the London-Brighton Railway were opened in later years, in particular at Hurstpierpoint, Burgess Hill and Hassocks.

The main line was opened from London to Haywards Heath in July 1841 and in its entirety two months later. The opening ceremony on 21 September proved to be an even more spectacular event with crowds around the terminus and on every vantage point along the line. In his speech John Harman, the chairman of the railway company, expressed the opinion that Brighton would become 'the direct communication between the two great capitals of the two greatest kingdoms on the Earth'. He also indicated that at certain seasons the directors would run trains for first-class passengers only so that 'the most respectable and the highest families' would be able to travel to Brighton in the greatest comfort; they had no desire, he said, to shut out any parties, but they wanted to benefit the town by providing these trains for persons who brought most wealth to the town.

Initially, there were seven 'up' passenger trains and six 'down' each day, some of which were first-class only—except for special compartments for servants! The fast trains, intended for businessmen, completed the journey in two hours or less. The single fare to London was 14s. 6d. first-class and 9s. 6d. second-class, the respective fares for day returns being 20s. and 15s. By 1853 the number of 'up' trains had been increased to 12, including an 8.45 a.m. express, which actually completed the journey in just 80 minutes, a time not always matched even today!

Despite the chairman's sentiments, special excursion trains were introduced once the popularity and profitability of the Brighton line had been established. On Easter Monday 1844 a train consisting of at least 40 carriages hauled by four locomotives carried 1,100 passengers. By the end of that decade it was possible to enjoy a day at the seaside or at the races for a return fare of 3s. 6d. Travelling conditions, however, left much to be desired: whereas the first-class carriages were enclosed, having the appearance of the familiar road coaches, in fact, the second-class ones were mostly open wagons with no decent seats, their passengers being exposed to smoke, dust, noise and a rain of ash, especially in the tunnels. Umbrellas were frequently deployed! In the early years the weary travellers themselves were not allowed to smoke, either on the trains or in the stations.

Accidents were another hazard in those pioneering days. Only a few days after the opening of the Shoreham branch a man sitting on the tailboard of a luggage wagon was killed at Southwick when the train jerked and he was sent flying. In October 1841 the first accident occurred on the main line when a train was derailed at Haywards Heath and two passengers were killed. About the same time the southern end of the Patcham Tunnel collapsed, although there were no casualties. In his reminiscences, Nathaniel Blaker, who became house surgeon at the Royal Sussex County Hospital in Eastern Road, Brighton (which dates from 1828), recounts the harrowing experience of his first initiation into surgery as a pupil at the hospital. The casualty room was also the pupils' supper room, and in the evening of 21 September 1852 a tray of bread and cheese and beer was left on the table while Blaker was studying. A woman from Pyecombe, whom he knew, was brought in from the railway after an engine had passed over both her legs. The supper was duly cleared from the table and a mattress placed upon it. The surgeons amputated both limbs, after which the table was washed down and the supper replaced!

In the evening of 25 August 1861 came the worst accident that had so far occurred in Britain. Two excursion trains left Brighton only three minutes apart, followed just four minutes later by a regular train. The self-activated signal outside Clayton Tunnel failed to operate and confusion set in. The second train stopped in the tunnel and attempted to back out—only to be hit at speed by the third train. Steam and boiling water showered over a jumble of smashed carriages in the unlit tunnel. Sixty excursionists were killed or injured. Ironically, it is said that the splendid castellated entrance at the north end of Clayton Tunnel was built to reassure passengers; no such structure had been built at the southern end!

The projected branch line to Lewes was completed in 1846. It involved the construction across the London Road valley north of Preston Circus of a viaduct 400 yards in length with a central elliptical arch 67 ft. in height and 20 semi-circular arches. This structure, which

38 *The viaduct north of Preston Circus was completed in 1846 and built to carry the Lewes branch line from Brighton station across the London Road valley.*

attracted many an artist, was even more splendid before it became engulfed in urban development. As now, the railway passed under Ditchling Road through the Rose Hill Tunnel and crossed the Lewes Road at Moulsecombe (then a farmstead) by way of Skew Bridge to pass through a tunnel under the village of Falmer.

As it reached Lewes the railway was routed through the remains of the Cluniac Priory of St Pancras at Southover, which had been destroyed at the Reformation in the 16th century. William de Warenne and his wife Gundrada had founded the priory in 1078 and she had been the renowned prioress. As the navvies excavated the track they unearthed two leaden caskets: these bore the names of William and Gundrada. It is said that Mark Anthony Lower, the well-known Sussex antiquary, was summoned and the caskets opened in his presence. As the bones were deposited haphazardly, it was obvious that a second interment had taken place centuries before. However, there is an eerie tale that when the lid of Gundrada's casket was lifted one of the navvies saw for an instant—the face of Gundrada!

The Southover experience, which became known as 'the great discovery of 1845', led to the formation of the respected Sussex Archaeological Society. The caskets now stand in the Gundrada Chapel in the parish church of St John the Baptist at Southover, Lewes, although the remains are buried beneath the floor. For the author it is quite an awe-inspiring shrine: it is not often that one's Norman ancestors are exhumed in such a manner! The event is especially poignant as his great-grandfather, Robert Fines, was himself a railway labourer at the time!

In 1846 the London and Brighton Railway Co. amalgamated with the London and Croydon Railway Co. to form a new company, which was incorporated as the London, Brighton and South Coast Railway Co. (LBSCR). The expansion of the rail network proceeded apace. In the following year the projected branch line down the Ouse Valley to Newhaven was opened. By 1860 Brighton had connections through Shoreham along the coast to Southampton and northward to Horsham, and through Lewes to Eastbourne, Hastings, East Grinstead and Tunbridge Wells. So popular had Brighton become that about a quarter-of-a-million visitors came to the resort in that year. In fact, there was even pressure to construct rival lines between London and the coast.

One of the most far-reaching developments in the early years of the LBSCR was the establishment in 1852 of the locomotive works at Brighton. A site at Horley had originally been acquired for the purpose, but this was abandoned in favour of a site on the north-east side of Brighton station. It was a questionable choice because of the remoteness of the Sussex coast from the sources of raw materials and the limited space available; as the works expanded over the years the buildings had to be supported by piers on the hillside to the east (the remains of which can still be seen).

Nevertheless, the Brighton line became famous for its locomotives and their designers. Even before the opening of the local works there were some well-known locomotives in operation: the firm of Sharp and Roberts built the 'Sharpies', and the E.B. Wilson Company the 'Jenny Linds', named after the famous singer (who performed at Brighton Town Hall). In 1847 John Chester Craven was appointed locomotive superintendent and was to rule the roost at the new Brighton works as something of a despot until his resignation in 1869.

Although he and his son William built some fine express locomotives, the works was apparently left in a shambolic state.

The next superintendent was William Stroudley, who came from the Highland Railway. Although he was strong-willed and highly efficient, he was a complete contrast to Craven in his fair-mindedness and the great respect he was to earn from the workforce. In fact, Stroudley's name is writ large in Brighton's roll of honour, being closely identified with a series of famous locomotives in their livery of 'new railway green', such as the small and powerful 'Terriers', which were 0-6-0 tank engines (six coupled driving wheels) and the renowned 'Gladstone' class 0-4-2 express locomotives with tenders. Something of a mystery hangs over the description of the livery as it was not green at all but a rich golden ochre: one theory is that Stroudley was colour blind; another that he gave the wrong specimen autumn leaf to the paint shop—or perhaps it just changed colour! Stroudley introduced luxury saloon coaches on the Brighton line; also the famous American Pullman cars. In about 1875 extensive Pullman works were constructed on the west side of the main line south of Preston village.

In the 1880s Brighton station and its forecourt were extensively redeveloped. The fine Mocatta station-house was retained, but obscured by an elaborate cast-iron canopy. Rastrick's original wooden roof over the platforms was replaced by the present spacious and more extensive iron and glass roof (recently renewed by Railtrack at great cost). An unusual feature was a carriage road, which ran underneath the station from an entrance in Trafalgar Street at a low level up to the platforms.

During Stroudley's time a separate line was constructed to serve a goods yard on the east side of the station with a new cast-iron bridge over New England Road. In 1869 a branch line was constructed to serve Kemp Town (by then a name applied generally to the eastern part of Brighton), a remarkable and expensive engineering feat. This branch, which was less than two miles long, left the Lewes line east of the Rose Hill Tunnel, crossed the Lewes Road valley on a long viaduct and embankment, and then passed by way of a deep cutting into a tunnel over 1,000 yards long, which disgorged immediately into a wide cutting (east of the present Freshfield Road) containing the Kemp Town station and goods yard. In 1879 the Cliftonville Spur was constructed on the west side of Brighton so as to provide a direct link between the coast line at Hove and the London line at Preston, thus by-passing the Central Station. This involved a deep cutting and a tunnel underneath Dyke Road.

Stroudley died in 1889 from bronchitis, having caught a chill while demonstrating one of his famous locomotives in France. His place was occupied until 1904 by R.J. Billinton, one of a line of superintendents who continued the great tradition of Brighton-built locomotives into the 20th century. A few years ago the author helped a good friend and neighbour, Peter Love, to trace his family history. His great-grandfather, William Love, was a locomotive superintendent at Brighton and must have succeeded Billinton. But the history really came to life when it was found that previously William had been an engine driver and his actual Stroudley locomotive was discovered in the York Railway Museum, with a plaque in the cab bearing his name!

The Building Boom of the Victorian Era

In 1845 Brighton lost its royal patronage altogether. In February that year Queen Victoria wrote in a letter from the Pavilion: 'The people are very indiscreet and troublesome here really, which makes this place quite a prison.' She promptly deserted the royal palace. She returned to London by train, accompanied to the station by a troop of dragoons, a symbolic occasion marking, unintentionally, the hand-over of royal patronage to rail patronage. Brighton almost lost its beloved Pavilion as a unique symbol. The interior was virtually gutted and the building destined for demolition and replacement with houses to be built by Thomas Cubitt of London. In the nick of time, however, another of those great Brightonians intervened—Lewis Slight, Clerk of the Town Commissioners. He demonstrated that local government officers could be entrepreneurs when by 'sleight of hand' he ensured that the Pavilion became public property. The transfer was secured in 1851, three years before Brighton received its charter of incorporation as a borough. It has remained a tremendous asset to the town to this day. After a £10 million refurbishment in the 1980s it is now incorporated symbolically in the logo of the new city of Brighton and Hove.

Rail patronage lifted Brighton from the doldrums of the 1830s and initiated the second phase of the town's growth, not only promoting development on an unprecedented scale but also influencing the form it was to take. Hitherto, there had been a gulf in the social scale between the nobility and gentry of fashionable Brighton and the labouring classes of the impoverished back streets and alleyways. The railways led to a much broader social spectrum. At the fashionable end came the *nouveaux riches*, who had made their fortunes in the Industrial Revolution and could now retire to the coast, while keeping in touch with their businesses and entertaining their house-guests. They were reinforced by the professional classes and retired army 'top brass'. It was this class which by and large was to colonise the parish of Hove and the adjoining heights of Montpelier and Clifton Hill in Brighton. At the other end came thousands of clerks, artisans, labourers and servants to fill the jobs created directly by the railways and indirectly by the phenomenal growth of the holiday and service industries. The gap between was filled by the so-called middle classes—moneyed or otherwise—who settled on the coast to establish or manage the new businesses, commute to London or enjoy a modest retirement. They, too, could afford servants; and so could just a few working-class families with a steady income, who, as the censuses of the Victorian period testify, might take in a young waif or orphan girl to help out with a large family.

One of the first railway-inspired (and financed) developments was the construction in the mid-1840s of a spacious thoroughfare, appropriately named Queen's Road, connecting Brighton station to West Street, thus providing a direct route, not only to the seafront, but also to Western Road, which was already becoming a shopping centre. This development involved what was probably the first slum clearance in the town, as an overcrowded warren known as Durham and Petty France blocked the North Street end of the new road.

The Clock Tower at the southern end of Queen's Road, which could lay claim to being Brighton's second best-known—if contentious—symbol, was not erected until 1887-8. It was

THE
ROYAL EVACUATION OF BRIGHTON.

The BRIGHTON folks all look so black,
Hotels and lodgings minus—
Because the QUEEN has turned her back,
And shews them so much shyness !

We say the Queen—but join, of course,
Her most Illustrious Mother,
Who sways, with mild maternal force,
The movements of the other !

But, what's the reason they thus turn
Their royal rumps on Brighton ?
PAUL PRY has *not* the cause to learn,
And so will name the right one !

From Brighthelmstone, to London Town,
The distance is full fifty—
Whereas from town, to WINDSOR down,
Just twenty-one will lift ye.

And, therefore, it affords, 'tis clear,
(Which is a serious matter,
Full twice the time for the PREMIER
To languish at the latter !

He knows a *move*—and thinks KENT *hops*
A *step* to royal favour—
While her kind Highness loves LENT *chops*,
'Cause they've a *minty* flavour !

And there goes he—his *mutton-fist*
A fine large shoulder showing—
While they, it seems, cannot resist,
But after it are going !

Yet, don't despair, ye Brighton folk—
PAUL PRY support the million—
Will give the queen himself a poke—
She SHAN'T *rump* the PAVILION !

39 *The Royal Evacuation, 1845.*

40 *Goldstone Villas, Hove, and we can see the change in styles between Goldstone Villas (similar to Cowper Street—see page 71—but larger) and Eaton Villas to the right, built in brick with gables.*

41 *The Clock Tower, c.1900.*

provided by James Willing, a local businessman, at a cost of £2,000 to commemorate Queen Victoria's Golden Jubilee in 1887. Magnus Volk was commissioned to design a time-ball on a mast at the top of the 76 ft. tower. This was operated by hydraulic power, the intention being that it would rise up the mast and fall at each hour. However, soon afterwards it had to be turned off because of complaints about the noise. Commendably, the city council is now endeavouring to restore this historical feature with electrical operation, but as time goes by there seems to be one thing missing—Magnus Volk himself!

In the 1840s streets comprising terraces of mainly working-class houses were built to the east and west of Queen's Road, followed by similar development further north between the station complex and London Road (the New England Street area). The latter offered ready access to the locomotive works, Brighton's first heavy industry, which, at peak, provided over 4,000 jobs. In the early years of the railway there was little further development east of the Valley Gardens or in the Kemp Town area. The new fashionable residents began to colonise the parish of Hove and the high ground in the nearby Montpelier and Clifton Hill area in the western part of Brighton. The development of Adelaide Crescent and its complement to the north, Palmeira Square, at last progressed. The Regency style of architecture, which persisted until later in Brighton than elsewhere, can be recognised in many of these fashionable developments, and is even reflected to an extent in some of the new working-class streets, which were generally of a higher standard than hitherto.

The first intermediate, or 'suburban', station was established on the Shoreham branch line in 1845. It was named 'Hove Station', but was on the east side of Upper Holland Road and not in the position of the present station, the intention being that it should serve the expanding Brunswick Town area in the parish of Hove, and, probably, the nearby St Ann's Well chalybeate spa. Related development soon took place northward between Western Road and Wick Road (now Lansdowne Road) nearer to the new station. In locating their stations the railway company had a shrewd grasp, not only of existing demand, but also of the potential for further development and revenue thus created.

In the 1850s another leap westwards took place when the development of the township of Cliftonville commenced about half-a-mile from Brunswick Town and nearer to the old village of Hove. This had its own shops and hostelries, and even a gas works next to the parish church of St Andrew. Cliftonville took its theme from the classical Italianate style of Osborne House on the Isle of Wight, which had just replaced the Royal Pavilion as the Queen's residence. This was reflected not only in a variety of architectural detail, such as squat towers or belvederes, arched windows and pitched roofs with corbelled eaves, but even in the Isle of Wight place-names for the streets. A notable exception was George Street, named after George Gallard the developer, which was a working-class street, later to become one of Hove's principal shopping centres. In 1865 a railway station named Cliftonville was built on the Shoreham line to serve the new township, which by the end of the 1870s had extended northwards to the railway line in a grid of mainly 'bye-law' working-class streets. The former Hove station was closed in 1873, the site being developed as a goods yard.

In about 1870 a new development, known as the West Brighton Estate, was commenced in the parish of Hove between Cliftonville and Brunswick Town. It was to be on a monumental scale with grand Victorian mansions set in exceptionally wide streets, or rather 'avenues', which in the contemporary New York manner were given numbers instead of names. In the central position was the widest of these, a fine boulevard named Grand Avenue, which was continued northwards as The Drive. By the 1880s similar fashionable development had taken place north of the West Brighton Estate up to the coastal railway line; the principal builder responsible for this development was the long-established firm of William Willett Ltd of Grand Avenue, who have now been commemorated in the naming of one of Hove's conservation areas. Most of the new houses in this period were in yellow brick instead of the familiar stucco and were embellished in the high Victorian manner with much more architectural ornamentation. In 1879 Cliftonville station was renamed West Brighton, a term then generally applied to all the development then in Hove Parish, even though it had come under the jurisdiction of the Hove Commissioners five years previously.

Around 1880 there was another leap to the west when building began on the Aldrington Estate just over the Hove parish boundary, again with fashionable houses leading down to the seafront and middle-class and working-class housing up to the railway line. In 1893 the parish of Aldrington was placed under the jurisdiction of the Hove Commissioners. In the same year the LBSCR Company was petitioned to change the name of the station again, from West Brighton to Hove, which was duly agreed and the station was also enlarged. However, the change was resented by Brighton Council, who continued to object strongly when Hove UDC decided to petition for a charter of incorporation as a municipal borough.

In the early 1870s Brighton was beginning to expand into the parish of Preston north of the Old Shoreham Road (east of Dyke Road) and what is now Preston Circus; so in 1873 by Act of Parliament that part of the parish to the east of Dyke Road, which included Preston village, was incorporated in the borough. Preston station (later Preston Park) had been opened a few years earlier on the main London line just to the north of the old village, undoubtedly in anticipation of the development that it would create. In the next few years new houses were built on each side of the railway. On the east side, between the village and the new station, these took the form of large detached villas and substantial terraces, while tucked away on the west side were mainly working-class terraces. The new residents had the opportunity of commuting the short distance to Brighton station or working in the new Pullman Works.

In the same period the northward expansion of urban Brighton proceeded apace. The 'township' of Prestonville, comprising working- and middle-class housing, was developed between Dyke Road and the railway, much of its employment being in the expanding railway works. To the east of the railway mainly middle-class houses were built north of Preston Circus and Viaduct Road. Preston Park, on the east side of Preston Road (London Road) north of the viaduct, was opened in 1883. Facing the park on the west side of Preston Road was a ribbon of large detached villas. Later in the century similar mansions in large grounds were built in the Withdean area north of Preston station and the old Preston village.

London Road station, which was opened on the Lewes line in 1877, promoted extensive development between Preston Park and Ditchling Road. Apart from the large houses in Stanford Avenue, most of this comprised terraces of middle-class housing. Round Hill, between Ditchling Road and Upper Lewes Road, which had long been within the Brighton Borough boundary, was developed in the 1870s as a fashionable suburb, while terraces of working-class houses were built to the east of Upper Lewes Road. This area was served by Lewes Road station on the Kemp Town branch line, located on the west side of the viaduct over Lewes Road with access from Richmond Road on Round Hill. A coal wharf adjoined this station.

42   *Fox's Little Toffee Shop, Church Street, Brighton, c.1900.*

43   *C.E. Bridle, Boot and Shoe Shop and Factory, Blatchington Road, Hove, c.1900.*

44   *A. Chatfield (later Adams), Confectioner and Tobacconist, Goldstone Street, Hove, c.1900.*

Development also proceeded apace on the steep hillside to the east of the Lewes Road valley. To the south of Elm Grove this comprised streets of mainly working-class terraced houses (now known as Hanover), while by the end of the century the area north of Elm Grove as far as the cemeteries was developed with a variety of houses. The latter area was served for a while by Hartington Road Halt on the Kemp Town branch line. Queen's Park was acquired and donated to the town in 1891 by the prosperous Race Stand Trustees. Large detached red-brick houses in the Victorian Gothic style were subsequently built facing the park in West Drive and East Drive, while new roads immediately to the north, between Queen's Park Road (originally named Park Road West) and Freshfield Road (originally named East Park Road), were developed with smaller middle-class terraces in a similar style. The Queen's Park area was conveniently served by Kemp Town station and its goods yard on the east side of Freshfield Road. A small area of associated working-class housing, built in the 1870s, was located just to the north of this station straddling the southern end of the tunnel (the side walls of which were brick, although the roof was bare chalk!).

By the turn of the century Brighton and its haughty neighbour Hove—with sponsorship from the LBSCR Company—had become a continuous urban area. Preston village had been captured and the developers were advancing over the Downs on all fronts. The population was of the order of 150,000, a threefold increase since the coming of the railway. This resulted from inward migration greatly exceeding outward migration and from a very high birth rate more than offsetting a high death rate.

Providing for the People

In the early years of Queen Victoria's reign there was a clash of opinions between the Brighton Town Commissioners, the Vestry, the ratepayers and others concerning the advisability of petitioning the Queen for a charter of incorporation as a borough. In 1853 a petition and a counter-petition were both submitted to the privy council; the former prevailed, and a charter was received in April 1854. For a while the Commissioners remained in being, but in the following year that body went out of existence. The Vestry continued to hold meetings on special matters, but in 1856 that body, too, was abolished. Incorporation meant that the new borough council could exercise a wider range of powers, particularly in the field of public health, sanitation and safety. The first mayor of Brighton was John Fawcett and the first town clerk Charles Sharwood, who had previously been a commissioner.

The last meeting of the Commissioners, which had been in existence since 1773, was held on 28 May 1855 under the chairmanship of John Patching. He was a member of a local family building business established by Robert Patching in 1774 in Duke Street in the Old Town. It moved to Portland Street off North Street in 1832 and remained there until 1992 when it moved to Westbourne Street, Hove. It is still there today with another John Patching as managing director. It is almost certain that after 228 years the firm of Patching and Son is the oldest business in the city. Over the years many builders have contributed to urban growth: in 1899 over 200 'builders and carpenters' were established in Brighton and Hove. However, the family of Patching deserves special recognition: they diversified in the mid-19th century to become, not only builders, but also builders' merchants, coal merchants, coffin makers and undertakers—and even collected the duty on coal being brought into Brighton! Many of their old records have been lost, but they were particularly known in Victorian times for building churches: in 1875 they built St James's Church between Chapel Street and High Street and 79 years later were engaged to demolish it— a time when they had become better known for building pubs! The late councillor Dudley Baker started work with Patching and Son as an office boy at 16 and went on to become their manager, a director, and mayor of Brighton.

The Local Government Act of 1888 introduced a major reform of local government that involved the establishment of administrative counties and county boroughs. In the case of the former, powers and duties were divided according to their territorial significance between county councils at the higher level and municipal borough councils, urban district councils and rural district councils at the lower level, the latter being further divided into civil parishes. The county borough councils were all-purpose authorities and these were confined to the largest and most important towns and cities. With its growth in population and importance over half a century, Brighton duly became a county borough. Hove, which in 1892 had become an urban district within the Administrative County of East Sussex, was granted a charter of incorporation as a municipal borough in 1898, but still within the administrative county. Portslade-by-Sea also became an urban district: this was initially confined to the coastal area, but was subsequently extended to cover the northern part, including the village of Old Portslade.

The parishes of Hangleton, West Blatchington and Patcham, which were still undeveloped, were in Steyning (East) Rural District, a rather peculiar administrative area which had its offices at Shoreham in West Sussex. The parishes of Rottingdean and Ovingdean, with their similarly isolated villages, were in Newhaven Rural District. This situation remained until a major revision of boundaries in 1928. The overall structure of local government generally was not altered again until the local government reorganisation of 1974.

The great increase in population over the second half of the 19th century necessitated a corresponding increase in the provision of commercial and other services. The town centres began to assume the familiar pattern of today. In Brighton, shops and other services extended along Western Road into Hove, along London Road towards Preston Circus and along Lewes Road and St James's Street. In the Lanes of the Old Town fishermen's cottages were converted into small shops, and the now famous antiques trade began to be established there. Premises in Queen's Road and West Street tended to be converted into shops to attract the visitors arriving at the railway station. In Hove, the main commercial development took place in George Street, Blatchington Road and Church Road; while in Portslade (and West Hove) the area was similarly served by Boundary Road, Station Road and also North Street (since redeveloped mainly for industry). Many premises originally built as houses were converted into shops with residential accommodation or storage above, while in some places where there was space 'bungalow' shops were even erected in front of houses: these can be seen today in Western Road west of Hampton Place. Within the residential areas the familiar small centres and corner shops made their appearance.

Another feature of the commercial development was the inordinate number of drinking-houses, from hotels (sometimes with working-men's 'shades' discretely hidden round the back) to public houses and beer houses: in 1899 there were over 600 in Brighton and Hove. Some of the more select ones were strategically sited near railway stations where they could serve travellers as well as the high density housing in the vicinity. Surviving examples of these are the *Railway Hotel* (now *Finnegan's Wake*), *The Railway Bell*, *Queen's Head Hotel* and *The Prince Albert* at Brighton station; the *Station Hotel* at Preston Park station; the *Cliftonville Hotel* (now *The Station*) at Hove station; the *Palmeira Hotel*, which was probably intended to serve the original Hove station in Holland Road; the *Queen Victoria* at Portslade station; and *The Railway Hotel* at London Road station. Most of the smaller hostelries were located in the new working-class areas, such as the 'Railwaymen's Quarter' between Brighton station and London Road which was particularly well-endowed. At the heart of this area was the *Fitters' Arms*, where 'Blind Wally', the son of

45 *The Wheeler Band in the Pavilion grounds, c.1895. Brighton's Victorian and Edwardian buskers were regarded as celebrities.*

the licensee, Walter Chapman, entertained the patrons on the piano and sometimes busked on the streets with the piano on a horse-drawn cart! Some establishments in Brighton, known as 'penny gaffs', were just small music halls. Needless to say, drunkenness was a serious problem in relation to crime and health.

In contrast were the Victorian schools. Before 1870 the education of the working classes was dependent upon the churches and voluntary bodies. However, following political agitation the Elementary Education Act of 1870 was passed, providing for School Boards to be elected where there was found to be a deficiency. This *ad hoc* system was abolished by the Education Act of 1902, and replaced by local education authorities comprising, for elementary education, the county boroughs, municipal boroughs with a population above 10,000, urban districts with a population above 20,000, and elsewhere the county councils, and for higher education the county boroughs and the county councils. Accordingly, Brighton became the authority for both elementary and higher education, and Hove for elementary education only.

Some fine elementary schools were built in Brighton and Hove around the turn of the century in the romantic Gothic revival/ Arts and Crafts style in red brick and terracotta characteristic of the period. Some have since been demolished or converted, but three of the best architecturally in Brighton still remain: Elm Grove, Stanford Road and St Luke's (near Queen's Park), all of which contribute to Brighton's townscape as well as to the town's education. The first is now both primary and secondary while the others are primary only. In the field of higher education, Brighton's old Municipal Technical College in Waterloo Place near St Peter's Church is another fine building in the same architectural style that still remains in use. The old Municipal School of Art in Grand Parade, which was demolished in the 1960s and replaced by an unsympathetic modern building, was built in 1876-7 in the earlier Italianate style.

In his intriguing book *The Climate of Brighton* (1859) William Kebble, physician to the Sussex County Hospital, writes of the salubrious climate of the town, despite its many sanitary defects. He even refers to variations between one part and another. There can be no doubt that, sheltered by the South Downs and soothed by the sea, Brighton and Hove had—and still has—a climate particularly mild in winter, suited to invalids, convalescents and young children. This is evidenced by the number of private schools, nursing and convalescent homes that were established locally in Victorian times. The decennial censuses reveal that many of the larger Regency and Victorian houses were in use as preparatory schools. In fact, one of Hove's most famous pupils was the young Winston Churchill, who in 1883-5 attended the Misses Thompson's Preparatory School at Lansworth House, 29-30 Brunswick Road, where a commemorative plaque can be seen today. In 1947 Churchill received the freedom of the borough of Brighton and gave a humorous account of his experiences as a boy. Perhaps Hove can make a modest claim to have helped win the war!

Several well-known independent schools for older pupils were also established in Brighton, some of which still remain. Roedean Girls' School, which stands proudly above the cliffs east of Kemp Town, is known worldwide. This splendid Gothic revival pile designed by John Simpson was opened in 1898 and subsequently extended, but it had its

46 *Brighton and Hove Dispensary (later Hove Hospital) in Sackville Road, c.1900.*

origins as a small school founded in Kemp Town by three Lawrence sisters in 1885. A feature of the present building was a tunnel with a long flight of steps down to the beach with a changing room at the bottom. Although no longer used, it can still be seen through a grill along the Undercliff Walk. For the duration of the Second World War Roedean School became a naval establishment, HMS *Vernon*.

St Mary's Hall in Eastern Road, Brighton, which caters for girls of all ages as well as infant boys, is a complete contrast to Roedean in that it is hidden away behind its walls: in fact, a member of staff refers to it as 'one of Brighton's best kept secrets'. It was built as a school in 1836 by the Elliott family, daughters of a clergyman, to the designs of the architect George Basevi in an early Tudor style. The school, which still has descendants of the founders on its Board, is particularly proud of its history and multi-national tradition.

Brighton College, also in Eastern Road, is another well-known independent school. From 1848, when the first buildings were erected to the design of the prolific architect George Gilbert Scott, until 1973 it was entirely for boys, but thereafter it became progressively co-educational for juniors and seniors. The range of buildings along the Eastern Road frontage was built in 1886-7 to the design of Sir Thomas Graham Jackson, who had worked in Scott's office. The whole assembly of impressive buildings is essentially Gothic in style, Scott's being in flint and stone and Jackson's in brick and terracotta. Among the more famous old boys are the explorer Sir Vivian Fuchs, the suave actor George Sanders (who refers to the College in his *Memoirs of a Professional Cad*), actor Sir Michael Horden, and author Peter Mayle, who apparently did not appreciate his time there!

The Brighton and Hove High School for Girls in Montpelier Road occupies the former home of the lord of the manor, Thomas Read Kemp. Believed to have been designed and built by Amon Wilds senior, it was called The Temple, probably because it conformed to the measurements of Solomon's Temple. Its dome and tall corner chimneys have since been removed, but it is still one of Brighton's gems, although also rather retiring behind its cobbled walls.

Brighton Grammar School was founded in the 1870s in a large terraced house in Buckingham Road. One of its best-known pupils was the famous and, sometimes, controversial artist Aubrey Beardsley, who was born in the same road. Before the First World War it was intended that the school be moved to a new building to be erected at the junction of Dyke Road and Old Shoreham Road, but no sooner was this fine red brick building occupied than war intervened and it was taken over as the 2nd Eastern General Hospital. It is said that the injuries of the wounded soldiers brought home the horrors of war to the townsfolk. After the war the school finally took possession and it became the Brighton, Hove and Sussex Grammar School. It is now the Brighton and Hove Sixth Form College.

The splendid Hove Town Hall, built in 1882 but destroyed by fire in 1966, was designed for the Hove Town Commissioners by Alfred Waterhouse in a style derived from the Gothic revival and also from the Arts and Crafts movement inspired by William Morris and John Ruskin. A special feature was the clock tower replete with a carillon of

47 *Brighton Town Hall and the Wholesale Fruit and Vegetable Market, Bartholomews, c.1890.*

48 *Hove Town Hall, Church Road, was built in 1882.*

bells that played well-known tunes automatically at midday. The building was very much a symbol of Hove, and the Great Hall with its organ was a focus of community life. Its more romantic style of architecture was to influence the design of much of the subsequent development in Hove—and Brighton—during the late Victorian and the Edwardian periods. Some of the new houses were advertised as 'Elizabethan'. After the 1966 fire, while the council were using Brooker Hall (the home of Hove Museum) in New Church Road as temporary offices, there was a debate as to whether the Town Hall should be restored or replaced. The latter view prevailed and the present Town Hall was built in the 1960s idiom of glass and concrete. It is perhaps ironic that the Town Commissioners' original town hall in Brunswick Street West still stands, being now in commercial use. The Portslade Urban District Council had their offices in Station Street until premises in Victoria Road, previously owned by the firm of Ronuk, were acquired as Portslade Town Hall.

In the late 1840s the Brighton Guardians came to the conclusion that the workhouse on Church Hill was no longer adequate and decided that a new one with an associated industrial school for children should be built. In 1859 the latter, which became known as the Warren Farm Industrial Schools, was erected on a site fronting Warren Road, east of the race course, to the design of the parish surveyor, George Maynard. The building, which had rendered walls and a slate roof, comprised two storeys, except for a central section, extending to the rear of three storeys. It was not at all pretentious. Both it and the workhouse would be in need of a water supply, and in 1858 work commenced on a hand dug well in the chalk on the Industrial School site. This was expected to yield water 400 ft. down, but when none was discovered digging continued for four years, until at a depth of 1,285 ft. water broke through in a torrent which filled the well to 340 ft. from the surface. As this happened during a change of shift there were no casualties, but one can only marvel at the endurance of those labourers. Church bells were rung all over the town in celebration! This was to be another first for Brighton, as it is regarded as the deepest hand dug well in the world. It remained in use until 1878 when mains water was supplied.

The new workhouse, also designed by George Maynard, was built in 1866 together with a range of associated buildings, including an infirmary, nursery, and lunatic, fever and foul wards. The former site in Dyke Road was redeveloped with large houses in the high Victorian manner, with roads named in honour of the royal family. The new main workhouse building fronting Elm Grove was—and still is—a simple rendered structure but imposing for all that with its central clock tower and cupola. In 1914 the establishment was renamed the Brighton Poor Law Institution, but after the outbreak of war it was taken over as the Kitchener Field Hospital, and did not revert to its previous use until 1920. However, since it was built there were many changes in the poor laws, with reliance in the 20th century again on outdoor relief until the system was eventually abolished under the National Assistance Act, 1948, which created the welfare state. In 1935 some of the buildings were taken over as the Brighton Municipal Hospital; then, in 1948, the whole establishment assumed its present status as the Brighton General Hospital, now administered by the South Downs Health NHS Trust. Several additional buildings have been erected over the

49 *The Lake in Queen's Park, Brighton.*

50 *Cowper Street in Poet's Corner, Hove, was built c.1875-90 between Sackville Road and Tamworth Road and is typical of High Victorian terraced development. The stucco houses have cant (splayed) bays, in the classical idiom, but often with more ornamentation than the Regency style. The houses were built after the Public Health Act of 1875 which introduced by-laws to regulate standards. The development from Tamworth Road westwards marked the change in the late 19th century when houses were built in red brick in a more 'romantic' idiom derived from the Gothic revival and the Arts and Crafts Movement. This view was taken in 1911 and shows the street decorated to celebrate the coronation of George V.*

years, including the 1948 ambulance station. The establishment is not only a respected hospital, but still forms a striking feature on the Brighton skyline. The Industrial Schools became a children's home in the 1930s, then the Fitzherbert R.C. Secondary School until it finally closed in 1987. The building was subsequently demolished and a private Nuffield Hospital built on the site. It was then that the old well was discovered.

Brighton General complements the equally respected Sussex County Hospital in Eastern Road. The latter, which is now administered together with the nearby Sussex Eye Hospital by the Brighton Health Care NHS Trust, has been greatly extended over the years, including the erection of a tower block, but the original part, designed by Charles Barry, which was opened in 1828, can still be seen on the road frontage. The fine Royal Alexandra Hospital for Sick Children in Dyke Road was opened in 1890: built in red brick in the idiom of the time, it forms another striking feature on the skyline. Unlike the Brighton Hospitals, Hove Hospital in Sackville Road (originally Brighton and Hove Dispensary) is no more, but the 1880s building still remains and has been cleverly converted into flats as Tennyson Court, a name chosen to complement the names of other streets in what is now known as 'Poet's Corner'. A polyclinic and a day hospital have been built on the old smallholdings site south of Nevill Avenue.

In the Victorian period infectious diseases were rife, particularly in the overcrowded slums, so that isolation hospitals became essential under the Public Health Acts. Bevendean Hospital, near the top of Bear Road in Brighton, and Hove Sanatorium (later Foredown Hospital) in Foredown Road, Portslade were built in the late 19th century well outside the built-up area. Both have been redeveloped for housing in recent years, but the water tower of the latter, which forms a prominent landscape feature, was commendably retained and converted by the former Hove Borough Council into a heritage centre with a 'camera obscura' affording views over the city, the Channel and the Downs as far as the Isle of Wight. There was also a smallpox hospital in a far more isolated spot on the ridge of the Downs north of Portslade known as Fulking Grange, the foundations of which can still be found on the South Downs Way between Fulking Hill and Perching Hill. Supplies had to be transported along the ridge from Dyke station or by mule up the hollow-way from Fulking! Unfortunately, no photograph of this hospital seems to have survived.

The Wagners, Churches, and Religious and Political Dissenters

The building boom of the Victorian era was accompanied by a religious revival and the construction of many splendid churches, mostly in the soaring Gothic style, which had already seen a revival in the 1820s with the construction of St Peter's Church. This took over the role of Brighton's parish church from St Nicholas in 1873. The Rev. Henry Michell Wagner, a High Churchman, was the incumbent for over forty years and he and his son, the Rev. Arthur Douglas Wagner, were responsible for many of the Victorian churches, commencing in 1848 with St Paul's in West Street, which the former built at his own expense for £14,000. The architect was Richard Carpenter, a leading protagonist of the Gothic revival. His design cleverly respected the Brighton vernacular with the use of local flint, but the intended spire surmounting the tower was never built; instead the present octagonal timber bell-stage with a spirelet was substituted.

The Rev. Arthur Wagner continued his father's philanthropy, and in particular strove to bring the gospel into the working-class areas of Brighton by first constructing two modest mission churches at his own expense: St Mary's in St James's Street and the Church of the Annunciation in Washington Street. Arthur is said to have summoned his flock to worship at St Mary's by walking around the streets ringing a handbell! In complete contrast was the incredible church of St Bartholomew in Ann Street, just to the west of London Road. Built in 1872-4 to the design of Edmund Scott, on the site of an earlier mission church of the same name (derived from the dedication of the 11th-century priory), it soared above the neighbouring working-class terraces to such an extent that it was likened to an immense Noah's Ark. It is still one of Brighton's finest landmarks and is seen to great effect from the railway viaduct to the north. It is said to have the tallest nave of any parish church in the country, higher even than Westminster Abbey. The interior, in what might be called the Byzantine style, is equally impressive. When it was built the church was the subject of much criticism from some of Arthur's Protestant colleagues, which may have been due, not so much to the rituals, but to the fact that all the seats were free to worshippers whatever their social class. A more serious complaint was that the vast building caused a down-draught that

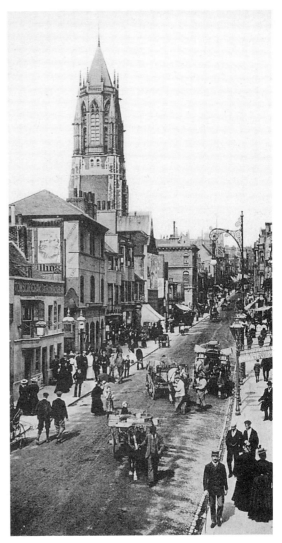

51 *St Paul's Church in West Street, c.1900. West Street was widened on the west side around c.1930. A swimming stadium was built south of the church in 1934, and was believed to be the largest covered sea-water swimming pool in the world. However, just over a year later it was converted into an ice rink and became the home of the famous Brighton Tigers Ice Hockey Team. The building was demolished in the 1960s.*

prevented smoke escaping from neighbouring chimneys, which the Rev. Arthur rectified at his own expense. However, as one of the most glorious Anglo-Catholic churches in the country, St Bartholomew's became famous as the focus of what became known as the 'London, Brighton and South Coast Religion'!

52 *St Martin's Church in Lewes Road, Brighton, as originally proposed. The tower was never built as it was too expensive.*

St Bartholomew's Church was followed by St Martin's in Lewes Road, which the Rev. Wagner built as a memorial to his father's long service as vicar of Brighton. Designed by Somers Clark in a simple Gothic style, it has perhaps the most sumptuous interior of any church in Brighton, with furnishings donated by the founder's brother Henry.

Brighton and Hove also have a wealth of Victorian places of worship belonging to other denominations and faiths. Brighton had a strong nonconformist tradition, which contrasted with its renowned Anglo-Catholicism. Two of its finest nonconformist churches have been demolished in more recent years. The Dials Congregational Church, built in 1870, which stood on high ground in Dyke Road at its junction with Clifton Road, had a tower that was one of the finest landmarks on Brighton's skyline. The other was the Countess of Huntingdon's Church on the south side of North Street near the entrance to The Lanes, which dated from 1871; built in Gothic style with a spire it was a handsome feature in the street scene. It was also of historic significance as it replaced a chapel originally built in 1761 in the grounds of the house of Selina, Countess of Huntingdon, who had been converted to Methodism and founded a prominent branch of the faith known as 'Lady Huntingdon's Connexion'.

Hove, too, has some fine Victorian churches, three of which deserve special mention, one Roman Catholic and two Anglican. St Peter's in Portland Road, which was built at the turn of the century, is in red brick and has a splendid Italian-style campanile. All Saints at the junction of The Drive and Eaton Road was built in the early 1890s to the design of J.L. Pearson, echoing his Truro Cathedral, but still lacking its intended spire. It became the parish church of Hove instead of St Andrew's. St John's at the eastern end of Church Road, with its flint walls and spire, complements the Palmeira Lawn, with its trees and well-loved Floral Clock, and with the surrounding Victorian buildings forms a fine urban square.

It is worth noting here that the name Palmeira commemorates Sir Isaac Lyon Goldsmid, who lived at nearby Wick House (1838-59), the grounds of which then included the chalybeate spa of St Ann. He was the first Jewish baronet and also held the title of Baron de Goldsmide da Palmeira granted to him by Portugal after he settled a dispute between that country and Brazil. Quite a number of the roads in the eastern part of Hove, once the Manor of Wick, are named after members of the family or places where they lived. The Jewish community is well represented in this area and today has three local synagogues.

53 *All Saints parish church at the juction of Eaton Road and The Drive, Hove.*

54 *St John's Church, Church Road, Hove.*

Brighton has traditionally been a seedbed for dissent and radical ideas, both religious and secular. The oldest nonconformist church still standing is the Union Chapel at the corner of Union Street and Meeting House Lane, which dates from 1683. The first meeting house of the Quakers was built in North Street about 1700, but this was demolished about a century later, when the present meeting house between Ship Street and Meeting House Lane was built, this being enlarged in 1876.

Thomas Read Kemp founded a dissenting religious sect and as early as 1817 built the independent Trinity Chapel at the junction of Ship Street and Duke Street. Kemp later realised that he was not a particularly good preacher, so handed over his chapel to a friend, George Faithful, a solicitor by profession. On his return to the Church of England Kemp sold the freehold to the Rev. Robert Anderson and the chapel duly became part of the establishment of the Church of England. In 1855 it was rebuilt in the Gothic style with flint and stone and renamed the Church of the Holy Trinity. It became the seat of the ministry of a fervent preacher, the famous Rev. F.W. Robertson, whose sermons were acclaimed worldwide. Apart from some changes consequent upon the widening of Duke Street, Holy Trinity still remains as a feature of the Old Town.

George Faithful, who remained a nonconformist, left Holy Trinity to build a chapel in Church Street (opposite the Museum) that became the Trinity Independent Presbyterian Church, later the Pavilion Baptist Chapel. The building was demolished early in the 20th century. Faithful became one of Brighton's first MPs in the Reformed Parliament of Whig Prime Minister Earl Grey, following the Act of 1832 which abolished the 'Rotten' Boroughs.

In the early Victorian period a charismatic nonconformist minister was preaching a highly controversial doctrine of 'spiritual marriage between soul mates'. The Rev. Henry James Prince, sometimes nicknamed 'Prinny', was ordained about 1840 and, having been forbidden to preach elsewhere, became minister of the Adullam Chapel in Windsor Street off North Street. This chapel was demolished when the Regent Cinema was built.

A Co-operative Benevolent Fund was established in the town in 1827, followed in 1828 by a Co-operative Trading Association with shops in West Street and Queen's Place. These were based on the communal ideas of Robert Owen, the owner of cotton mills in Lanark, who had put them into practice in his factories. There was, indeed, much poverty in Brighton following the Napoleonic Wars. For some thirty years Dr William King devoted much of his life to the Co-operative Movement. He was supported by Lady Byron, the widow of the famous poet, who had a house near the Chain Pier and engaged Dr King as a tutor for her daughter. Lady Byron also became a great supporter of the Rev. F.W. Robertson in his evangelical work. For a time, Dr King was a member of the Town Commissioners and enthusiastically supported their acquisition of the Royal Pavilion. He was appointed physician to the newly opened Sussex County Hospital (the prefix Royal was added later) and also to the Brighton Provident and Self-supporting Dispensary in Queen's Road.

The railways and, later, the building boom attracted hundreds of workers from the north of England and from Scotland who had been supporters of Robert Owen: George Henderson, an engineer from East Lothian, was a disciple of his. He founded a Brighton branch of the mechanics' institutes with a library and reading-room that helped educate workers before the Educa-tion Act of 1870 led to the establishment of free schools. A local working men's institute was established in 1848 with an initial membership of around one thousand. Through these establishments Henderson and others were able to organise the working classes. Another early pioneer of the labour movement was George Jacob Holyoake, a passionate orator who founded a religious 'disbelief' called Secularism which, in 1841, led him to become the last person to be imprisoned for atheism.

55 *Probably Henry James Prince, 'Minister' of the Adullam Chapel, Windsor Street, Brighton. He believed in the marriage of 'soul mates' regardless of their existing marital status. The preacher was identified by the reference to 'Prinny' on the reverse of the photograph.*

56   *Brighton Trades and Labour Council.*

In 1889 a branch of the Social Democratic Federation was formed in Brighton and in 1890 the Brighton Trades Council was created, inspired by another engineer, Will Evans, a modest self-educated man who, nevertheless, could inspire the workers with his passionate oratory. Several speakers at the meetings of the Trades Council and their annual May Day demonstrations on the Level became well known nationally. One of these was Margaret Bondfield, who in 1887 had started work as a draper's assistant in Western Road, Brighton, where the girls had little spare time and slept in bare dormitories. Her experiences spurred her on to make her mark in the labour movement. She eventually became Minister of Labour in Ramsey MacDonald's Labour Government, which was elected in 1929, and the first woman to serve in the cabinet. By the time of the General Strike of 1926 the movement had become so strong that industries and services were brought to a standstill in Brighton. With all the political agitation in the town it is perhaps no wonder that Hove always tried to keep its neighbour at arm's length.

In the 19th century the political complexion of the councils bore little relation to the aspirations of the adult population as a whole, for until householders and lodgers were enabled to vote in 1867 the franchise was dependent on the ownership of property. Until 1918 women were denied the vote altogether; even then they had to wait until they were 30 years of age. It was not until 1928 that men and women obtained equal rights. Right up until the Second World War local councils generally had no formal political structures: many aldermen and councillors professed to be Independents, but in the privacy of their gentlemen's clubs it was undoubtedly, in many cases, another story. It is likely that many members of the ruling class were more interested in personal preferment than local politics. Mortimer Collins in his 'Winter in Brighton' (1868) wrote:

> Politics nobody cares about. Spurn a
> Topic whereby all our happiness suffers.
> Dolts in back streets of Brighton return a
> Couple of duffers.
> Fawcett and White in the Westminster Hades
> Strive the reporters' misfortunes to heighten
> What does it matter? Delicious young ladies
> Winter in Brighton!

Professor Henry Fawcett and James White, to whom reference is made, were Liberals elected as MPs for Brighton in 1865 and re-elected in 1868. They were certainly no duffers. Professor Fawcett was a celebrated Cambridge economist influenced by the radical philosopher John Stuart Mill, who held that systems of laws and morals should promote the greatest happiness of the greatest number. The professor subsequently became Postmaster General in Gladstone's Liberal government, remarkably given that he had been blinded in an accident in 1858; this, at least, he had in common with Brighton's busker 'Blind Harry' of the *Fitters' Arms*!

Brighton had several Liberal and Liberal-Conservative members of Parliament in Victorian times, but it was not until 1964, when Dennis Hobden won the Brighton Kemp Town constituency seat by seven votes after seven recounts, that a Labour Party member was returned to Parliament locally. Amazingly, in 1995 not only did the party secure a majority on Brighton Council, but also on Hove Council. Then, at the general election in 1997, Labour members were elected in all three of the local Parliamentary seats: Ivor Caplin in Hove (including Portslade), David Lepper in Brighton Pavilion, and Des Turner in Brighton Kemp Town. The Burgesses of old must have turned in their graves!

Hotels, the Lift and the Birth of High Rise

Probably no form of transport has had a more profound influence on the structure of cities than the humble lift or elevator. The principle of the lift is undoubtedly as old as the block and tackle of the sailing ships, which could be used to haul mariners as well as sails aloft. In the Brighton area donkey power had long been used to draw water from deep wells: examples of old donkey wheels, within which the animals laboured, can still be seen at

Stanmer and Saddlescombe. But the history of the mechanical lift is obscure. There is reference to a lift carrying up to eight passengers to a viewing gallery at the Regent's Park Coliseum as early as 1829 but, apparently, no record of its power source. It is generally regarded that the first hydraulic lift was installed at the Paris Exhibition of 1867, and the first electric lift at the Mannheim Industrial Exhibition of 1880. Nevertheless, there is no doubt that the first mechanical lift in Brighton was in use at the *Grand Hotel* when it was opened in 1864. In fact, it can be said that this 'Palace by the Sea', designed in the Italian Renaissance style by J.H. Whichcord with 150 rooms in nine tiers, owes its very existence to its lifts for passengers and goods. The *Grand Hotel*'s passenger lift was actually referred to as an 'ascending omnibus', but its power was hydraulic, the down-pressure of a 60-ft. column of water driving a ram which raised the lift platform.

The *Brighton Herald* published a eulogy for the *Grand Hotel* on its opening day, 23 July 1864, taking its readers on a tour of the building which, it said, 'stands on our cliffs like Saul amidst the men of Israel, a head and shoulders taller than the tallest'. Having

57 *The Elms in Rottingdean and Rudyard Kipling's home, 1897-1902. In some respects a dissenter, Kipling left Rottingdean for Burwash because he felt there was a lack of privacy so near to Brighton.*

58 *The* Metropole *and* Grand Hotels *from the West Pier,* c.*1900.*

described the magnificence of the ground floor, the reporter enthused about the magical quality of the new-fangled vertical transport:

> We will now mount the staircase, or if the visitor please, he may ascend to what storey he please, in the 'lift'. He has only to take his seat (with half a dozen others) if he pleases, in a comfortable little room, and his commands will be obeyed with as much facility as were those of the Master of the Lamp or the Ring. Unless he look at the adjacent wall he will not know that he is in motion and even then he will think, not that he is rising, but that the adjacent wall is going down. The particular storey at which he will alight is 'set' by an index inside, the door is then unlocked, also from the inside; the uplifted visitor steps on to a level floor; the machine descends; et en voila tout.

Other splendid Victorian hotels dependent upon the lift followed the *Grand* along the Brighton seafront, such as the *Norfolk* (1865) in a similar style and the *Metropole* (1888). The latter was designed by Alfred Waterhouse (architect of Hove Town Hall) in his contrasting Victorian Gothic style using red brick and terracotta: it was regarded as brash at the time, but there can be no doubting its contribution to Brighton's image and character. It is a pity, however, that its delightful little landmark spire was removed in more recent times to make way for extra rooms: it gave a sense of loftiness that even Sussex Heights, the 1960s tower block behind the hotel—and twice the height—fails to achieve. Hove's former *Prince's Hotel* (1874), on the seafront at the corner of Grand Avenue, is another good example: reflecting the Italianate style of Cliftonville, but in yellow brick, it is now known as King's House, and has been chosen as the headquarters of the new unitary authority.

For some time before Volk's Electric Railway was extended to Paston Place in 1884 (see page 104), Brighton Corporation had been considering the possibility of constructing a lift up the 50 ft.sea wall of East Cliff but had been thwarted by engineering and financial difficulties. Now, Magnus Volk, anxious to attract customers from fashionable Kemp Town,

59 *Regency Square from the West Pier, c.1925.*

60 Prince's Hotel, *Hove,* c.*1900.*

offered to provide a lift at his own expense. His ingenious scheme involved laying a double track down one of the long flights of steps near his arch opposite Paston Place. On this would run two five-seat cars, one going up and the other down, connected by a cable around a pulley at the top. The cars would be operated by adjusting the water level in tanks underneath each of them. Construction actually commenced at the same time as the extension of VER, but it attracted so much hostility from the residents above that the project had to be abandoned. Apparently the greatest fear was an invasion by the 'hoi-polloi' from below the cliff.

In 1896 Brighton Corporation at last achieved its ambition to erect a lift at Paston Place. The design was far more splendid than Magnus Volk's abortive scheme, involving a red-brick tower rising from a long, glazed shelter incorporated into the Madeira Terrace development and echoing the same Oriental theme. The top section of the tower, capped by a dome clad in copper 'fish scales' and ornamented by griffins and dolphins, was designed to form an elegant entrance and belvedere in Marine Parade. The lift was hydraulically operated by water from the mains supply, the ornate lift cage able to carry up to 15 passengers. Some residents of Kemp Town may have regarded the structure more as a siege tower, but it is still there today (like most lifts, now electrically operated), a tribute to the Victorian city fathers and their borough surveyor, Philip Lockwood.

Water, Sewerage and Scavenging

The growth of Brighton and Hove after the coming of the railway could not have been sustained without the provision of a piped water supply and sewerage. Even in the mid-19th century wells and cesspits in close proximity were a notorious source of disease. There was a rudimentary system of drainage in some older parts of Brighton, chiefly for storm water, with an outlet on the beach near the *Royal Albion Hotel*. Nathaniel Blaker of the Royal Sussex County Hospital tells in his memoirs of the black slugs that used to come into his basement

61 *Inspection of the Goldstone Waterworks in 1874. A second engine house was added subsequently. This is now the Hove Engineerium.*

at 29 Old Steine from cracks in the defective brickwork of the sewer and of the smell from the 'gulley-holes'. He also states that the water from his well had a peculiar taste due to a 'communication' between the well and the cesspool next door!

The first public waterworks was constructed in Lewes Road south of Preston Barracks following the formation of the Brighton, Hove and Preston Waterworks Company in 1834. In 1853 the Brighton, Hove and Preston Constant Service Waterworks was formed and this absorbed the older company at a time when supply was limited to about 7,000 of the larger houses. In 1866 the Goldstone Waterworks was constructed in the western part of Preston parish (later incorporated into Hove), water being abstracted from a well 160 ft. deep in the chalk. This splendid example of Victorian industrial engineering, with its beam engines housed in buildings of multi-coloured brick and a truly monumental chimney, is now the Hove Engineerium created by Jonathan Minns.

In 1872 Brighton Corporation purchased the company's undertaking. They proceeded to acquire other companies and during the next 30 years constructed additional waterworks at Patcham, Mile Oak and Falmer. Progress was now rapid, and 24,000 properties were receiving a good piped supply by 1881. This enabled a system of drainage for foul sewage and surface water run-off to be provided in parallel. Inter-authority co-operation in the field of sewage disposal was initiated under the Brighton Intercepting and Outfall Sewers Board Act of 1870, under which an intercepting sewer was constructed along the seafront of Brighton and Hove with an outfall into the sea at Portobello at Telscombe Cliffs to the east.

Nathaniel Blaker would undoubtedly be surprised to learn that in modern times Brighton Council has been proud to organise tours of the sewers beneath the Old Steine as yet another tourist attraction!

In the days of wells and cesspits the Brighton Town Commissioners argued endlessly concerning the employment of private scavengers to clean the streets with their carts and to remove rubbish and what was politely called 'night soil'—the contents of cesspits often sold on as fertiliser. A favourite place to tip rubbish was over the cliff at Black Rock but with improvements in sanitation, refuse incinerators were built on the, then, outskirts of the urban area—at Hollingdean in Brighton and at Leighton Road in Hove. Both had associated council works depots and the former also an abbatoir. In more recent times incineration has been replaced by landfill but, with sites becoming full, proposals for incineration are once more on the cards.

Victorian Roads, Horse Buses and Bicycles

The railways had had a devastating effect on the coach services. In the late 1830s there were 36 coaches, licensed to carry 3,400 passengers a week, running between London and Brighton as well as services to and from Windsor and Oxford, and the mail coaches, which also carried passengers. Despite reductions in fares, services were cut drastically after the opening of the railways and the coach offices around Castle Square were closed; it is believed that the last stage-coach to run regularly on the Brighton Road finally called it a day in 1862, although there was a nightly mail coach carrying parcels between London and Brighton until the turn of the century. As a consequence of the decrease in traffic, the turnpike trusts had been forced into debt and the condition of the roads deteriorated.

However, as with the demise of the regular steam trains a century later, the amateur enthusiasts came to the rescue. The Brighton Road established its world-wide reputation as a fifty-mile long sports arena when the amateur coachmen raced one another or attempted to beat the clock. In 1888 James Selby drove the *Old Times* on a return journey from London to Brighton in a record time of 7 hours and 50 minutes. Even during the coaching era the Brighton Road had been the venue for walking races: there is a long newspaper report of a

62 *A horse omnibus which ran from Brighton to Rottingdean in the late 19th century.*

London to Brighton 'pedestrian match' for a £50 wager between a Mr Townsend, a Lewes man distinguished for his 'ten-toed talent', and a Mr Berry from Lancashire on 30 January 1837. The race, which was witnessed by a multitude of spectators, was won by the Sussex man in a time of 8 hours and 35 minutes. In June 1903 Mademoiselle Florence made the journey on what must surely be the most unusual form of transport ever to be seen on the Brighton Road—a 2-ft. diameter globe. The 'Lady Globe Walker' made what was claimed to be 'The Greatest Walk in the World' in 3 days and 22 hours!

The railway may have led to the demise of commercial coaches, but it actually fostered the horse-drawn omnibuses. An enterprising coach proprietor, Edmond Strevens, anticipating a threat to his business, introduced an omnibus service from Kemp Town to Brighton station as soon as the branch line to Shoreham opened in 1840. He also ran a combined coach and omnibus service between Haywards Heath and Brighton until the completion of the main line in the following year. Strevens then provided an additional omnibus from Brunswick Town to Brighton station. In 1853 horse-drawn omnibus services from the new suburb of Cliftonville were being advertised, running to the station and to Kemp Town. Two years

63 *Mademoiselle Florence, 'Lady Globe Walker', 1903. Who needs a car to get from London to Brighton?*

later services by 'Gallards' and 'Steers and Gallard' (George Gallard was the developer of Cliftonville) charged a fare of fourpence. It has been suggested that the expansion of services may have been encouraged by the repeal of the Corn Laws allowing the import of cheaper horse feed!

In 1869 excise duties on omnibus services were removed with the result that, until local authority licensing was introduced in 1876, there were no controls operating. Walter Tilley, a local corn merchant and innkeeper, was one of the first to take advantage: for about thirty years Tilley's Brighton Buses ran along Lewes Road from Castle Square to the *Gladstone Arms* (near Preston Barracks), Round Hill and the cemeteries, thus fostering development in the area. In 1872 Tilley was advertising handsome three-horse omnibuses with first- and second-class compartments. At first the service was hourly, but in the 1880s the buses ran every quarter hour, the fares being threepence first-class and twopence second-class. Following the opening of the station at Preston, Henry Thomas operated an omnibus service along London Road to both Preston and Patcham. He later ran an out-of-town service to Rottingdean in competition with Steven Welfare.

In 1884 the Brighton Carriage Company applied for licences to operate services to a wider area than hitherto using one-horse omnibuses seating 12 passengers and with a basic fare of only one penny. However, before operating they were bought out by a new Brighton General Omnibus Company. Horse buses were now becoming big business, so the smaller independent operators merged to form the rival Brighton, Hove and Preston United Omnibus Company Ltd (BHP) with 30 buses and 150 horses, their garage being in Conway Street, Hove. Few of the new one-horse buses appeared, mainly because of fierce competition and opposition from animal lovers. The BHP company soon became the dominant operator, although Walter Tilley withdrew and continued to ply his own Lewes Road and other routes until 1902.

The formation of BHP coincided with the introduction of a superior vehicle: it had plush upholstery, glass panels in the front as well as the sides and an interior lamp; but the main improvement was the replacement of long 'knife-board' seating on the roof with more comfortable 'garden seats' approached by a semi-spiral staircase at the rear. This design, in fact, continued as the model for the later motor buses until the 1920s. With the establishment of BHP the number of routes and the frequency of buses increased considerably, a penny fare being a popular innovation. Much of the new mileage was in Hove, where the roads were not so steep and the clientele wealthier, services being provided to the station, the shopping streets and the seafront. Nevertheless, not all the wealthy residents were appreciative. Another change was the removal of the bus terminus from the congested Castle Square to the Old Steine-Aquarium site. A measure of the early success of BHP is that in 1885 the company became one of the first subscribers to the South of England Telephone Company.

64 *A steam coach designed by Sir M. Goldsworthy Gurney. A steam carriage built on the same principle arrived in Brighton from Essex long before the motor car; and a steam-driven vehicle was the first to arrive in the town in the 1896 Emancipation Run.*

65 *Preston Road (part of the Brighton to London Road), c.1900. Preston Park is on the right behind the high railings that were not removed until 1928.*

The omnibuses benefited from the late arrival of the tramways, one of the reasons for which was Hove's vehement opposition to the latter. The first local public tramway actually opened in 1884 from the Hove/Aldrington boundary along what is now New Church Road (at that time in course of development only at the eastern end) to Shoreham via the coast road, passing through Portslade and Southwick. It was an unlikely venture in competition with the railway. Initially the trams were drawn by steam engines, but they were so accident-prone that horses were substituted. There was no way in which Hove would allow an extension of the service eastwards from Aldrington, even after that parish was merged with its dominant neighbour. The service ceased shortly before the First World War.

Of course, the well-to-do seldom had the need of public transport in any form. Private carriages in variety, as well as riding horses, were commonplace, and mews continued to be built as part of the new prestige developments, especially in Hove. In addition, horses and carriages with drivers could be hired from livery stables, such as those attached to the *Sussex Hotel* on the coast road at Cliftonville. There were also a number of local riding schools, one of the best known being Dupont's, which occupied Brunswick Town's old market hall (now the Old Market Arts Centre) in 1854. Horse-drawn cabs were available on stands at the principal stations and in the main streets. These included four-wheeled landaus and 'Victorias', as well as the sprightly two-wheeled Hansom cabs or 'flys' with the cabbie sitting aloft. From 1876 these all required a hackney carriage licence from the local authority, as did the horse-omnibuses and those speciality conveyances seen mainly on the seafront: the hand-drawn Bath chair, which was Brighton's 'rickshaw' for the elderly, and the odd little goat-cart for children. Not requiring a licence were the nanny-powered, coach-built perambulators for babies seen in increasing numbers along the promenade.

The second half of the 19th century saw the development through many variations of what many claim to be the most versatile of all forms of transport—the bicycle. Its antecedent was the hobby-horse propelled by foot power. This enjoyed a revival in the 1860s when cranks and pedals were fitted directly to the front wheel. This led in turn to a taller version with steel tyres capable of being steered, such as the unstable 'boneshaker' bicycles with parallel or displaced wheels, and even tricycles, all of which were generally marketed under the name 'velocipedes'. These tended to be replaced in the 1870s by the well-known 'ordinary bicycle', nicknamed the 'penny-farthing' because of its peculiar wheel configuration. These early versions were mainly novelties for the wealthier sporting types, who were known to take their contraptions on the Brighton Road, and even race against the horse-drawn coaches. The breakthrough came in 1885 with the invention at Coventry of the modern safety bicycle by J.K. Starley (born at Albourne, north of Brighton), the rear wheel of which was chain driven. This was further improved by the invention three years later of the pneumatic tyre by a Scottish veterinary surgeon, J.B. Dunlop. The bicycle subsequently enjoyed a great boom, with fierce competition between many new manufacturers. Starley's son, John M. Starley, later set up a manufacturing business in Hythe Road, Brighton. In recent years the latter's son occupied the premises as Starley's Garage.

With mass production, the bicycle was to become the transport of the people, used by women as well as men for the journey to and from work and for social and sporting purposes. By the end of the 19th century it was a familiar sight on the streets of Brighton and Hove, and also, with the formation of cycling clubs, on the Brighton Road and the byways of Sussex. The bicycle was also provided by those firms whose employees needed to travel the streets, such as rent collectors, tallymen, lamplighters, window cleaners and site supervisors. In the police forces the cycling 'Bobby' complemented the established mounted officers where mobility was required, and the errand boy on his special carrier bicycle played an important role in retail trade, ferrying his orders between shop and privileged account customers.

The errand boy's bike joined a plethora of hand-carts and barrows at the lower end of the commercial supply chain. Dairies and bakers were particularly proud of their fleets of hand-carts with smart deliverymen. At the next level, horse-drawn carts and wagons were still prolific; but a feature of the Victorian age was the development of a variety of specialised conveyances, mostly horse-drawn, but some hauled by steam traction engines in the form of 'road trains'. The brewer's dray, drawn by a team of powerful shire horses—descendants of medieval war horses—was a familiar sight in Brighton and Hove; large breweries in Kemp Town, Lewes Road, the Old Town and Cliftonville supplied an inordinate number of hotels, pubs and beer houses. Some magnificent furniture depositories were built at the turn of the century and their large horse-drawn vans were commonplace; some were designed to be loaded onto flat-bed railway wagons and even shipped abroad. Amongst other familiar horse-drawn commercial vehicles was the ultra-smart laundry van plying between the burgeoning laundries and the hotels and the homes of the well-to-do.

Perhaps the most sophisticated of all the Victorian specialised transports was the ornate glass-plated or open hearse drawn by fine plumed horses: a funeral cortège of hearse and carriages processing solemnly into Brighton's Extra-Mural Cemetery in Lewes Road, with its lavish monuments and mausoleums, or into Hove's new cemetery in Old Shoreham

Road at Aldrington, was indeed an awesome sight. With so many vehicles of different sizes and speeds on the roads, and little in the way of traffic regulation, it is not surprising that at times there was congestion in the centre of Brighton. As a result, some of the narrow streets in the Old Town, such as Duke Street and Black Lion Street, were widened and the new Prince Albert Street was constructed. Some of the worst congestion was in the main Western Road, but it was well into the 20th century before widening was to take place. Hove was in a much better situation because of its exceptionally wide roads, but even here there was a notorious bottleneck, known as 'the Bunion', formed by the Brighton Brewery in Cliftonville, which jutted out into Church Road. This was at last demolished in 1902 as a result of a deal with the new Hove Borough Council.

Victorian Emergency Services

The Town Commissioners of Brighton and Hove had properly organised police forces in Victorian times, their headquarters being in the respective town halls in Bartholomews and Brunswick Street West. Normal police work meant 'plodding the beat' and, where necessary, frog-marching drunken or unruly prisoners. However, horses were hired from livery stables, particularly for special events: in 1889, for instance, Hove's chief constable was required to provide four mounted officers for a visit by the Shah of Persia! Only the top brass would have had the use of a horse-drawn carriage or cab for official duties but their job had risks as well as privileges: in 1844 Brighton's first police chief, the popular Henry Solomon, was murdered in his own station in the basement of the town hall by a thief who had been brought there for stealing a roll of carpet in St James's Street.

Brighton's fire-fighting capability seems to have evolved as the result of a number of serious conflagrations. The Town Commissioners had a 'fire establishment' of sorts from 1831, but with the growth of the town the facilities were quite inadequate, so in 1867, with great ceremony, the Volunteer Fire Brigade was inaugurated. Their first station was in Upper Russell Street, south of Western Road, but in 1875 the brigade acquired premises at 4 Duke Street in the Old Town, where they were to remain until their dissolution in 1921. According to a contemporary photograph, one of the first appliances was a horse-drawn, manually operated fire engine called *Ocean Wave*, which was made available on loan. In 1885 the Volunteers acquired a smart steam-powered fire engine made by Shand, Mason and Co., which they called *The Alert*—although it still took some time to get up steam. A Hove Volunteer Fire Brigade was formed in 1879, with a fire station at 85 George Street (a coat-of-arms can still be seen on the building). Their fire engine was horse-drawn with a steam pump, but the horses were inconveniently stabled in a mews near the seafront.

On 19 June 1880 occurred the worst fire ever experienced in Brighton, starting in the premises of an upholsterer in Queen's Road. It was fought not only by the volunteer brigades and the police from both Brighton and Hove, but by the railway fire brigade, the coastguards and a contingent of lancers from Preston Barracks! In the following year the Brighton Police Fire Brigade was formed under Thomas Gibbs from the Metropolitan Brigade. He was succeeded in 1888 by Louis Victor La Croix, a flamboyant fire chief with a waxed moustache and a chest full of medals, who for over thirty years was one of the town's best-known characters with a reputation for derring-do: on one occasion he personally drove a horse-drawn fire engine at speed along New Road, only to crash into shop premises in North Street! The professional police brigade and the volunteers were to co-exist in Brighton until the latter's dissolution.

Maritime Brighton and Shoreham Harbour

The railway network of the LBSCR spelt disaster for the cross-Channel steam packets. The company wanted to establish a rail port with an interconnection between train and ship but Brighton had no sheltered harbour and the terminus was too far inland. The Chain Pier was often battered by storms, and there was insufficient water at low tide for the larger steamers then being built. A scheme to erect a breakwater at the seaward end of the pier had come to naught. The alternatives open to the company were Shoreham and Newhaven. The former, where the packets were berthed, was the most prosperous of the two harbours and much nearer to Brighton, but the LBSCR failed to reach agreement with the harbour commissioners, and so opted for Newhaven harbour, which in 1823 had been referred to as 'little more than a ditch'. A series of improvements were effected culminating in the construction of the half-mile-long breakwater in the 1880s.

In 1847 a railway line was opened from the Brighton line south of Haywards Heath to Lewes. This coincided with the opening of the branch down the Ouse Valley from

66 *King's Road, c.1900, showing the* Metropole Hotel *and the entrance to the West Pier.*

67 *Lower Promenade and King's Road arches, c.1890, showing young Brightonians playing 'pitch and toss' and marbles. They appear to be watched by a postman: nevertheless, as some old postcards reveal, mail was sometimes received on the day of posting! The arches conceal the former low cliff.*

Lewes to Newhaven, so that passengers from London bound for the continent were able to by-pass Brighton altogether. A cross-Channel service from Newhaven to Dieppe commenced in 1849 and the service from Brighton ceased. Thereafter the Chain Pier continued to fulfil its secondary role as a popular promenade, a prototype for the seaside pleasure piers that were to follow. The new locomotive works were also used for marine engineering until 1880 when workshops were built at Newhaven. Shortly before his death in 1889 William Stroudley designed the last two paddle-steamers for the company, one of which, the *Rouen*, made a record crossing for this type of vessel from Newhaven to Dieppe in 3 hours and 20 minutes.

Brighton's second pier was opened opposite Regency Square in 1866. Designed by the engineer Eugenius Birch, the new West Pier (the Chain Pier was, of course, the pier to the east at that time) was intended to serve the fashionable west end of the town; nevertheless, it attracted much opposition from the 'nimbies' of the Square—an ironical historical note bearing in mind the recent valiant efforts to restore the rusting hulk of what is now the country's only Grade I listed pier. Initially, the pier was little more than a promenade about 370 yards in length, only a little longer than the Chain Pier, but solidly built on steel piles. In 1894 it was greatly extended by the addition of new landing stages and the erection of a large concert hall. Once again paddle steamers began to ply from Brighton, but mainly to other Sussex resorts and the Isle of Wight, there being only occasional excursions to France.

The opening of the West Pier was followed by another of Brighton's great tourist attractions, the Aquarium, cleverly sited in a strategic position at the western end of Marine Parade near the Old Steine. It was built in a romantic Gothic style by Birch, and was clearly influenced by Paxton's iron and glass Crystal Palace, with its successful aquarium. Brighton Council insisted that in order to maintain the sea views no part of the vast structure should rise above the level of Marine Parade, with the result that the Aquarium was sunk below ground; it was likened to an undersea cathedral. Below ground there were also a restaurant and reading rooms, while on the roof were fine uncluttered terrace gardens. An attractive clock tower with a spire dominated the entrance at the west end, which led to a flight of steps down to the underworld. The Brighton Aquarium was opened to great acclaim on 10 August 1872 to coincide with a meeting of the British Association for the Advancement of Science. Early in the 20th century the Aquarium became run down, but in 1929-30 the

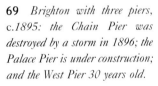

68 *The Chain Pier and a firework display to celebrate the Peace of Paris that ended the Crimean War in 1856.*

69 *Brighton with three piers, c.1895: the Chain Pier was destroyed by a storm in 1896; the Palace Pier is under construction; and the West Pier 30 years old.*

70 *The Aquarium, c.1895.*

exterior was redeveloped in the contemporary Art Deco style, with a restaurant and band-stand added on the roof, although still below the level of Marine Parade. The clock tower was removed, but the clock itself was installed in a simple tower at the entrance to the Palace Pier. The Aquarium has now been named the Sealife Centre, but visitors are still able to descend into that haunting undersea wonderland where they can even walk along a glazed tunnel through the shark pool!

The popularity of the West Pier had an adverse effect on the fortunes of the old Chain Pier, which continued to suffer storm damage. In 1891 it was sold to the Marine Palace and Pier Company, who began the construction of a new pier opposite the southern end of the Old Steine. The Board of Trade imposed a condition that the Chain Pier should be demolished as soon as the new pier was completed. However, progress was slow, and in 1896 the old pier was declared unsafe and duly closed. Two months later, on 4 December, it was destroyed by a mighty storm, its wreckage exacting a costly revenge on the West Pier and on the upstart under construction nearby. In 1899 the new Palace Pier, as it became known, was finally opened as a promenade deck about 570 yards long supported on steel piles. The magnificent superstructures, reflecting the Oriental design of the Royal Pavilion, were added during the first decade of the new century, as were the landing stages for the paddle steamers.

An early lesson from Brighton's piers was that leisurely promenading, which combines walking—the most basic mode of transport—with maritime sightseeing, lies at the heart of the seaside experience. In fact, visitors would even pay to walk over water without getting seasick! After the incorporation of Brighton as a borough in 1854 the council, with foresight, widened the promenade between the Old Steine and the Hove boundary, taking advantage of the low cliff to create a linear grandstand from which to observe the kaleidoscopic activity of the beach and the sea. The famous cast-iron railings, bearing the town's dolphin emblem, and the King's Road Arches on the lower promenade below date from that time.

71   *Brighton beach, c.1857.*

72   *Brighton beach, c.1859.*

73 *Launch of the Brighton RNLI lifeboat, c.1875. This was probably the* Robert Raikes *which was housed near the West Pier.*

The coming and going of the luggers and hog-boats of the fishing fleet from the beach of the Old Town and the bustle of the fishmarket between Ship Street and East Street were always a source of fascination for visitors—although some of the more fashionable promenaders preferred not to linger in these parts. There were private yachts and sailing dinghies galore, and sometimes regattas run by the new sailing clubs based on the King's Road Arches. Sailors touted for intrepid passengers to take to the sea in rowing or sailing boats or on board the famous schooner-yachts owned by Captain Collins, whose cry 'Any more for the Skylark?' became a Brighton catchphrase. In the 1860s there were over 300 bathing machines in Brighton alone and an increasing number of bathing tents for the less-modest; the antics of the bathers and paddlers could always be guaranteed to amuse the *voyeurs* along the promenade railings. There were in addition bands, minstrels, donkey rides, performing animals and vendors of every description.

Local sailors and their customers were undoubtedly reassured by the presence of the lifeboat *Robert Raikes*, which was housed in an arch near the West Pier. A local branch of the Royal National Lifeboat Institution had been formed as a result of the foundering of the brig *Pilgrim* at Brighton in 1857. The purchase of their boat, powered by sail and oar, was made possible by the contributions of London Sunday school children, its name being that of the philanthropist and founder of the national Sunday school movement.

In the 1890s, despite opposition from some residents, Brighton Corporation embarked upon an even more imaginative promenade development at the eastern, fashionable end of the town. This involved the construction of an ironwork terrace halfway up the lofty sea wall between the Aquarium and Duke's Mound, providing an open promenade at the higher level and a sheltered walkway beneath. 'Madeira Terrace', with its rhythmic pattern of latticework arches graced by the moulded heads of Neptune and Aphrodite, still forms a splendid complement to Madeira Drive. The whole concept was clearly inspired by the filigree stonework of the Royal Pavilion, the Oriental idiom being continued by the concurrent erection along Marine Parade above of the tall cast-iron lampposts with their Chinese-style lanterns, again symbolic of the 'Queen of Watering Places'.

The seafront westward of the Old Town was another popular area for the more fashionable promenaders. By the end of the 19th century a wide promenade had been constructed along the length of the Hove seafront, complemented at the Brighton end by the Brunswick Lawns and at Aldrington by the first of the new Western Lawns. The former became virtually the exclusive territory of the well-to-do on Sunday mornings, when they flaunted their finery after church in the 'Peacock Parade'.

At this time there was still over half-a-mile of shingle beach, with open fields to the north, separating the Western Lawns and Shoreham Harbour. A survey by Lieutenant William Roy in 1760 shows that this gap in the parish of Aldrington had been occupied by the mouth of the River Adur, forced eastwards by the drift of shingle along the coast. From time to time the shingle spit was breached, so that the shifting river-mouth forming the harbour entrance and also the channel up to the port of Shoreham presented navigational problems. The present protected entrance at Kingston between Southwick and Shoreham was opened by January 1818, leaving the former river-bed to the east as a tidal creek. Some 35 years later the section between Southwick and Aldrington was reconstructed as a broad canal with a lock at the western end, thus allowing ships to lie afloat throughout the tidal cycle. The opening took place on 20 February 1855. In 1870 a large gas works was erected on the shingle spit between the canal and the sea. This replaced the gas works at Black Rock, Brighton and at Church Road, Hove, which became holder stations. Thus coal, mainly from the north-east of England, became the principal bulk import into the canal, although there was also a considerable trade in timber and building materials.

74 *Wreck of the* Atlantique *of Nantes west of the Chain Pier, 1860.*

75 *Madeira Lift, c.1905, showing Volk's Railway. Horses were used to haul bathing machines up and down the beach. There was an accident which involved a horse and one of the electric cars.*

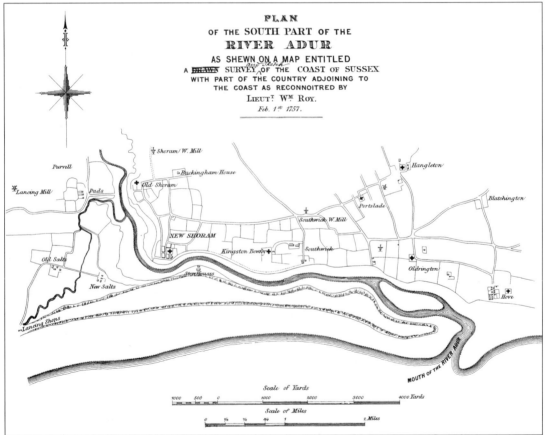

PLAN
OF THE SOUTH PART OF THE
RIVER ADUR
AS SHEWN ON A MAP ENTITLED
A ~~DRAWN~~ SURVEY OF THE COAST OF SUSSEX
WITH PART OF THE COUNTRY ADJOINING TO
THE COAST AS RECONNOITRED BY
Lieut. W.ᵐ Roy.
Feb. 1ˢᵗ 1757.

76 *Survey of the River Adur by Lieut. William Roy, 1757. The mouth of the river is near the village of Hove (now Hove Street).*

It was the canal and, in particular, the gas works that led to the development of the mainly working-class township of Portslade-by-Sea on the north bank between Copperas Gap and Aldrington Drove (now Boundary Road/Station Road). Two ferries carried workers across the canal. Portslade station in Aldrington Drove had been built to serve the inland village of Old Portslade when the Shoreham branch line opened in 1840. By the end of the century development, mainly of middle-class housing, had extended northward to the station and the Old Shoreham Road, and eastwards into Aldrington. There was also a nucleus of working-class housing at Southern Cross to the north of Copperas Gap, and another at Fishersgate to the west in the parish of Southwick, an area which is still served by Fishersgate Halt on the railway line.

The Devil's Dyke—Brighton's Victorian Theme Park

The closing years of the 19th century saw the construction of a number of incredibly eccentric and innovative 'leisure-time' railways in the Brighton and Hove area. The Devil's Dyke, which in Regency times had become popular for its spectacular gorge and panoramic views, was to develop in Victorian times as a veritable theme park. A permanent inn had been built on the site of the present hotel on the summit in 1831; four years later this was taken over by William Thacker, who was to remain landlord at the Dyke for well over fifty years. He must have been successful, as in 1871 he erected a larger hotel on the site. By 1876 there was a public road transport service in operation: a guide published in that year states, 'Waggonettes, Coaches and other Carriages, run to the Dyke and back daily, from the *King's Head Inn*, West Street, Brighton'. A waggonette was an up-market sprung wagon with a canopy, having seats for about fifteen passengers and a driver. It was normally hauled by two horses, but a third could be attached to surmount the hills on the route.

In 1873 came the first of a series of ambitious but abortive schemes to construct a railway from Brighton to the Dyke on the part of promoters independent of the LBSCR. Various routes were suggested, including one that branched from the main line south of Patcham Tunnel and followed the long downland ridge right to the summit near the hotel at a height of 700 ft. Eventually the Brighton and Dyke Railway Company obtained parliamentary approval to construct a railway with the agreement of the LBSCR and, with due ceremony, the first sod was turned at the Dyke on 2 June 1883. It was expected that the line would be completed in 1885, but because of engineering and other difficulties the formal ceremonious opening was delayed until 1 September 1887. Appropriately, the first train was hauled by a Stroudley 'Terrier' tank engine named *Piccadilly*.

In the scheme as completed, trains from Brighton to the Dyke shared the LBSCR coastal line from Brighton Central station to a junction in the parish of Aldrington (just to the west of the present Aldrington Halt). From there a new single-track standard-gauge branch line curved northwards, passing underneath the Old Shoreham Road and over Hangleton Road (then a country lane) to follow the west flank of Round Hill to a small terminus at the Dyke, which was 500 ft. above sea level, but 200 ft. below the summit. There were plans to extend the line, but these never came to fruition. For most of its three-

77 *Devil's Dyke (the gorge).*

78 *Devil's Dyke and Poynings looking west from Newtimber Hill. Watercolour by the author before the hurricane of 1987 which felled much of the clump of trees on Chanctonbury Ring in the distance.*

79 *Dyke Approach, c.1900. Showing the hotel, Elephant Gates and switchback.*

80 & 81 *Devil's Dyke Steep Grade Railway.*

mile length the gradient was a strenuous 1 in 40, and at busy times trains had to be hauled by two locomotives. It has been claimed that passengers were known to disembark and pick wildflowers while the train was struggling on its way up the hill!

In 1891 the bizarre private Golf Club Halt, which never appeared on the timetable, was built to serve the recently opened Brighton and Hove Golf Club, which had its club house at Skeleton Hovel on Round Hill. It was a 'request stop', and when the train left Devil's Dyke a bell would ring in the club house to alert golfers. There seems to be some uncertainty as to where it was located: it was not on the track leading past the club house to Dyke Road, now marked as 'the site' of Golf Club Halt, but some one hundred yards further to the north where the single brick platform can still be found lost in scrub. The railway also served the Dyke Golf Club, which in those days had a separate ladies golf course!

After a most encouraging start, the fortunes of the Brighton and Dyke Railway Company were at times precarious—not least because of the contribution that had to be paid to the LBSCR; but the increase in the number of visitors brought undoubted prosperity to the new landlord at the Dyke, James Hubbard, a Canadian entrepreneur who acquired the estate from the veteran Thacker. He set about developing his property as a major tourist attraction with bandstands, a 'camera obscura', an observatory and a coffee room for 275 people. There were also various sideshows and fairground rides—probably the first of any consequence to be seen in the Brighton area. These rides included a switchback railway, boat swings and a circular bicycle railway.

On Whit Monday 1893 Hubbard had some 30,000 visitors. So successful had the Dyke become that in that year he joined forces with William Brewer, a civil engineer from 'the land of cuteness and dollars', to plan a number of real transport innovations. One of these

82 *Devil's Dyke aerial cableway, c.1900. The author's impression of the scene as it might have been on a fine bank holiday at the turn of the century.*

involved the construction of a cable tramway—similar to the San Francisco cable-cars—from the Dyke railway station to the summit, but this was not to materialise. However, in the following year, to much acclaim, an aerial cableway across the gorge was opened. The track cables were suspended from a catenary cable supported by iron lattice-work towers, one on each side of the gorge. The track cables carrying cage-work cars passed through the centre of these towers and into small north and south stations, the distance between them being about 1,100 ft. The cars, each seating four passengers, were hauled by an endless cable, traction being provided by a Crossley's patent oil engine located at the north station. For a single fare of sixpence passengers could experience the thrill of an 'aerial flight' 230 ft. above the floor of the gorge. Sometimes, when in mid-flight, an attendant would drop a lump of chalk overboard, so that—as some photographs show—a pile of chalk gradually accumulated below. Attendants were also known to traverse the cables by hand and foot, thus adding to the excitement of a trip to the Dyke.

The last of Hubbard's transport ventures, opened in 1897, was the Steep Grade Railway, a funicular down the 'Shepherd's Steps' in a shallow combe on the escarpment just to the north-east of the hotel. The double-track 3 ft.-gauge lines were laid on longitudinal sleepers fixed to piles driven into the chalk. The 840 ft. long railway rose 395 ft., the steepest gradient being 1 in 1.5. Traction was provided by a Hornsby-Ackroyd oil engine located in a low brick building at the top, which also served as a station, which had open platforms on trestles. A small platform and buffers were provided at the bottom. There were two cars hauled by steel cables around a pulley wheel driven by the engine. Each could seat 12 passengers on a floor that sloped at an angle of 30 degrees, there being a horizontal platform at each end for the conductor. Brakes were applied automatically if the cable tension were relaxed. This remarkable railway not only enabled passengers to visit the scarp-foot village of Poynings, where cottagers enjoyed an unexpected trade in cream teas, but carried goods as well.

In the early years of the 20th century Hubbard was in financial difficulties, and in 1907 he returned to Canada. The aerial cableway and the funicular ceased to operate about two years later (but remains of both can still be found). Hubbard's Dyke Estate was subsequently taken over by the Army, as the nation had more serious matters to contend with. After the war, when housing development threatened, the Dyke Estate was acquired by Brighton County Borough Council, thanks to the endeavours of Alderman Sir Herbert Carden, a wartime mayor and proponent of municipal enterprise. In recent years ownership has passed to the National Trust and today it is still one of the city's great tourist attractions. The Victorian amusements are no more, but it is intriguing to seek out the evidence that remains (although it must be said that a descent of the 'Shepherd's Steps' can be hazardous!). However, the real attractions of the Dyke that led to its popularity in the first place are still there: the impressive gorge, the Iron-Age earthworks (the Poor Man's Wall) and the breathtaking view over six counties. The hotel was rebuilt again after the Second World War and has a good bar and restaurant to serve the needs of tourists, ramblers and hang-glider pilots.

Magnus Volk—Inventive Genius

Magnus Volk was an inventive genius who proclaimed that 'Brighton should be first in everything'. He was born at 35 Western Road, Brighton on 19 October 1851 (he deserves to have his birthday and parentage precisely recorded). His father—also named Magnus— was a clockmaker who had emigrated from the Black Forest in troublesome times 10 years previously. He sailed from Rotterdam aboard a famous paddle-steamer, the *Batavia*, bound for the Pool of London. He was able to travel by train on the Brighton line as far as Haywards Heath, from where the journey had to be continued by coach (probably the one run by Edmond Strevens) as the railway would not be opened all the way for another 11 days. The elder Magnus worked hard at his trade, and in 1850 he married a Sussex girl, Sarah Maynard, at the old parish church of St Nicholas in Brighton.

The young Magnus inherited his father's technical skills and, in particular, became profoundly involved in the new technology of electricity, including telegraphy and telephony. In 1879 he too married a Sussex girl, Anna Banfield, at the Baptist Providence Chapel in Burgess Hill. They set up home at 40 Preston Road, Brighton, and in the following year he installed a dynamo powered by a gas engine in order to provide electric light. It was to be another two years before there was a public electricity supply (from a generating station in North Road). Before long, Magnus Volk was deeply involved in the potential for electric traction, fully aware that at the Berlin Trades Exhibition of 1879 Ernst Werner Von Seimens had demonstrated a small electric locomotive hauling trucks.

With the railways bringing visitors to Brighton in ever-increasing numbers it had become necessary to expand the seafront attractions. The crumbling East Cliff from the Old Steine to the Kemp Town slopes had already been enclosed by a sea wall. In the 1860s this was improved, thus enabling Marine Parade at the upper level to be widened and a new road, Madeira Road (later to be renamed Madeira Drive), to be constructed at the lower level. In between these roads at the Old Steine end was built the Brighton Aquarium, the mainly subterranean Gothic marine extravaganza opened in 1872.

Once Magnus had made up his mind to add an electric railway to Brighton's attractions events moved at astonishing speed. On 14 June 1883 he wrote to the Town Clerk seeking permission to construct a narrow (2 ft.) gauge line along the beach from the Aquarium to the Chain Pier. His proposal was considered at two meetings of the Works Committee, and despite some objections—particularly from one councillor who thought that the new Madeira Road should be primarily for equestrians—verbal approval was given two weeks later. Magnus did not wait for the formal agreement (which was secured on 25 July), but went ahead regardless. Amazingly, he was officially able to open his little passenger railway with due ceremony on 4 August 1883 in time for the bank holiday weekend! In his book *Magnus Volk of Brighton* (1972) the inventor's youngest son Conrad expressed it succinctly in one short paragraph: 'Those were the days'!

It may fairly be claimed that Volk's Electric Railway (VER) was the first public electric railway in the world. The quarter-mile long track, constructed by the firm of J.T. Chappell, was laid well above high-water level, the rails being fixed to longitudinal sleepers on shingle ballast, which was also used to form low embankments to clear two groynes. The car, which was about 12 ft. in length, had seats for up to 12 passengers and a footboard at each end for the driver. It was constructed to Volk's design by Pollard's, a local coach-building firm. The generating plant, which incorporated an Otto gas engine and a Seimens' dynamo, was housed in a sea wall arch. From there, cables supplied electricity to the two track rails and then to a motor under a seat in the car providing belt drive to the axles. The speed thus obtained was about six miles per hour.

The council had required that VER should be dismantled at the end of the season. However, despite storm damage and some mischievous tampering with the live rails, the indefatigable Magnus applied for permission to extend his popular railway westwards to the borough boundary. When this was refused he promptly applied to extend eastwards as far as Paston Place, Kemp Town. This time permission was granted, subject to a requirement that the whole railway should be removed if the council so required. Technical problems had to be overcome inasmuch as the new line had to pass under the Chain Pier at quite a steep gradient and then to surmount more groynes on its route to a new station just to the west of the Banjo Groyne, a jetty (still existing) which had been nicknamed 'The Free Pier'.

Magnus re-laid the whole track to a gauge of 2 ft. 8½ in. and ordered a larger car with an overall length of 19 ft. built of solid mahogany and capable of seating 30 passengers. A second car was added later. He also leased an arch in the sea wall at Paston Place where, in the basement, he installed a larger Otto gas engine and Siemens' dynamo, a more powerful motor being attached beneath the new car. He later used the ground floor as a workshop and the first floor as an office with a balcony from which he could survey his transport undertaking. The extended line, now 1,400 yards in length, was opened informally on 4 April 1884, only some three months after construction began. As always, there was considerable opposition to the new project, not only from those who felt their livelihood—and even their lives—were threatened, but also from the 'fashionable' residents of Kemp Town who feared the eastwards drift of the 'hoi polloi' into their exclusive domain.

83 *The opening ceremony of Volk's Electric Railway, 4 August 1883. Magnus is standing on the left at the back of the carriage wearing his working clothes as he was working right up until the last minute. Alderman Cox, the Mayor, is at the front of the carriage and Magnus's wife, Anna, is sitting in the left-hand corner.*

84 *An 1896 poster advertising Volk's Daddy-long-legs Railway.*

85 *Volk's Daddy-long-legs Railway, 1896-1901, at the landing stage at Banjo Groyne. Magnus's 'Arch' can be seen to the left of the steps.*

86 *Rottingdean Pier, c.1900.*

By 1887, the year of Queen Victoria's golden jubilee, Magnus was in considerable financial difficulty, but in that year he came up with another brilliant invention: a horseless carriage in the form of an electric passenger 'dog-cart' powered by batteries. It had two large driving wheels and a tiller-steered front wheel. In the following year he actually constructed a larger four-wheeled version for the Sultan of Turkey. This was almost certainly the first car to be exported—even before the petrol driven version arrived in this country!

The year 1892 saw the birth of what can only be described as the 'Magnus Opus', a veritable transport dinosaur officially entitled 'The Brighton and Rottingdean Seashore Electric Tramroad' but soon to earn the sobriquet 'the Daddy-long-legs Railway'. The pretty fishing, farming and smuggling village of Rottingdean, tucked away in its own valley or dene leading between chalk cliffs to the sea, was now becoming an attraction to trippers from Brighton. The provision of a railway link became a challenge to Magnus Volk. The cliff-top was much too undulating and could not easily be reached by an extension of VER. At high tide the sea lapped, and at times ravaged, the foot of the cliffs. There was only one solution: to lay a railway along the rocky foreshore, which for much of the tidal cycle would be submerged.

The scheme involved two narrow-gauge tracks or 'roads' with an overall width of 18 ft. Ballast could not be used as the base, so each track was secured to a line of large concrete blocks embedded in the chalk. The vehicle itself comprised a luxurious enclosed saloon with plate-glass windows, surrounded by an open deck with space for the driver, and another open deck on the roof. The saloon was even equipped with an ottoman and potted palms! The overall dimensions were 50 ft. in length and 22 ft. in width. Up to 150 passengers could be carried seated or standing. The significant feature, however, was that the vehicle was carried on four 24-ft.-long legs—hence the nickname. Each leg ended in a bogie with four wheels.

The line ran for about three miles from a landing stage attached to Banjo Groyne at the end of VER to a new jetty at Rottingdean, which became known as 'Rottingdean Pier'. Beneath this jetty was installed a 60 kilowatt dynamo driven by a special steam engine of 100 brake horsepower made by Sissons and Company of Gloucester. The furnace for the boiler burnt 'anthracite peas'. This time the current had to be supplied via overhead cables carried on a line of wood poles. Trolley poles on the saloon fed the current down the legs to a pair of 25h.p. motors in the bogies. A maximum speed of eight miles per hour was intended.

This almost unbelievable railway took some four years to plan and build, being fraught with problems from the outset. Magnus had to seek financial backers and obtain parliamentary as well as council approval. Construction was formidable, as materials had to be lowered by ropes down the cliffs at various points. The generating plant had to be transported through Rottingdean in a large dray hauled by a team of horses; it was said that Magnus placated some of the gentry by supplying their houses with electric light!

The railway was eventually granted a Board of Trade certificate. *Pioneer*, as the vehicle was named, was required to carry a lifeboat and lifebuoys; in fact, its travels even became known as 'voyages'! The official opening ceremony took place on 28 November 1896 when a full complement of civic dignitaries, directors and Members of Parliament were taken on a return 'voyage' to Rottingdean. One enthusiast opined that one day such a railway might even be constructed across the Channel! However, on 4 December, just a week after the opening, a terrible storm lashed the coast. It utterly destroyed the Chain Pier and almost put an end to both VER and the new seashore railway. *Pioneer* itself was wrecked, probably by debris from the Chain Pier.

The indomitable Magnus Volk was undeterred and his railways were duly restored. He even constructed an intermediate landing-stage at Ovingdean Gap as a request stop. On 28 February 1898 'Daddy-long-legs' was honoured by conveying Edward Prince of Wales on a short trip. However, Magnus continued to be beset by problems. In 1900 sea defence works at Kemp Town caused scour, which forced the temporary closure of the seashore railway; he was even faced with the possibility of a diversion or, alternatively, of building a landing stage at Black Rock and closing the Kemp Town section altogether. Eventually, in 1901, *Pioneer* made its last voyage. It remained moored to the jetty at Ovingdean until 1910 when it was sold with the rails as scrap to a continental firm and removed in barges hauled by a tug. One might imagine wryly that it returned as bombs or shells a little later!

87 *Kemp Town Private Esplanade and Slopes, c.1890. This shows Volk's Electric Railway, but Madeira Road (Drive) had yet to be built.*

Remains of the line of concrete blocks and stumps of the landing stages at Rottingdean and Ovingdean can still be seen at low tide; also some ironwork of the landing stage at Banjo Groyne.

In the meantime, VER was not only restored but improved with new rolling-stock and a connection to Brighton's main direct-current electricity supply, the generator in the 'Arch' being replaced by a transformer and back-up batteries. In 1902, despite opposition, Magnus extended VER from Paston Place to Black Rock, with a contentious crossing over Banjo Groyne and a short viaduct on wooden piles across the scoured beach beyond. Remarkably, apart from the Aquarium Station being moved a short distance to the east, the jolly little cars of VER still trundle along the same line today, thanks to a successful rearguard action that ensured that this feature of Brighton's heritage was not closed down on its centenary in 1983.

Magnus Volk will appear again in later sections of this book; but it is appropriate to record here that he passed away peacefully at the age of 85 on 20 May 1937 at 38 Dyke Road, Brighton, which had been the family home since 1914. This semi-detached late-Regency house just to the north of Seven Dials still exists and bears a commemorative plaque, although it is now numbered 138 Dyke Road. Until recently one could still see the workshop that he built in the back garden backing onto Russell Crescent—appropriately above the railway tunnel under the Dyke Road ridge. A significant feature of the workshop was that Magnus built it around a sycamore tree that he could not bear to fell. Although the structure has been demolished, his beloved tree still remains. Magnus retained an active interest in VER and many other local projects throughout his life. During the First World War he fashioned surgical appliances for war victims in his workshop and even served as a radiographer. It is fitting that this great Brighton inventor is buried in the tranquil churchyard in Ovingdean village—just half-a-mile inland from the route of his Daddy-long-legs Railway.

Six

Motor Cars, Aeroplanes and the Suburban 'Woodby-Happeys'

Petroleum is King (American Slogan)

The end of the Victorian era was another watershed for Brighton and Hove. The twin towns were now in competition with many up-and-coming seaside resorts within easy reach of London by rail, and more and more of the affluent were choosing to travel in luxury by train to the flesh-pots of the French Riviera and Switzerland, or even aboard the new twin-screw floating hotels of the Cunard and White Star lines to America. The necessary shot in the arm came in the form of the motor vehicle, coupled with the lure of the Brighton Road and the initiative of an enterprising hotelier by the name of Harry Preston.

In the 19th century horseless carriages, driven by steam and even electricity, gas and compressed air, were comparatively rare and often regarded as unreliable satanic contraptions. By law their speed was limited to a walking pace (2 m.p.h. in town, 4 m.p.h.

88 *Motor Track, Madeira Road (Drive), c.1910.*

89 *London Road just north of Mill Road, Patcham, c.1914.*

in the country) and a person was required to walk in front carrying a red flag! The 1880s saw the development of the first successful petrol-engine vehicles by the Germans Karl Benz and Gottlieb Daimler. In 1894 one of the Benz models was imported into this country by Walter Arnold of London and used by him as the basis for the first motor car made in England. The new horseless carriage was the ideal plaything for the affluent classes, and its increasing popularity soon led to the Locomotives on the Highways Act, 1896, which raised the speed limit to 12 m.p.h. and removed the humiliating requirement of the red flag.

In jubilation, Harry Lawson's short-lived Motor Car Club staged their historic 'Emancipation Run' on 14 November 1896. By choosing the famous, but neglected, Brighton Road they put the resort firmly back on the map, this time as a fashionable motoring centre. The participants assembled for breakfast at the *Metropole Hotel* in Whitehall and, after the Earl of Winchelsea had symbolically torn up a red flag, they set off in 30 vehicles on their epic journey from Hyde Park to Brighton headed by a pilot car driven by Harry Lawson. Each entrant was provided with an instruction leaflet entitled 'Motor Car Tour to Brighton', which stated that a supply of motor oil (petrol) and lubricating oil would be available at the *White Hart*, Reigate and water at various inns on route. They were also instructed not to pass each other. However, the orderly procession, which was to have been greeted by the mayor of Brighton at Preston Park, did not quite materialise, as due to atrocious weather only 17 vehicles safely completed the journey, with long intervals in between. Ironically, the first vehicle to arrive was a Bollee steam-car, which completed the journey in 2 hours and 30 minutes. The next vehicle took twice as long!

Nevertheless, the event was an exciting spectacle, witnessed by thousands of people in London, Brighton and along the road. As more and more motor cars were imported and also manufactured in the country the concept of a convenient drive down to Brighton, with all its attractions, became firmly established. In 1901, Harry Preston (later Sir Harry), who happened to be a motoring enthusiast, restored the derelict *Royal York Hotel* in the Old

Steine, one of Brighton's oldest. Four years later he promoted a scheme to lay a tarmac surface on the Madeira Road (Drive) from the Palace Pier to Kemp Town to provide a motor-racing track nearly a mile in length. Hitherto, Brighton's streets had been mainly surfaced in crushed stone (Macadam) or wood blocks, which being dusty and stony were not ideal materials for the faster motor vehicles. Harry Preston's visionary proposal met with initial opposition from Brighton Corporation, but it was quite irresistible, not least because the new Madeira Terrace and the promenade above in Marine Parade provided a splendid grandstand.

The scheme was duly implemented, and in July 1905 Brighton's first Motor Race Week was held, set off by a magnificent display of Edwardian fashion on Ladies' Day. Many famous enthusiasts participated, including Theodore Schneider, C.S. Rolls and J.T.C. Brabazon. The main event, the 'Flying Race' for the most powerful cars, was won by the well-known Clifford Earp with a 90h.p. Napier at an incredible speed of 97 m.p.h., which astounded the thousands of spectators. An intrepid lady motorist, Miss Levitt, delighted everyone by coming fourth in the same make of car at over 77 m.p.h. The event was heralded as a triumph and established Brighton's Madeira Drive as a venue for motor sports, even to the present day.

The Brighton motor races undoubtedly had an impact on the incidence of car, and also motor cycle, ownership amongst wealthy residents and visitors, as did the gradual improvement in performance, reliability and design. Many of the earliest motor vehicles to be seen in Brighton and Hove were remarkably similar in design to the traditional horse-drawn carriages, which were supplanted over the years as the rich man's personal transport. As Lord Montagu said of the 1896 Lutzman (a primitive horseless car in the Benz idiom with solid tyres): 'one looks in vain for shafts and a quadruped'. With no registration or licensing, there are no statistics to indicate the growth in vehicle ownership in the early 20th century, but entries in the trades section of the local street directories do give a general impression. *Pike's Directory* of 1905, the year of Brighton's first Motor Race Week, lists seven firms under the heading 'Motor Manufacturers' (which included repairs and sales), whereas the equivalent in 1913 (prior to the restrictions imposed during the First World War) lists 61 such firms.

The most prominent establishment in both lists was the Grand Hotel Garage run by the Brighton, Sussex Motor and Carriage Works Ltd, who also had a carriage works in Conway Street, Hove and a showroom in King's Road, Brighton. A comprehensive range of services was advertised, including repairs, accessories, tuition in driving and 'mechanism', as well as the hire of the popular French Panhards. A significant feature was 'Carless Capel's petrol' and Pratt's motor spirit: in the early days of motoring there were few opportunities to refuel on the road, so that spare cans of petrol had to be transported on a long journey.

Many other carriage works, livery stables and blacksmiths saw fit to diversify into the new motor trade, although private and commercial horse-drawn vehicles were still prominent until well after the First World War. A rare traffic census taken at the constricted Sackville Road railway bridge in Hove on 28 August 1911 showed that 634 horse-drawn vehicles, 600 cycles, 215 hand barrows and 70 motors passed under this important bridge in one day. This also gives an indication of how popular the bicycle had become as the transport of the working and middle classes and as an economical form of commercial transport.

War is recognised as a forcing-house for technology. Once the world had recovered from the trauma of the First World War there was a tremendous leap forward by a viciously competitive motor industry in America, Britain and the continent. Mass production brought standardised, economical models within the reach of the middle classes. One of the first of these was the Model-T Ford, originally introduced in 1908, which remained in production in England and America until 1926, when Ford tooled up for the new Model-A, launched the following year. The British Austin Seven, also launched in the mid-1920s, proved to be another efficient and economical small car with an exceptionally long life.

The late 1920s and the '30s, however, saw the introduction of regular model changes with 'stylistic obsolescence', accompanied by aggressive marketing and advertising, which presented the motor car as a status symbol. One effect was the creation of a huge second-hand market, which spread motor-car ownership even further down the social scale, although it was not until after the Second World War that it was to make any serious impact on working-class transportation. In 1940, the year after petrol rationing was introduced, there were about 1.4 million cars registered in Great Britain.

The rapid development of the motor car in the inter-war period was paralleled by that of the motorised commercial vehicle: vans and lorries gradually replaced the ubiquitous carts and wagons on the streets of Brighton and Hove, while a new generation of specialised mechanical transports came into existence. Although some horse-drawn vehicles were to return during the years of petrol rationing, petroleum was indeed king by the mid-1930s, not only in the towns, but also on the downland farms, where the motor tractor eventually ousted the faithful quadruped and the steam traction engine.

In Edwardian days motorists on the Brighton Road could still encounter the occasional coach-and-four of the amateur enthusiast. The most famous was undoubtedly the millionaire Alfred Vanderbilt, who on 4 May 1908 actually inaugurated a commercial run from London to Brighton with his coach *Venture*. This nostalgic event brought enthusiastic crowds to greet his arrival at the *Metropole Hotel*. He later complemented his service with the renowned coach *Old Times*, and also introduced American trotting horses, which could cope with the better road surfaces.

Remarkably, however, mass production after the First World War brought a wave of nostalgia for those hand-built and custom-made marvels, and for the equestrian-like freedom of the open road of pre-war days. Thus, after a comparatively short period, the concept of the 'veteran car' was born. In 1927 the *Daily Sketch* sponsored a veteran car run from London to Brighton in commemoration of the famous Emancipation Run of 1896, a stipulation being that the cars entered had to be at least 21 years old. It was rather an amateurish event and the pedigree of some of the cars was suspect. Nevertheless, the run was repeated in 1928 and again in 1929, sponsored by the *Autocar* magazine and the *Daily Sketch* respectively.

In 1930 the Veteran Car Run was given a further boost when it was sponsored by the Royal Automobile Club, the oldest motoring organisation in Britain (second only to the

90 *London Road, Brighton with tram lines, c.1905.*

French club in the world). The RAC has organised the world-famous run ever since, the annual event being interrupted only by the Second World War and, also, by the petrol shortage in 1947. The event has sometimes been referred to as the 'Old Crocks' Race' and in the early years there was an element of truth in this misnomer, as until 1933 average times had been recorded: for example, in 1930 a de Dietrich achieved an average speed of 30.3 m.p.h.

Other events were to boost the Veteran Car Run. In 1930 a number of enthusiasts met at Brighton's famous *Old Ship Hotel* and formed the Veteran Car Club ('of Great Britain' was added later). This led to a frantic search for veteran models to restore to their former glory (the term now refers generally to pre-1919 vehicles; pre-1905 models being the most sought after). The seriously rich enthusiast was able to build up a collection of veteran cars while keeping up with the latest powerful models to come off the production line. In 1938 the last Brighton run before the Second World War attracted as many as 105 starters.

Around this time it was generally considered that the answer to the increase in traffic was to build more and more roads, irrespective of cost or the effect on the environment. In 1932 a plan prepared by a joint committee comprising representatives of Brighton, Hove and neighbouring authorities actually proposed a by-pass north of the Downs plus two downland 'ring roads'! Only the western section of the proposed inner ring road from Patcham to West

Hove was subsequently constructed, in effect a major improvement of Mill Road, Snakey Hill (renamed King George VI Avenue) and Hangleton Road, which previously were country lanes. A proposed new direct link from Black Rock to Roedean was also constructed, this being part of the improvement of the coast road from Brighton to Rottingdean and beyond. Although not included in the 1932 plan, a western by-pass to Patcham Village was constructed in the early 1930s as part of the improvement of the main London Road; it is interesting to note that the *Black Lion*, formerly a small inn on the Old London Road, Patcham, was rebuilt at the northern end of this by-pass as a 'roadhouse', the modern equivalent of the old coaching inn. The *Grenadier Hotel* was built as a similar hostelry on the improved Hangleton Road.

One can only conjecture how many other by-passes and ring roads might have been built across the Downs had the Second World War not interrupted the roads programme of the Ministry of Transport, which had assumed responsibility for trunk roads in 1936.

Buses, Trams, Trolleys and Taxis

It was not long after the turn of the century that public road transport turned to new-age technology. The Brighton, Hove and Preston United Omnibus Company Ltd (BHP) acquired their first experimental motor bus in 1903, and on 1 January 1904 began a service from Hove to Portslade, one of the first outside London. The vehicle was a 24h.p. Milnes-Daimler double-decker, the first of 25 which the company was to acquire in the next five years. However, in 1909, because of complaints about the noise of these motor vehicles, they supplemented their fleet with a Hallford petro-electric bus and also three Electrobuses, which could travel 30 miles without recharging. The latter were particularly successful, so 12 more were acquired the next year.

On 12 July 1906 BHP was involved in a dramatic rescue. A Vanguard bus of the London Motor Omnibus Company Ltd, on its way to Brighton, crashed on Handcross Hill with the loss of 10 lives. A BHP director, E.A. Eager, picked up doctors and equipment in one of his Milnes-Daimler buses and drove this improvised ambulance to the scene of the accident, from where he transported casualties to hospital. In those days there was no organised emergency transport service. The accident, which echoed the early railway disaster in Clayton Tunnel, provoked serious doubts in the public mind about the new motor buses.

Gradually, however, the famous horse-drawn bus services of Brighton and Hove were superseded; but partly because of wartime restrictions and the requisitioning of vehicles by the military it was not until 1916 that the last service—to Brighton station, like the first in 1840—was withdrawn. Competition from the motor buses ended the horse-drawn tramway from Aldrington to Shoreham in 1912. However, in the early war years BHP itself was exposed to competition from other operators. In 1915 the Southdown Motor Service Ltd was formed, taking over excursions, tours and country routes operated by BHP. In the same year Thomas Tilling Ltd, a successful London-based company, obtained licences from Hove Corporation to operate 12 buses, although only five were used initially because of the refusal of Brighton Corporation to allow the company to pick up passengers over the boundary

91 *Brighton station—transport interchange, c.1905. A Brighton tram at its terminus, a horse-bus and a private carriage are serving railway passengers.*

unless they had a return ticket issued in Hove! These buses operated from premises in Lower Holland Road, Hove. In 1916 BHP was purchased by Thomas Tilling, thus disappearing in the same year as its horse-drawn buses.

Brighton Corporation's initial reluctance to allow Thomas Tilling to ply for hire in the borough was undoubtedly the result, in part, of the protection from competition for their own cherished tramways, inaugurated on 25 November 1901 and virtually completed by 1904. Initially the central tram terminus was at the southern end of the Valley Gardens opposite Church Street, but in 1903 the tramlines were extended to the so-called 'Aquarium' terminus at the southern end of the Old Steine. From there the completed network fanned out to the extremities of Brighton's built-up area, providing seven regular services from the new terminus via Valley Gardens, as follows: Brighton Station via North Road and Queen's Road; Tivoli Crescent North via London Road, New England Road, Seven Dials and Dyke Road; Ditchling Road (Five Ways) Circular via Ditchling Road, Preston Drove, Beaconsfield Road and London Road; Ditchling Road (Five Ways) Circular, the reverse of the above; Lewes Road (Preston Barracks) via Lewes Road (the depot, workshops and offices were sited near the end of this route); Race Hill via Elm Grove; and Upper Rock Gardens via Elm Grove, Queen's Park Road and Egremont Place.

In addition, there was a regular 'cross-country' service from Seven Dials to Upper Rock Gardens via New England Road, Viaduct Road, Union Road, Elm Grove, Queen's Park Road and Egremont Place. On race days, there were special services from Brighton station to the Race Hill, as well as from the Aquarium terminus; and in the summer a special tourist service ran, complete with a guide. There were no direct east-west routes through the main town centre: Western Road, North Street and St James's Street were judged to be too narrow, while King's Road and Marine Parade were considered to be too 'environmentally sensitive'. The Corporation hoped to extend the tramway into Hove from

92 *Brighton Corporation trams at the Racehill terminus, c.1905. There was a cross-town service for race-goers from the railway station.*

Seven Dials along Goldsmid Road, and provision was made in the track layout, but this route never materialised.

Direct current electricity at 550 volts was fed to a 40/50h.p. motor on each tramcar by way of overhead wires supported by iron standards, the supply being collected by a trolley arm, which had to be reversed by means of a rope when the tram reached the end of a journey. The 3ft. 6in. gauge tracks were laid double, except on some particularly narrow sections of road. The tramcars, which were nearly 30 ft. in length, were open-topped and painted in an attractive livery of chocolate-brown and cream, although liberal advertising was incorporated on the 'modesty' panel surrounding the upper deck, with its reversible lattice seats.

The Brighton trams contributed to the demise of the horse-drawn omnibuses, especially as they could tackle hills that were too steep for the quadrupeds. However, in the inter-war period the trams were increasingly challenged by the motor vehicles that shared their routes, passengers often having to negotiate a line of vehicle traffic to gain access. Cyclists were also known to get stuck in the recessed tramlines! In 1938 Brighton Corporation secured an Act of Parliament to replace their trams with trolley-buses and diesel motor buses. The former still required an overhead supply of electricity but were free to manoeuvre within the limits of their trolley-arms. The changeover took several months, the last of the trams making a sentimental journey from the Aquarium terminus to the Lewes Road Depot on 1 September 1939, just two days before war was declared.

Both Brighton and Hove Corporations had earlier experimented with trolley-buses—in 1913 and 1914 respectively—probably influenced by the BHP company's successful battery-electric buses. A special wired circuit was provided for an RET 'Railless' trolley on a part of the Ditchling Road tramway, while overhead wires on standards were erected on a route from Hove station to Church Road (St Aubyns) via Goldstone Villas and George Street for an ultra-smart 'gearless, trackless' trolley-bus provided by the Cedes-Stoll Company. Probably because of the First World War, neither system proceeded beyond the experimental stage. The equipment in Hove, which gave every indication of permanence, was dismantled in 1915.

During the inter-war period Thomas Tilling greatly extended its motor-bus network throughout Greater Brighton, with a variety of vehicle types. It operated over some roads covered by Brighton Tramways, although the tram routes themselves were exclusive territory. In 1929 Tilling experimented with a number of new double-decker buses with covered tops, and in the following year began to replace its fleet of Tilling-Stevens open-topped vehicles, still reminiscent of the old horse-buses, with AEC Regent buses, streamlined in the current idiom and resplendent in red and cream livery. A number of single-deck Dennis Dart 'mini-buses' were also added to the fleet in the 1930s, these providing a more flexible service on routes such as that from Portslade station to the fringe of the Downs at Mile Oak, which was still largely open country.

In 1935 Thomas Tilling formed a wholly owned subsidiary, the Brighton, Hove and District Omnibus Company Ltd (BHD), with headquarters, workshops and main garages

93 *Waggonette to Devil's Dyke, c.1905.*

94 *Charabanc outing from* The Eclipse, *Montgomery Street, Hove, 1913. Charlie Povey has the concertina.*

95 *Hove Corporation experimental trolley-bus, 1914, at the bottom of Goldstone Villas. Note the proliferation of bicycles, including the ubiquitous errand boy's bike.*

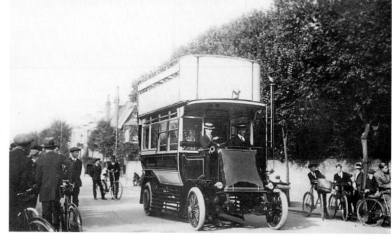

96 *The Paddocks, Mile Oak, Portslade, c.1905. Such pleasure gardens were popular venues for outings and treats. Note that this was out in the country before development commenced. Later, Mile Oak could be reached by a single-decker bus from Portslade station.*

at Tilling's Conway Street premises in Hove, and another garage at Whitehawk Road, Brighton. The new company subsequently negotiated a 21-year agreement with Brighton Corporation to pool local services. This was incorporated in a 1938 Act of Parliament, under which the Corporation would operate 27½ per cent of the total vehicle mileage and the new BHD company the rest. It was a significant step towards a system of integrated public transport after years of wasteful competition and dispute.

In parallel with the urban bus services of Tilling/BHD, Southdown extended their stage-carriage country services from Brighton. Their double- and single-deckers in a livery of apple green and butter yellow with ornate lettering became a familiar sight in Sussex and beyond. In 1921 there were services to Portsmouth, Worthing, Eastbourne, Lewes, Uckfield, Lingfield, Horsham and Petworth, as well as a joint service with the Maidstone and District Company to Hawkhurst. In the summer of that year it was possible to travel to London by stage-carriage buses: by Southdown to Handcross, by the East Surrey Company onto Reigate, and from there by London General to the capital. The overall journey took over five hours but the total fare (6s. 8d.) was cheaper than both rail and the open-topped charabanc through-services. Southdown also ran many excursions and tours from Brighton by coach and charabanc. Many other operators brought visitors into the town, Madeira Drive being used as a convenient seaside coach and charabanc park.

Until 1933 Southdown had no bus station in Brighton for its extensive country services, but had to operate from the roadside at the Aquarium near its offices and coach station in Steine Street. It had wanted to build a bus station at the east end of the Aquarium in 1922, but the proposal was rejected at a Borough Council meeting by one vote. In 1933 agreement was reached to use Pool Valley off the Old Steine, with terminal facilities at the rear of the former *Royal York Hotel*, which had been acquired by the council for office purposes. Thus, the site of the Saxon harbour on the Wellesbourne was once again in use as a transport facility! At the time Southdown also had garages and workshops in Freshfield Road and Edward Street in Brighton, and in Victoria Road, Portslade.

Motor buses brought about the demise of the horse-drawn buses in the First World War, but it took much longer for the motorised taxi-cabs to do the same to the horse-drawn cabs, which still had a certain fashionable image (the author can recall them still plying for hire at Hove station from a rank at the top of Goldstone Villas in the early 1930s). The first motorised taxi-cabs appeared about 1908, an early operator being the Provincial Taxi Cab Co. with a garage on the east side of Queen's Road near Brighton station, their taxis mainly British Siddeleys and Wolseleys. By 1914 several firms were operating from garages in Brighton, but many of their vehicles were subsequently commandeered for war service.

After the war many ex-servicemen used their gratuities and savings to enter the taxi-cab business, encouraged by Brighton Council's readiness to issue licences; but fierce competition coupled with the Depression in the late 1920s brought disaster, especially as many of the vehicles were uneconomic motors dumped on the second-hand market by the wealthy. The Brighton and Hove Taxicab Association was duly formed and convinced the

97 *A Vanguard London to Brighton bus has crashed on Handcross Hill, 1906.*

98 *Traffic congestion in Western Road, c.1934, with the road being widened on the north side.*

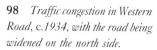

99 *Western Road, c.1905. From near Hampton Place westwards into Hove the road was wider than the section to the east, so that there was no need for widening in the 1930s; consequently, apart from the traffic, the street can still be identified today.*

council to limit the number of licences. In the mid-1930s Britax, a private hire firm that did not need a licence, entered the market with a fleet of new 12h.p. Austins offering competitive fares and no charge prior to coming to a customer's door. In the face of the new competition the independent 'cabbies' met at the instigation of one of their number, Gordon Moody, and formed a co-operative organisation, the Streamline Association, Brighton, which made an application to the council to downgrade their own licences from first- to second-class. The former covered the superior limousine type of vehicle with a partition between the driver and the passengers. Progress was slow at first, as the public at large were not particularly keen on taxis, but in the following year Streamline reached a successful agreement giving them the sole right to operate from Brighton station. In 1938 this association established new headquarters in Middle Street, with a telephone switchboard and petrol pumps, and gradually replaced the members' individual vehicles with Standard Flying 14's with distinctive black and cream bonnets. Despite the trials and tribulations of war, competition and deregulation, Streamline survived to celebrate its diamond jubilee.

Like the railways, buses and taxis played a vital role in the Second World War, despite many adversities such as petrol rationing, blackout working, air raids, lack of vehicle replacements, operating curfews and staff shortages—the latter being alleviated by the infallible lady 'clippies'. A few buses were even equipped for producer-gas operation, supplemented by petrol, the gas being produced by burning anthracite. The first bus to be converted had its equipment installed under the rear staircase, but when this later exploded at the Patcham terminus the bus was restored to diesel operation. Trailers were subsequently introduced, but even then there was an objection that the blackout was being infringed!

The agreement between BHD and Brighton Corporation undoubtedly benefited both organisations during the war, although the company had to defer its participation in trolley-bus operation until 1944. Southdown suffered the loss of its express services, but continued to operate local stage-carriage services to parts of Brighton that were previously outside the borough, such as Moulsecombe. This company actually provided coaches for the war effort and even formed its own 'Dads' Army' (Home Guard) unit!

Emergency Services: Police, Fire, Ambulance

At the beginning of the 20th century the Brighton Borough Police Force had five sub-stations in addition to their headquarters at the Town Hall. The first record of mechanised transport for normal police duties involved the purchase of a pedal cycle in 1907 for the use of patrol sergeants, and in 1912 a cycle was provided for each of the six stations—for emergency use! Soon after the First World War, which saw the introduction of women special constables to augment a depleted force, motor vehicles were being used for normal duties. In 1922 there is a record of a motor cycle and, also, a motor car for the permanent use of the chief constable; by 1929 there was, in addition, a Morris van and one 'fast' car in use. The fleet had only increased to eight motor vehicles (excluding ambulances) by 1937, but this restricted mobility was offset by the fact that four years previously some thirty patrols had been equipped with wireless transmitters/receivers—this, surprisingly, being regarded as a world

100 *Wounded Indian soldiers from the First World War outside the Royal Pavilion. The Pavilion was said to be the most picturesque hospital in the world.*

101 *The Prince of Wales unveiling The Chattri, 1 February 1921. This fine monument to Indian soldiers who died at the Royal Pavilion still stands proudly on the Downs north of Patcham at the site of the burning ghat where many who had died were cremated.*

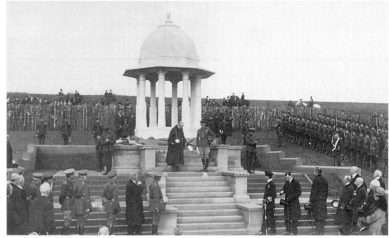

102 *The 2nd Eastern General Hospital, Stanford Road School in the First World War. Although not as luxurious as the Royal Pavilion, this school was another of the buildings taken over as an emergency hospital for the war wounded.*

first for Brighton. At the same time 163 members of the force had learnt to drive in a second-hand car.

The Hove Borough Police Force seems to have become mechanised earlier than their Brighton counterparts, as there is a record of a pedal cycle being acquired in 1902. However, the first motor vehicle was, apparently, not purchased until 1926: a VSA model G26 De-Luxe motor cycle and sidecar, which shortly afterwards was used by a patrol to apprehend a gang of housebreakers in a getaway car after a break-in in New Church Road. The first motor car, a Crossley, was acquired in the following year. More motor vehicles were obtained in the 1930s, and by 1938 one of these had been equipped with wireless. Communication was improved shortly afterwards by the erection of telephone pillars and kiosks linked to the police station at Hove Town Hall in Church Road.

In the early years of the 20th century the Brighton Police and Volunteer Fire Brigades replaced their horse-drawn and steam fire engines with motorised appliances, some of which were actually designed by Brighton's fire chief La Croix and partly built at the brigade's headquarters. The two brigades continued to share responsibilities until after the First World War. However, on Christmas night 1920 there was the greatest conflagration since the Queen's Road fire of 1880. This led to another reappraisal of the fire-fighting arrangements, as a result of which, in 1921, a full-time professional fire brigade was established with its fire station at Preston Circus. The police lost their brigade and, amidst much controversy, the volunteer brigade was disbanded. The fire station at Preston Circus, headquarters of the police fire brigade since 1901 following the reconstruction of this major junction when the tram lines were laid, was rebuilt in 1938 and still remains the headquarters, augmented by a local station in Roedean Road.

The full-time Hove Corporation Fire Service superseded the volunteer brigade in 1913, and in the following year the first motorised fire engine was acquired to replace a 'steamer' which had been in use for about ten years. The new brigade continued to use the inadequate fire station in George Street until 1926, when new premises were opened in Hove Street. At that time Portslade-by-Sea Urban District Council had a fire station in Church Road, Portslade, and the building can still be identified.

Before the Second World War there was no properly organised public ambulance service. Such arrangements as did exist—apart from private hire facilities—were on an *ad hoc* basis between the police and the ever-ready volunteers of the St John Ambulance Brigade and the Red Cross. Brighton police acquired an early type of motor ambulance in 1902, apparently to replace a 'litter' which was little more than a hand-barrow comprising a stretcher on wheels and sometimes used to transport legless drunks! In the late 1920s they also had a 'combined ambulance and prison van'. In addition, some hospitals, such as Brighton General and Bevendean, had ambulances to transport their patients.

The Second World War saw the emergency services placed on a wartime footing, with the formation of the Civil Defence Ambulance Service (mainly to deal with air-raid casualties), the nationalisation of all the fire brigades, and the amalgamation of the local police forces into a Sussex Police Force.

Traffic Control and Management

As the number of vehicles increased so the police became more and more involved in traffic control. Initially this was limited to enforcing the 12 m.p.h. speed limit, but the Motor Car Act 1903 required cars to be registered and motorists to be at least 17 and licensed; no test was required, but dangerous driving became an indictable offence. In Hove the wide Kingsway along the seafront positively encouraged speeding, and this had to be monitored by the mounted police. A bizarre edict of Hove Watch Committee in 1905 was that the police should also stop persons 'driving' perambulators two abreast on the pavement! Macho motorists resented the restrictions on their freedom, and for a time an informal 'Brighton Road Motor Patrol' with a fleet of cars and cycles carried red flags to warn motorists of police traps. The Automobile Association had a similar function when it was formed in 1905: after explicit warnings were declared illegal, members were advised to question AA scouts who failed to salute!

During the inter-war period the rapid increase in the number of motor vehicles (which reached the one million mark in 1923) necessitated the introduction of a series of traffic regulation measures, which further taxed the resources of the police. In Brighton, officers were on point duty in many of the main streets from the early 1920s, and in 1925 gyratory systems had to be introduced at major junctions, such as the Aquarium, Preston Circus and Seven Dials. In 1927 Brighton's well-known semaphore system was introduced at the West Street/King's Road junction and in the next two years at Preston Circus, Seven Dials and Old Steine: this involved a constable in a central stand operating signal arms showing a stop sign. By 1935 the semaphores had been superseded by traffic lights, 14 sets being in operation in that year. Parking was also beginning to contribute to traffic congestion and road hazards, and the first unilateral waiting system was introduced in the narrow East Street about the same time. In Hove, traffic congestion was less of a problem because of the exceptionally wide streets, but in 1921 police were on point duty at the Holland Road/ Western Road and Sackville Road/New Church Road junctions, and in 1930 the first traffic lights were installed at the latter intersection.

After nearly sixty years of complaint, serious traffic congestion eventually led to the widening of Brighton's Western Road and West Street during the period 1926-35: this necessitated the demolition of buildings on the north and west sides respectively. Other widening took place in North Street and Castle Square; and Junction Road was formed between Queen's Road and Surrey Street outside Brighton Central station. Despite many proposals to demolish the Victorian Clock Tower, this monument is a survivor of the road-widening era.

Building Development of the Motor Era

In Edwardian times Brighton continued to expand northwards on a wide front into its new Preston territory from Dyke Road to Lewes Road. The influence of motor vehicles was not then significant, so the new housing tended to be urban in character, sited within walking distance of Preston Park station or the trams in Dyke Road, Ditchling Road (Five Ways) and Lewes Road (Preston Barracks). Except for some larger properties in the Harrington

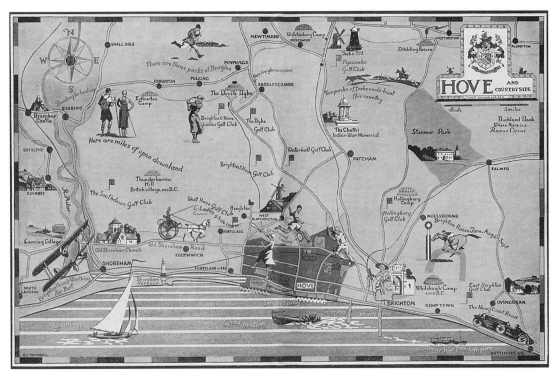

103 *Publicity map for Hove, 1935-6. These were the days of competition between Hove and Brighton, which is why Hove is shown much larger that its rival, which hardly exists east of the Palace Pier! There was even a scheme for a pier at Hove in the 1930s.*

Road area north of Preston Park, the new streets comprised mainly terraces or semi-detached pairs of middle-class red-brick houses in the decorative style popular at this time. The need for private garages was seldom anticipated. Similar development took place in East Hove south and north of the railway line up to the Old Shoreham Road, as well as in the Aldrington area where the gap between Hove and Portslade-by-Sea was narrowed. As a result of this expansion two new railway halts were opened: Holland Road (west side) and Aldrington Halt (replacing Dyke Junction) at the top of Tamworth Road.

After the First World War the pattern of development was increasingly influenced by the motor car and motor bus. In layout and character it was to some extent inspired by the Garden City movement initiated by Ebenezer Howard. Thousands of people of modest means aspired to live in a semi-detached house or bungalow in a leafy suburb or 'dormitory' village. An informal layout of winding roads, culs-de-sac and abundant greenery became the vogue. Nevertheless, there was some reluctance on the part of estate developers to provide space for the car, with the result that garages were often squeezed in at the back of houses accessed from that common cause of neighbour dispute, the shared driveway.

The post-war government of Lloyd George established the principle that housing— particularly for the working classes—was a social problem that should be the concern of

104 *Advert by Braybons the builders to attract the 'Woodby-Happeys', 1935-6. A house for less than £1 a week would surely have attracted anyone!*

local authorities, supported by government subsidies. This led to the development of several council estates in Brighton and Hove, which to varying degree reflected the new trend in style and layout. Brighton's first estate, at Moulsecombe on the Lewes road, was commenced in 1923: this necessitated a part of Patcham parish (then in Steyning East Rural District) being transferred to the borough. The estate earned praise as a 'garden suburb' closely related to its downland setting and complemented by the superb Moulsecombe Wild Park. It was, however, something of a dormitory settlement, some three miles from the town centre and dependent upon a bus service which some residents found expensive, particularly during the Depression (it was to be 50 years before Moulsecombe station was constructed). Other council estates followed, the largest being Whitehawk and Manor Farm on the eastern outskirts of Brighton. The new estates were associated with slum clearance and the relief of overcrowding, particularly in the Carlton Hill district. Hove Council's Knoll Estate in West Hove was commenced in the mid-1920s in that part of Aldrington situated north of Old Shoreham Road.

Pressure for private housing across the existing boundaries of Brighton and Hove and around the downland villages of Patcham, Rottingdean and Ovingdean led to a large-scale revision of local authority areas in 1928. The rather peculiar Steyning East Rural District Council was abolished and its constituent parishes reallocated to adjoining authorities: Patcham was added to Brighton Borough; Preston Rural, West Blatchington and Hangleton to Hove Borough; and Portslade (Rural), which included the old village, to Portslade-by-Sea Urban District. The parishes of Rottingdean, Ovingdean and Falmer (southern part only) in Newhaven Rural District were also added to Brighton, which increased its land area more than threefold. In addition, largely through the initiative of alderman Sir Herbert Carden, who was responsible for many improvements over the years, more than 10,000 acres of farmland, within and outside the new borough boundaries, came into the freehold of Brighton Corporation. Much of this land, such as the Devil's Dyke Estate, was acquired to protect both the downland and the water catchment area.

Between the wars, particularly in the 1930s, low-density suburbia spread rapidly into the downland fringe thanks to the flexibility offered by the car and motor bus. By the

Second World War, when house building virtually ceased, the western flank of Hollingbury Hill was in course of development above the critical 300 ft.contour, as was the Tongdean area west of the London-Brighton railway line. In the same period development took place at Hollingdean and Roedean; the villages of Rottingdean and Ovingdean became linked by new suburban development; and virtually new suburban settlements came into being at Woodingdean and Saltdean, the former having its origin as a pioneering community of shack-type dwellings.

In Hove, by 1939, the Shirley Drive area east and north of Hove Park, which included the Stanford Estate, was substantially developed with larger houses to form a contiguous built-up area with Brighton along Dyke Road. Further to the west, Hove had extended northwards as far as the hamlet of West Blatchington, and even beyond Hangleton Road (part of the ring road) in the vicinity of the *Grenadier Hotel*. Only five years before the branch line closed, the suburban Rowan Halt (south of Rowan Avenue) was built on the Dyke Railway to serve the new Aldrington Manor Estate and, thereby attract a new clientele.

105 *Cromwell Road and Davigdor Road, Hove, c.1905. At the junction with Holland Road can be seen Davigdor Road School, the power station,* Palmeira Hotel *and the newly built Presbyterian church. The junction was dubbed 'Education, Illumination, Intoxication and Damnation Corner'! Only the hotel now survives.*

106 *Hove Manor, Hove Street, 1914. The house, built c.1785 by John Vallance, was demolished in the 1930s and Hove Manor flats were built. The family name lives on in the nearby Vallance Road and Gardens. The range of farm buildings to the north was demolished in the 1920s and replaced by Hove Fire Station (now flats) and offices.*

107 *Expanding Preston, c.1914. Looking north-east from a point above Millers Road towards Hollingbury Hill. In the foreground is Preston Grammar School, built in 1899, and behind the school is the London–Brighton railway. St Peter's Church, Preston Manor and the old village are amongst the trees. Preston Drove can be seen climbing the hill to Fiveways in Ditchling Road.*

108 *Aerial view of Hove, c.1935. In the foreground is Adelaide Crescent and Palmeira Square, and in the distance can be seen development on the Downs in the Shirley Drive area.*

109 *St Helen's Church, Hangleton, c.1910. The church, seen from the south, dates from Norman times, and until the early 1950s was comparatively isolated. The site of the ancient village located north of the church was excavated by the Brighton and Hove Archaeological Society before and during suburban development. The results confirmed the probability that the already impoverished village was finally deserted as a result of the Black Death in 1348 (report by E.W. Holden in Vol. 101, Sussex Archaeological Collections). The church, St Helen's Park (where the dewpond was located) and Hangleton Manor to the south now form a conservation area.*

It is said that one estate agent even advertised a bogus 'Hangleton Halt' further up the line! Portslade-by-Sea also developed extensively during the inter-war period, initially linking up with Fishersgate (part of Southwick) and Southern Cross, and eventually with Old Portslade Village north of Old Shoreham Road.

Much of the modern development in Brighton and Hove, both before and after the Second World War, took the form of estates with their own schools, shops, open spaces and other community facilities. Although most are commendable from a design and functional point of view, the buildings are rarely as striking in the wider townscape as their Victorian counterparts. One of the exceptions is Varndean School (originally the Girls' Secondary School built in 1926, but now, with recent additions, a Community Comprehensive Technology College), which, although long and low, stands in a dominating position on high ground at the top of Balfour Road overlooking extensive playing fields. Varndean Boys' Secondary School in Surrenden Road (now the Varndean Sixth Form College) was built in 1931, sharing a campus of 55 acres with the Girls' School. Together with Moulsecoomb Senior School, which was built about the same time, it was attractively designed as long two-storey buildings with open arched aisles in a 1930s idiom. The provision of playing fields has been an important feature of modern schools compared with those of the Victorian era, whose pupils had—and in some cases still have—to use public recreation grounds often located at some distance.

The extensive development during the first four decades of the 20th century put pressure on water supply and sewerage, necessitating improvements to the system, including the construction of additional pumping stations at Mile Oak (1900), Saltdean (1924) and Balsdean (1936).

In parallel with the new suburban development social changes began to take place within the old urban area. As early as the First World War some of the erstwhile fashionable houses in Kemp Town and Hove proved to be too large to run as the days of cheap domestic staff receded. As a result such properties have been progressively converted into flats and class distinctions blurred. By the 1920s new light industries were providing employment opportunities for young people who would formerly have entered domestic service, in particular the Dubarry Perfumery Co. and the Standard Tablet Co. on the north side of Hove station.

At the time of the first post-war census in 1951, taken before the impetus for development started once more, the population of Brighton, Hove and Portslade was 239,447, compared with 165,227 in 1901 (excluding a small population in the areas added in 1928), an increase of about 45 per cent; but this does not tell the whole story, as much of the new housing in settlements beyond the administrative boundaries, such as Peacehaven, Telscombe Cliffs, Southwick and Hassocks, was occupied by people who worked in the seaside towns or had retired from there.

Cinemas, Dance Halls and Variety Theatres

If churches and chapels were a prominent feature of the building boom of the Victorian era, then the equivalent in the first half of the 20th century must surely have been the palaces of entertainment. Without undue exaggeration, it can be said that Hove was the forerunner of Hollywood! James Williamson, a chemist at 44 Church Road, Hove, was a pioneer of the motion picture at the turn of the century and made a number of short films. The monthly *Hove Parish Magazines* for 1897 show that as early as 19 January that year he gave a demonstration of his 'cinematograph' in Hove Town Hall on the occasion of the annual prize-giving to children of the day and Sunday schools. Then at a similar children's treat on 23 September in the same venue he gave a more extensive demonstration. As the report states:

> Three of these living photographs were from the London Jubilee procession, the first showing the Naval Brigade, the next the Colonial troops, and the last the Queen's carriage. Another picture showed the Hove Jubilee procession going up The Drive; another, the Hove sea-wall in rough weather, and another the sea-going car on its way to Rottingdean. Mr. Butler played suitable selections [on the organ] during the exhibition of the pictures, and the patriotic airs accompanying the Jubilee procession were taken up vociferously ... More living pictures followed [an interlude by a ventriloquist!], Mr. Williamson shewing scenes on Westminster Bridge, and at a bull fight, at the Hove Regatta, cutlass drill by the Hove Coastguard, cricket and football, and children at play.

The excellent Hove Museum has a special room where short films made by Williamson and other pioneers are shown.

A few years later James Williamson built a small studio off Wilbury Road, Hove, which was taken over by another pioneer, George Albert Smith, a lecturer in astronomy, who became well known as the inventor of the colour system. The word 'Kinemacolor' can still be seen on the north wall of the studio from the railway line just to the west of the Wilbury

Road bridge. George Smith had earlier built a film studio in St Ann's Well Gardens, Hove, said to have been the first of its kind in the world. He even exported many of his short films to America! His name is associated with that of a Brighton resident, George Darling, who made Smith's first movie camera. Made at a small factory in Preston Village, Darling's cameras became standard for the new industry, and were even used to film the Boer War.

Another pioneer, William Frieze-Green, took out a patent on a movie camera in 1898 when he lived in London, but he subsequently moved to Brighton and is commemorated by a plaque at 20b Middle Street. He probably came to the town, like other film makers, because of the favourable atmospheric conditions. The story of his life was told in the 1951 Festival of Britain film *The Magic Box* starring Robert Donat. Brighton has featured in many films over the years, not only because of its atmospheric conditions and setting, but also on account of its raffish reputation, particularly as the place for an easy divorce (aided by the professional correspondent!), a theme which was exploited in *The Gay Divorcee* (1934) starring Fred Astaire and Ginger Rogers and, more recently, in *The End of the Affair* (2000) starring Ralph Fiennes and Julianne Moore. More films with a location in Brighton are referred to later in the book.

As the film industry progressed in the early 20th century many small independent cinemas opened up in Brighton and Hove, some adapting existing premises and others purpose-built. The only one surviving from that era is the Duke of York's at Preston Circus. The first of a new breed of super-cinema, The Regent, was opened in 1921 on the east side of Queen's Road near the Clock Tower. In a way, it was ahead of its time, as it was the development of the 'talkies' in the late 1920s that really inaugurated the era of these luxury cinemas, veritable Art Deco palaces where the patrons were really pampered. In Brighton came the Savoy in East Street (built on the site of the old Brill's Baths), the Astoria in Gloucester Place, the Odeon in West Street and another Odeon in Kemp Town, which suffered bomb damage in the Second World War. In Hove there was the Lido, at the top of Denmark Villas near the railway station, and the Granada in Portland Road. A feature of these modern cinemas was the organ interlude featuring the 'mighty Wurlitzer', which rose majestically with its organist from a pit in front of the screen.

Ballroom dancing paralleled the popularity of the cinema and the two

110 *Advertisement for the Lido Cinema, Ballroom and Café, 1935-6.*

111 *Jack Sheppard's Entertainers, Brighton seafront, 1919. Brighton's own 'Cheekie Chappy', Max Miller, is on the far right. Concert parties were a popular entertainment on the seafront and the piers in the early part of the 20th century.*

sometimes went hand-in-hand. For example, the Regent Dance Hall above the cinema in Queen's Road had a national reputation and will always be associated with the name of Sid Dean and his Band. Hove's Lido Cinema, which actually started life as an ice-rink, had a ballroom at the rear, where in the early war years the author played sax and clarinet with Den Francis and his Maestros of Melody. This was at a time when many professional musicians had been called up and there were opportunities for teenage amateurs to play for people anxious to find refuge from the wretched 'blackout'. However, perhaps the most famous of Brighton's dance halls was Sherry's in West Street, which had a gallery where one could listen to the band and watch the dancing over afternoon tea. It is all a far cry from the frenetic discos and nightclubs in Brighton today!

The variety theatres of Brighton, successors to the music halls and 'penny gaffs' of the Victorian era, were also widely known. One of these, in New Road near the Theatre Royal, has an incredible history. It started life in 1854 as Wright's Music Hall, but after a fire in 1867 it was rebuilt as the New Oxford, said to be the last to have a 'chairman' to compère the performances. It was burnt down again in 1892 and rebuilt as the Empire; but in 1905 it became the Coliseum of Varieties, only to be renamed the Court Theatre in 1907. This flourished until the late 1930s when it changed to a cinema of the same name. After the war it became the Dolphin Theatre, then Her Majesty's Theatre and finally the Paris Cinema until it was demolished in 1963 and replaced by an office block! The most famous variety theatre in Brighton throughout the first half of the 20th century was undoubtedly the Hippodrome in Middle Street, which opened in 1901, although in

112 *A carnival procession along Madeira Drive in the 1920s. Such events, now organised by the Lions and other charities, are still popular.*

113 *Backstage at the Palace Pier Theatre, c.1936. Stage electrician Bob Fines is seated on the right. Between the wars there was dancing at the end of the pier to the music of the Bert Green Band.*

114 *Tommy Trinder, star of Jimmy Hunter's* Brighton Follies *at the Palace Pier, c.1936.*

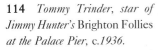

the previous few years the building had been an ice-rink. Many well-known artists performed there, including Brighton's own celebrated comedian Max Miller and the famous Crazy Gang. Sadly, the theatre closed in 1965 and became a bingo hall, but the ornate interior is still intact and one hopes, perhaps in vain, that it might once again bring variety to Brighton. This was not the first Hippodrome in the town, as the French Ginnett circus family had opened their Royal Hippodrome in Park Crescent in 1876. It was some way from the town centre, but Tilling's stables were opposite and their horse-buses carried visitors to the circus for free. Magnus Volk is believed to have helped Fred Ginnett introduce electric lighting, even before it was brought to the London theatres. Ginnett later built a new Hippodrome in North Road, renamed the Eden Theatre in 1894, and later the Grand Theatre, which, like other establishments, became known for both cinema and variety shows.

Both the Palace Pier and the West Pier had theatres at the seaward end that staged popular variety shows and plays, despite the rather long walk in inclement weather. During the summer and pantomime seasons between the wars the author's father, Bob Fines, was stage electrician on the Palace Pier. In their boyhoods, the author and his brother Bob spent many happy hours on their Dad's 'perch' backstage, watching shows such as Jimmy Hunter's *Brighton Follies*, starring Tommy Trinder and introducing a young songbird by the name of Betty Driver, better known today for her appearances in Granada Television's *Coronation Street*.

The Railways Fight Back

Although the LBSCR company lost some of its first-class clientèle in Edwardian times, it was not until after the First World War that the company experienced serious competition from 'King Petroleum'; the trippers and holidaymakers continued to flock down Queen's Road from Brighton station to a seafront which in those glorious summers was as crowded as ever. Even in the war years Brighton thrived at the expense, not only of the Continental resorts but also of the North Sea ones, perceived to be at risk from shelling and Zeppelin raids.

In the aftermath of the war the coalition government led by Lloyd George was faced with a disorganised national rail system comprising some 120 independent undertakings, some in serious financial difficulty. The possibility of nationalisation was rejected in favour of amalgamating the undertakings into four regional companies. Thus, in 1923, the famous LBSCR name disappeared when the network was absorbed by the new Southern Railway Company (SR). The Brighton Works continued to build locomotives and rolling stock but in a new livery of dark green.

Faced with increasing competition from motor cars and coaches on the Brighton Road, SR invested in the electrification of the main lines to the coast. By 1925 electric trains powered by an overhead line were running from London to Coulsdon. Four years later this section was converted to the third-rail system of supply, and in 1931 work began on continuing this system (coupled with new signalling) down to Brighton and along the coast. Electric trains replaced the steam trains on 1 January 1933: it was regarded as a revolutionary step

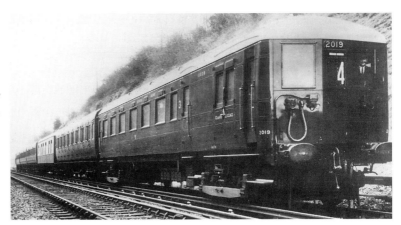

115 *'Southern Electric', 1933, the first of the electric trains and Southern Railway's answer to the motor car.*

and attracted much attention from the press. The new service was considered to be fast, frequent, clean and reliable, one of the notable advantages being the smooth acceleration of trains out of the stations. On the following Easter Monday some 129,000 visitors came to Brighton by train.

At the same time SR set out to encourage Londoners to live at the seaside whilst still working in the capital by offering competitive season ticket rates. The war had already given commuting a boost, as many London businessmen had thought it safer to move their families to the seaside. The local authorities encouraged the trend, motivated by what many councillors considered to be a prestigious growth in population and rateable value. This attitude was exemplified by Hove Corporation's lavish publicity guides in the 1930s, in which Wilhelmina Stitch told the story of a middle-class family, the 'Woodby-Happeys', who came to Hove on holiday by Pullman train only to become privileged residents in the new leafy Suburbia-by-the-Sea: 'and when they stepped forth into the bright sunshine after a grey day in London, they did indeed feel they had entered fairyland'! In those days Hove Council actually envisaged that the town could expand northwards into the downland valleys leading towards the Devil's Dyke: downland preservation at best meant limiting development to the 300 ft. contour. And we never learnt what happened to the Woodby-Happeys after Hitler interrupted their seaside idyll!

The SR Company also helped promote the hiking boom of the 1930s by offering 'Go as you Please' and other cheap tickets to clubs and individuals. Their evocative Art Deco posters and walking guides (written by S.P.B. Mais) have become treasured railway memorabilia. However, not all lines could match the competition of the motor vehicle. On 2 January 1933 the urban Kemp Town branch was closed, except for freight; and on 31 December 1938 the Devil's Dyke railway was closed, unable to compete with the motor buses that ran all the way to the summit. A small one-man-operated steam 'railbus' with automatic stoking had been introduced on the line in the latter years, but to no avail.

Long-distance freight was one area in which the railway remained dominant. In the first decade of the 20th century the main goods yards at Brighton station (Cheapside) and Kemp Town station were augmented by the construction of new goods yards at Sackville

Road and Holland Road in Hove. These goods yards, together with sidings at Portslade and Lewes Road stations, were magnets for local commercial road transport. Various undertakings, in particular coal and builders' merchants, established depots on the sites. It was an integrated system that exploited the particular advantages of rail and road: in those days only an 'old India hand' would have known the meaning of the word 'juggernaut'.

The Brighton Railway Works experienced a decline in the first half of the 20th century. In 1901 marine engineering was transferred to Newhaven and in 1912 carriage construction was moved to new works at Lancing. Then, in the late 1920s, much of the locomotive engineering was transferred to Eastleigh and Ashford. However, there was a revival during the Second World War when the first steam locomotives for about twenty years were built at Brighton, including *Fighter Command*, one of the famous 'Battle of Britain' class, weighing 128 tons (the first engine built at the works weighed only about 25 tons). Some 850 workers were still employed at the end of the war.

Maritime Brighton, Hove and Portslade

The Brighton seafront continued to be a source of fascination, at least in peacetime. One of the great local innovations of the early 20th century was the introduction of the paddle-steamers of P. and A. Campbell's White Funnel Fleet, such as the famous *Brighton Queen* and *Brighton Belle*, made possible by the construction of extensive landing stages at the seaward end of the West Pier and Palace Pier. Popular excursions were run to resorts along the coast, including the Isle of Wight, and to Boulogne and other Channel ports in France. For thousands of people it was a once-in-a-lifetime chance to go abroad—even if only to the Isle of Wight! For a period before the First World War regular cross-Channel services from Brighton led to customs facilities being provided on the West Pier. In fact, so successful were Brighton's piers that several schemes were advanced over the years to provide one in genteel Hove, although none came to fruition.

The bathing at Brighton is grand.

Spindrift

116 *The saucy postcard—the epitome of the Brighton seaside.*

117   *King Edward VII on his favourite seat in Hove, c.1905. This was a shelter in private gardens south of Grand Avenue. The King used to visit the Sassoon family in nearby King's Gardens.*

118   *Brunswick Lawns, Hove, and the 'Peacock Parade' after church, c.1905.*

119 *Western Lawns, Hove in the 1930s. A popular miniature railway can be seen in the foreground.*

120 *West Pier, Brighton, c.1905.*

121 *Palace Pier, Brighton, c.1930.*

122 *Palace Pier Theatre, c.1910.*

The internal combustion engine did not have the revolutionary impact on marine transport that it did on road transport. The first ocean-going motor ship in the world was not operational until 1912; and it was not until the 1960s that the tonnage of motor ships registered in the UK exceeded that of steam ships. Motor boats with petrol engines began to replace sailing boats at the turn of the century, although recreational sailing—with or without auxiliary engines—has never been more popular than it is today. Harry Preston, of car racing fame, acquired a motor yacht, *Lady Ada*, soon after moving to Brighton in 1901, and in 1906 actually made it available to the mayor as a 'flagship' when a naval flotilla visited the town. Shortly afterwards, Harry took possession of a more powerful yacht, *My Lady Molly*, 60ft. in length with a 75h.p. engine, which was built at Shoreham. This probably inspired the creation of the Sussex Motor Yacht Club, which introduced motor yacht racing to Brighton. Among the novel features of the inter-war period were the red speedboats that provided hair-raising trips from the Palace Pier.

It is believed that fishing or pleasure boats, fitted with a petrol engine, first operated from Brighton beach in 1909, although such propulsion was not the norm until the 1920s. In the early days, because the fishermen were used to stowing their nets and gear at the back of the hold in the luggers, the engine was installed in the forward 'cuddy', thus requiring an extra-long shaft; later, however, engines were normally fitted centrally.

Despite various proposals over the years, Brighton still had no harbour where ships and larger boats could be moored or anchored, so locally owned vessels were usually based at Shoreham Harbour, which continued to prosper. The tonnage of shipping using the canal there increased in 1906 when Brighton Corporation built a coal-fired power station to the west of the gas works (on the Southwick side of the county boundary). Towards the end of the First World War two concrete towers, known locally as 'mystery ships', were fabricated on the south side of the canal west of the power station. After the war it was revealed that the intention had been to tow them to the straits of Dover to be anchored there as defence towers. The conclusion of hostilities made the monsters redundant, but in 1920 one was towed to the Solent and partly submerged as a defensive tower off The Nab.

123 *Brighton seafront west of the Palace Pier, 1930. The new Savoy Cinema can be seen on the site of the old Brill's Baths at the bottom of East Street.*

124 *Brighton seafront east of the Palace Pier, 1930. This shows the reconstruction of the Aquarium which had just been completed.*

In 1933 the Shoreham Harbour Trustees constructed the larger Prince George Lock at the canal entrance alongside the original lock, which in the following year was converted into a dry dock. The attractive canal waterfront off Albion Street between the lock and the *Schooner Inn*, now the site of the Lady Bee Marina, was already becoming a focus for boating, with the Sussex Yacht Club, boat builders and chandlers established there.

East of Aldrington Basin at the Hove end of the canal there was a remnant of the old river-bed known as Wish Pond. In 1930 Hove Corporation, recognising the growing popularity of all forms of pleasure boating, constructed Hove Lagoon on the site, forming an extension to the Western Lawns. The guide-book acclaimed:

> One of the finest Model Yacht Lakes in the country. The Lake has been divided, setting apart a portion perfectly safe for children paddling or sailing boats. The larger Lake is available for the sailing of the larger model yachts, also for paddle-boats, rowing boats and canoes at very reasonable charges. As every provision has been made for the supply of refreshments, for shelters and for chairs, this is the place to spend a happy and restful day with the children.

The Lagoon is still popular today, although it has changed with the times: the sailors are now mainly trainee windsurfers and the model boats radio controlled. In recent years it has also become a famous rendezvous for animal rights protesters blocking the adjacent road into Shoreham Harbour!

By the mid-1930s a fine seafront promenade extended in one form or another for over seven miles from Hove Lagoon to the eastern boundary of Brighton at Saltdean, where a lido in the Art Deco style was built. The last section to be completed was the three-mile Undercliff Walk east of Black Rock, which combined a promenade with sea defences designed to protect the chalk cliffs, and hence the new coast road above. This project was an excellent example of municipal enterprise, which provided employment during the Depression.

125 *The seafront at Kemp Town, Brighton in the 1930s, showing the Black Rock open-air swimming pool (now demolished), Volk's Railway and the grand Regency development.*

Aviation—'Those Magnificent Men'

The internal combustion engine's integration with the heavier-than-air flying machine, introduced a new (but long-dreamt-of) mode of transport which eventually came to dominate the market in long-distance travel and facilitate the globalisation of commerce. It may reasonably be claimed that Brighton and Hove were in at the birth (well, at least the post-natal period!).

Gas and hot air balloons had been a spectacle over the twin resorts in the 19th century. As early as 1821, the year of the coronation of George IV, an 'aeronaut', Charles Green, made an intrepid ascent from Black Rock gas works in stormy weather and had to be rescued from the sea. After the works had been relegated to a holder station in the 1870s tethered ascents to view military manoeuvres in Whitehawk Bottom were advertised. There are also records of ascents from Ireland's Gardens, Devil's Dyke, St Ann's Well Gardens and Brooker Hall, Hove. (The latter fine Italianate building, originally the home of John Olliver Vallance, lord of the manor of Hove, became Hove Museum in 1926.)

In 1900 Count Ferdinand von Zeppelin made the first flight in his dirigible rigid airship, powered by two Daimler 16h.p. petrol engines, at Lake Constance. Three years later came the epic flight of the Wright brothers, Orville and Wilbur, in their twin-prop biplane, *The Flyer*, at Kitty Hawk, North Carolina; although it has been claimed that Gustave Weisskopf made the first heavier-than-air flight in America in 1899—in a steam-powered aeroplane! The first flight in the British Isles was made in 1908, probably by an American, Samuel F. Cody, although some give the credit to the English pioneer A.V. Roe. In 1909 the French aviator Louis Bleriot made the first successful cross-Channel flight from Baraques near Calais to Dover in a monoplane of his own design.

Shoreham Aerodrome on the west bank of the River Adur—later to become the Brighton, Hove and Worthing Municipal Airport—dates from 1910 and is regarded as Britain's oldest licensed airfield. Harold Hume Piffard ('Piff'), a former pupil of nearby Lancing College, built a 'pusher' biplane on the site and made his first 'hop' there in the May of that year; shortly afterwards he survived a crash, but by the September was making good controlled flights. Watching enthralled was young Stanley Vincent, whose father was a doctor of music: he used a tuning fork to help Piff adjust his engine—thereby originating the term 'tune-up'!

Harry Preston took a great interest not only in the motor car and motor yacht but also in the aeroplane. In 1910 a French pioneer, Andre Beaumont, brought a Bleriot monoplane in sections to Brighton, assembled it on the beach and took Harry as a passenger on the first ever flight from the town. The first flight actually to Brighton was made on 15 February 1911, when Oscar Morison flew a Bleriot monoplane from Brooklands and landed on the sands near Magnus Volk's Arch at Paston Place, only to break a propeller. Harry Preston entertained him at the *Royal York Hotel*, where the ill-fated 'prop' was subsequently put on display. After giving demonstration flights at Brighton, Morison flew to the Shoreham airfield and established his base there. On being invited to Lancing College he actually made the shortest of flights and landed on the cricket pitch! On 12 April 1911 Gustav Hamel, flying another Bleriot monoplane, made the first flight to

126 *A Fokker glider at Peacehaven in the 1920s.*

Hove, landing on the Brunswick Lawns, where an enthusiastic Harry Preston was waiting to greet him.

That eventful year in the annals of local aviation came to a climax on 6 May when the Grand Brooklands to Brighton Air Race was held, with Shoreham Aerodrome as the turning point. This event, which the *Sussex Daily News* referred to as 'the first aerial point-to-point race', was organised by Harry Preston and his brother in association with the Palace Pier Company. In publicity terms it was the aerial equivalent of the Madeira Drive speed trials—even though many competitors lost their way or were disqualified. Gustav Hamel won the race; but by all accounts the darling of the public was the 'magnificent' Graham Gilmour, who came second in his rear-engine Bristol biplane. Shortly afterwards he, too, landed on the Brunswick Lawns and, as the *Gazette* reported, 'Ladies in tight hobble-skirts performed the most extraordinary aerobatic feats in getting over the barrier'. However, on 13 May Morison beat Gilmour in a two-man race from Shoreham to the famous Roedean Girls' School above the cliffs between Kemp Town and Rottingdean, winning a £25 prize put up by Magnus Volk. Finally, on 4 July, came what is said to have been the world's first recorded air freight flight: Horatio Barber flew from Shoreham to Hove in a Valkyrie B tail-first canard two-seater with a cargo of Osram lamps for an Electric Congress, landing at Aldrington Recreation Ground.

In 1912 Magnus Volk's eldest son Herman (actually 'Magnus' Herman) booked a display for Paston Place by Claude Grahame White in a waterplane. As a consequence, Herman conceived the idea of establishing a seasonal seaplane base there, and forthwith designed a portable canvas hanger from which planes could be winched on a rail track to and from the sea. 'Volk's Seaplane Station' was opened in the summer of 1913 and attracted

127 *Shoreham airport terminal and control tower. This is a modern view, but the fine Art Deco building designed by Stavers H. Tilman has changed little since it was opened in 1936 as the contrepiece of the Brighton, Hove and Worthing Joint Municipal Airport (photograph courtesy of Shoreham Airport).*

many famous pilots, including Glenn Curtiss, who demonstrated the first Curtiss flying-boat to be seen in Britain. The project boosted the fortunes of Volk's Electric Railway and gave Brighton yet another attraction but it was short-lived, as in the following summer many of 'those magnificent men' were on more urgent business in the 'flying machines' of the Royal Flying Corps.

By the outbreak of war Shoreham Aerodrome was well established (despite a few 'prangs'), with an aero club, flying school and short joy flights in Eric and Cecil Pashley's Maurice Farman *Longhorn*. The Royal Flying Corps had taken an early interest in the aerodrome and in January 1915 took it over, mainly for use as a reserve base and flying school. Immediately after the war the Canadian Air Force were in occupation and it became the home for many captured German aircraft.

Shoreham was one of a number of military airfields established along the coast during the First World War, including that at Telscombe Cliffs east of Brighton. There is an intriguing reference in a 1919 edition of Ward Lock & Co.'s Brighton and Hove guidebook to 'Hangleton Aerodrome', which it stated could be seen from the Dyke Railway. It is possible that it was a similar wartime establishment, especially as, during the military occupation of the Devil's Dyke estate in the war, bombs were tested by dropping them from the old aerial cableway into the ravine: in fact, the ruined building which still stands like a legionnaire's fort west of the hotel was known in the 1920s as 'The Bomb House', so it may have been used to store the bombs. However, searches in the RFC and RAF documents at the Public Record Office at Kew have so far yielded no evidence. It now seems likely that the lost 'aerodrome' was in the neighbouring parish of West Blatchington—probably on the site of the present playing fields south of Court Farm Road—as there is a record that in October 1919 the 'Avro Air Fleet' was providing joy rides on a part of West Blatchington Farm.

In January 1920 the Canadians abandoned Shoreham Aerodrome and it reverted to grazing land—awaiting the blossoming of an extraordinary local young man, Frederick G. Miles, whose father was the proprietor of the Star Model Laundry in Wellington Road, Portslade-by-Sea. In 1916, while his father was in the army, Frederick left school at 13, bought an old motor cycle and hired it out to his friends. As his enterprise prospered he bought a Model-T Ford van and provided a local delivery service. Then, after going for a joy-flight in 1925, he became determined to progress to aviation. He soon designed and built a 'Gnat' biplane at his father's laundry, and, anxious to learn to fly, sought out Cecil Pashley, who had run joy-flights from Shoreham before the war. He discovered that the aviator had an Avro 504K stored at Croydon and persuaded him to go into partnership as the Gnat Aero Company. Pashley flew his Avro down to the coast, landing on the Downs near Southwick; it was then transported to the Star Laundry to be reconditioned by Fred Miles, his brothers and friends.

The next stage was to find an airfield. The answer was a field with a barn to the south of the abandoned Shoreham Aerodrome and on the other side of the railway line. Despite being initially refused an aerodrome licence, Fred Miles and his associates transported the Avro from Portslade and erected it in the barn. Pashley duly taught Fred to fly and before long they had a flying school in operation. More second-hand planes were acquired and then, in 1926, a new field north of the railway was leased, where the Southern Aero Club was formed and even a flying display held. The company, which was now Southern Aircraft Limited, continued to expand its activities. In 1930 they learnt that Sir Alan Cobham, the world-famous aviator, had been engaged to find a suitable location for a municipal airport for Brighton, Hove and Worthing. Realising that the adjacent site of the former Shoreham Aerodrome would be the best location, the company raised the money to acquire the land and then entered into protracted, but successful, negotiations with the three local authorities.

The Brighton, Hove and Worthing Joint Municipal Airport was officially opened by the three mayors on 13 June 1936. The centrepiece was the fine Art Deco terminal designed by Stavers H. Tilman, which is now a listed building and has been featured in a number of films, such as the BBC's *Tenko* series, in which it represented Singapore Airport. The consultant to the Joint Municipal Airport Committee was none other than Magnus Volk's son Herman. The opening was timed to coincide with an international rally, which included a demonstration of 'crazy flying' by Cecil Pashley. Subsequently, the King's Cup Air Race used the airport as a control point.

The closing years of the 1930s brought prosperity to the new airport with much aerial activity. The terminal building, with its customs facilities, encouraged operators, particularly Channel Island Airways, Jersey Airlines and Olley Air Services, to run scheduled services with twin-engine aircraft, such as the new de Havilland Rapides and Dragons, to the Channel Islands, Deauville and Le Touquet, as well as to many destinations throughout Britain. In addition, many single-engine club and private aircraft, including Tiger Moths, Puss Moths, Leopard Moths and Hornet Moths from the de Havilland stable, shared Shoreham's grass field. In 1937 the Martin School of Air Navigation was granted a contract to train RAF volunteer pilots there, as a result of which RAF Tiger Moths and other trainers became a familiar sight over Brighton and Hove. In fact, on 24 January 1938 a biplane actually 'pancaked' into a garden in Lyndhurst Road, Hove, the pilot baling out and landing with only minor injuries on the tram wires in Beaconsfield Road, Brighton. It was, sadly, a portent of things to come.

In 1939 Shoreham Airport was elevated to the status of an international airport; but it was to be a short-lived accolade, as once again war intervened and the airfield was taken over by the RAF for the duration. Its primary role was as a base for coastal patrols and air-sea rescue, but it also served as a refuelling point and emergency landing ground. In 1944 a wire-mesh strip was laid so that it could function as an advanced airfield for the Normandy invasion. Among the aircraft that landed there—successfully or otherwise—were four-engine Flying Fortresses and Liberators, as well as Spitfires and Hurricanes.

Brighton and Hove were in the front line of the war in the air. Although the towns were not subjected to massive bombing attacks, nearly 500 bombs were dropped in some 80 air raids. Many of these were carried out by 'sneak raiders' who targeted key installations, such as the London Road Viaduct and the locomotive works. Many casualties resulted from the indiscriminate dumping of bombs by raiders thwarted in their attempts to reach London. After the fall of France there was a serious prospect of invasion by air and sea: as a result, the beaches were closed and sections of the two piers were demolished in order to prevent their use by enemy ships. In fact, it was said that Hitler intended to make the Royal Pavilion his headquarters!

The author vividly recalls one baffling incident during the Battle of Britain in 1940. Before joining the RAF himself he was in the Hove Home Guard (said to have been the spitting image of 'young Pike' in the later TV classic *Dad's Army*). One day, when he was at work at Hove Town Hall, there was an almighty dog-fight overhead. Seeing a parachutist descending, he and a friend, Roy Shirley, set off in pursuit on their bikes, with no time to collect a rifle from home, but with all the enthusiasm of Captain Mainwaring, determined to capture their first enemy airman. They reached the top of the Three-cornered Copse on the outskirts of the town only to find that the parachutist had just been taken away in an ambulance. Afterwards they were informed that he was 'one of ours', a Polish pilot whose fighter had crashed into a vacant site in Portland Road, Hove. In 1996 the Southern Counties Aviation Club excavated the site and unexpectedly found not only the plane (a Hurricane) but also the remains of the pilot, who was identified as Sgt Richard Noble; yet records show that in 1940 his family had buried this same gallant airman in Yorkshire. The mystery of one single-seat fighter with three possible pilots has yet to be explained to the author's satisfaction!

Finally, it is worthy of note that Fred Miles, who built his first aircraft in a laundry at Portslade, and his youngest brother, George, went on to found Miles Aircraft (F.G. Miles Ltd) based at Woodley near Reading, a company that was to play an important role in the war in the air, producing a wide range of innovative training and other aircraft for the Royal Air Force.

Seven

The Road to the Millennium—and Gridlock

Post-war Crisis and Recovery

After the Second World War the twin resorts were once again in crisis, faced with a shattered economy and a serious housing shortage. Post-war austerity lingered into the 1950s, but as the nation's standard of living grew the pattern of leisure changed to the disadvantage of traditional seaside resorts. More and more people of all classes could afford to fly to the Costas and other exotic destinations on inexpensive package holidays: nationally, the proportion of holidays taken abroad increased from six per cent in 1951 to 16 per cent in 1969. At the same time, with increasing car ownership, informal holidays, such as touring, caravanning and camping, became immensely popular. In 1954 even the Brighton locomotive works—a major source of employment for a century— finally closed.

The response of Brighton County Borough Council, under the guidance of its charismatic Town Clerk Bill Dodd ('Dodd is God' as they used to say!) and his team of officers, was bold and imaginative: to promote the resort as a venue for national and international conferences and exhibitions; to encourage industrial development, taking advantage of their large land holdings; to capitalise on a trend towards second, usually shorter, holidays in late summer or autumn; to promote university and higher education; and to encourage language schools for overseas students—a development which also benefited Hove. By such means over a period of years the economy was diversified and in time Brighton and Hove came to be appreciated as a cosmopolitan resort, competing at an advantage with many other seaside towns. As will be seen later, trends in transport, particularly in aviation, once again played a major part in the transformation.

The Royal Pavilion became a potent symbol for Brighton's new image; and the Dome concert hall—once the Prince Regent's riding stables—functioned as a major conference venue until in 1977 the council's new Brighton Centre was opened on the seafront near the bottom of West Street. The hotels in Brighton and Hove played a vital role not only in providing accommodation but also in hosting conferences and exhibitions. In particular, extensive exhibition and conference halls were built at the rear of the *Metropole Hotel* in the 1960s.

Brighton Corporation continued its shrewd policy of land acquisition after the war when in 1947 it purchased the Stanmer Estate, formerly the seat of the Earls of Chichester. In 1952 the estate was embraced by an extension of the borough boundary to include the parish of Stanmer. These steps were the catalyst that led to the realisation of one of Brighton's recurrent dreams, to add a university to its cultural heritage. Much of the initiative was due to William Stone, the director of education. A university college was established with government approval in 1959; then, in 1963, by royal charter, this became the fully-fledged University of Sussex, the first building on the Stanmer campus having been opened the previous year to the design of Sir Basil Spence. The adjoining Stanmer Park, with its modest stately home and unspoilt downland village, became a splendid example of a publicly owned country park on the edge of a built-up area.

A College of Education was established on the other side of the Lewes Road close to Falmer station, which had a new lease of life as a major transport facility for both institutions. Although close by, Falmer Village (then in Chailey Rural District, but now in Lewes District) retained its delightful rural character. Also in the 1960s a new College of Technology was built on the west side of the Lewes Road at Moulsecombe, and a new College of Art in Grand Parade; all three colleges have since been amalgamated to form Brighton University.

Aviation

The importance of Gatwick Airport to the new diversified economy of Brighton and Hove—particularly with the development of the European Union and the trend towards the globalisation of commerce—cannot be over-stated. It facilitates not only business and leisure tourism but also industry and commerce generally. The airport also provides a market for local products, as well as a freight service. By 1997 some 25,000 people were employed there directly or indirectly, a significant number being Brighton and Hove residents.

Gatwick was founded as an aerodrome for private flying in 1930, 20 years after Shoreham, and was first licensed as a commercial airport in 1934. In 1952, after war service, it was designated for development as an alternative to London's Heathrow. Over the subsequent years terminal facilities were greatly improved and, with the increasing number of jet aircraft, the runway was progressively extended. Then in 1988 a second, North, Terminal was opened, the proposal having been supported by Brighton Borough Council at a previous public inquiry. In 1994 London Gatwick, to give the airport its official title, handled 21 million passengers, 190,000 aircraft movements and 227,000 tonnes of freight on its world-wide services. At that time, the forecasted growth in these sectors by 2008 was, respectively, in the ranges 43-67 per cent, 11-24 per cent and 72-94 per cent.

Shoreham Airport was certainly not as well placed as Gatwick after the war. The airfield was returned to civil flying in 1946, but restoration was a gradual process, and it was not until 1971 that it was at last reinstated as the joint Brighton, Hove and Worthing Municipal Airport. During the interim period the airfield was used for private flying and occasional small air shows. In 1952 the Daily Express South Coast Air Race started at Shoreham, one of the participants being the wartime hero, Douglas Bader. In the same year East Anglian Flying Services introduced a short-lived service with DH89A Rapides on a route from Ipswich and Southend to Portsmouth and the Channel Islands via Shoreham.

The year 1952 was also marked by the return of F.G. Miles Ltd to Shoreham, where the brothers designed and built a prototype jet trainer, the M.100 Student, seen as an economical replacement for the Percival jet Provost. Following a demonstration flight in 1957, production was proposed in South Africa for the South African Air Force, but the whole project was thwarted by the subsequent arms embargo. In 1961 the aircraft work of the company was acquired by British Executive and General Aviation and renamed Beagle-Miles Ltd, which in the following year became Beagle Aircraft Ltd. This company continued with the design and production of light aircraft at Shoreham until it was acquired and transferred in 1969. Meridian Airmaps Ltd, operating in the field of aerial photography, was another well-known company based at Shoreham during this post-war period.

During the twenty years after the reinstatement of the municipal airport in 1971 various attempts were made to operate scheduled services from Shoreham to the Channel Islands and France, but these were generally uneconomic. The last was in 1991 when Marinair operated a Saturday service to Jersey using 4-engine 46-seater DH Canada Dash 7s.

From the early days the grass airfield had been liable to flooding but, in 1981, after some 12 years of opposition from local residents and three public inquiries, the government approved the provision of a hard runway, imposing conditions that it be limited to 760 metres (830 yards) in length, with a maximum of 75,000 aircraft movements a year and no night flying. The new runway was officially opened on 18 September 1982. To mark the occasion a 150 ft. airship (Skyship 500) visited Shoreham.

Controversy continued to bedevil the Municipal Airport in the following years. In 1986 the Joint Committee actually invited tenders for its acquisition, but after receiving a number of serious offers it fortunately drew back at the last moment. Suggested alternative uses have included housing, a golf course, industry—and a new stadium for Brighton and Hove Albion FC. However, in 1987 English Heritage gave permission for the listed Art Deco terminal building to be altered so as to provide better air traffic control facilities. Coupled with the hard runway, this improvement allowed greater confidence for the future, despite the difficulties encountered in establishing scheduled services.

In September 1990 the airport celebrated its 80th birthday and the 50th anniversary of the Battle of Britain with one of its spectacular air displays. It was surpassed in 1995— 50 years after the end of the war—by a display that culminated with fly-pasts by many wartime and contemporary military aircraft, including a replica of Baron Von Richthofen's red Fokker triplane, a B17 Flying Fortress, an amphibious Catalina and a Miles Magister.

Today Shoreham Airport is once again thriving and set to regain its pre-war élan. It is not only the home of charter companies, flying clubs and schools, but various engineering firms; furthermore, with its regular air shows, attractive terminal building, archive collection and D-day Aviation Museum it has become an important tourist attraction for the seaside resorts. Private flying is increasingly within the means of a wider section of the public: one has only to see the microlites, hang gliders and paragliders surfing the thermals at the Devil's Dyke and elsewhere to realise the potential. However, it must be said that private flying is hardly likely to become the universal means of personal transport that was forecast in pre-war times, when six local airfields were planned!

The Roads—Surge and Gridlock

In the early post-war years few people could have predicted the impact that the motor vehicle was to have in the second half of the 20th century. By the time that British motor manufacturers had changed over from wartime production and were ready with their new designs they were caught up in the export drive of Clem Attlee's government. If the local motorist coveted one of the new British cars, such as the Hillman Minx or Standard Vanguard, he (or she) could even stay on a waiting list for five years. In any case, petrol rationing remained in force until 1950.

With the ending of restrictions and the rapid improvement in the standard of living, car or motor cycle ownership became a real possibility for the masses. This was facilitated by a series of small family cars coming off the production line, spearheaded by the renowned Morris Minor designed by Alec Issigonis, and the output of a prestigious motor cycle industry. In 1955 new car registrations alone exceeded 500,000 for the first time. The growing second-hand market began to spread vehicle ownership ever more widely across the social, gender and age spectrum. Another factor was the glamour of successful British motor racing.

The post-war years also saw a resurgence of interest in the vehicles of yesteryear—to Brighton's advantage. The London to Brighton Veteran Car Run was held again in 1946 and then continuously on the first Sunday in November from 1948 to the present day. In 1953 the famous event and its seaside destination were given worldwide publicity by the film *Genevieve* starring Kenneth More, Dinah Sheridan, John Gregson and Kay Kendall. Based on the Brighton Run, the film featured a 1904 Darracq, specially christened Genevieve after the patron saint of Paris where the car was built.

In 1956 the Suez crisis brought back petrol rationing until the following year. One of the consequences was the appearance on the local streets of an entirely different type of vehicle introduced from the continent, the bubble car. This was a small car, economical to run but vulnerable. Its short-lived popularity is said to have spurred the new British company BMC, formed by the merger of Morris and Austin, to commission Issigonis to design a rival small car. His answer was the front-wheel-drive Mini, which was to become a cult car of the 'swinging sixties'. Sales of the Mini helped to boost new car registrations to over 800,000 in 1960.

The early 1960s brought another motorised phenomenon to the streets of Brighton: the rival hordes of Mods and Rockers who descended on the resort astride their respective status symbols, the motor scooter and the motorbike. Their escapades have since been perpetuated in another Brighton-based film *Quadrophenia* (1979), like *Brighton Rock* reflecting the seamy side of local life, but good publicity for all that!

The formation of the Organisation of Petroleum Exporting Countries (OPEC) in 1973 led to petrol shortages and rocketing fuel prices and the emphasis in car design switched to fuel economy and safety. The past 20 years has seen a revolution in the motor industry and, indeed, in attitudes towards motoring. The development of the microchip has brought with it a variety of electronic devices to improve control, safety, security and communications in the vehicle. But at the same time, atmospheric pollution, global warming, traffic congestion and car crime have led increasingly to disenchantment, not only on the part of the green movement, but also of many habitual motorists: in fact, road rage is becoming endemic, not least in the centres of Brighton and Hove where both residents and visitors compete for road and parking space.

It is salutary to look back to September 1946, when a series of events was held in Brighton to celebrate 50 years of emancipated motoring. The souvenir programme proudly proclaimed: 'The stage is set, go forward British motors, new and fresh triumphs await you in your second fifty glorious years'. The number of cars (including private vans) registered in Great Britain at that time was probably little different from the 1940 figure, previously quoted, of 1.4 million. Even the most optimistic enthusiast would not have forecast that, aided by the globalisation of the motor industry, the number would reach 10 million by 1967 and 20 million three years before the 1996 centenary!

Buses, Trolleys, Taxis and Cycles

After the Second World War it took time for the local bus companies to renew their fleets and expand their services. However, in 1946 trolley wires were extended from the Race Hill terminus at the top of Elm Grove, down Manor Road to Black Rock, connecting with the Whitehawk Garage of the Brighton, Hove and District Omnibus Co. Ltd (BHD). This enabled the company to run a valuable cross-town trolley-bus service from Seven Dials to Black Rock in accordance with the joint agreement with Brighton Corporation. After 1946 all other trolley routes were operated by Brighton Corporation (there were none in Hove), and between 1949 and 1951 their services were extended northwards of the existing routes in Preston Drove to serve the expanding Hollingbury and East Patcham areas via Surrenden Road, Braybon Avenue, Carden Avenue, Carden Hill and Ditchling Road. In the late 1950s, with the advent of larger and more efficient Bristol diesel buses which could cope with the steeper gradients on these routes, it was agreed to phase out the trolley-buses altogether; this was finally completed in 1961.

The 1950s saw the heyday of the buses, with extended services and improved frequencies; but thereafter, with the growth of car ownership, decline set in. In the County Borough of Brighton car ownership per head of population doubled during the next decade, from 0.096 to 0.193. This meant not only fewer bus passengers but also greater congestion for the bus drivers to contend with in the town centres, often causing 'bunching', poor time-keeping and frustration.

In 1961, at the close of the previous 21-year agreement, a new Brighton Area Transport Services Agreement (BATS) came into effect. This time it included not only BHD and Brighton Corporation but also Southdown. The revenue and mileage were to be shared: BHD 50½ per cent, Southdown 29 per cent and the Corporation 20½ per cent. The licensing arrangements enabled the three undertakings to operate any of the local services in the area from Shoreham Beach to Telscombe Tye, northwards to the Devil's Dyke, Patcham and Falmer. The agreement was a major co-operative venture, which helped the buses meet the challenge of the motor car. In the same year the first forward-entrance 60-seat Bristol/ECW Lodekka buses were introduced, these electric folding doors operated by the driver. Later, these and other forward-entrance vehicles enabled the operators to change to one-man operation to meet staff shortages and increased running costs, Brighton Corporation pioneering the use of such a system in Great Britain in 1966. Although there were economic advantages to the operators and their drivers, one should set these against delays at bus stops, job losses, driver stress, lack of protection on late-night services—and an end to the social role of the erstwhile cheerful conductor.

The Transport Act 1968 authorised the formation in the following year of the National Bus Company (NBC), which embraced BHD and Southdown, but not the Brighton Corporation undertaking. In turn Southdown took over BHD, although the BATS agreement remained in effect. Southdown's Freshfield Road offices became the new headquarters, and major works were transferred from BHD's Conway Street depot to Southdown's works at Victoria Road, Portslade, leaving only servicing at the former. In 1972 NBC ordered a standard livery of red and green for its subsidiaries; Southdown opted to replace its traditional livery with a darker green with a white waistband. Independent Brighton Corporation Transport had repainted all of its 62 buses blue and white two years previously. Thus, there was an end—for the time being—of the familiar local red buses. On local government reorganisation on 1 April 1974 Brighton Corporation Transport was renamed Brighton Borough Transport.

In 1986, at a time when there was an urgent need for an integrated transport system, came yet another upheaval in bus operations. Nationalisation yielded to privatisation and deregulation and Southdown Motor Services, Southdown Engineering and a re-titled Brighton and Hove Bus and Coach Co. Ltd (B & H) became independent companies and the BATS agreement ceased. Southdown established its headquarters at Lewes and restored its traditional green and yellow livery, while B & H returned to Conway Street, reclaimed its red and cream livery, and also extended its operations into the hinterland. However, in 1989 Southdown was acquired by Stagecoach, and three years later its name and livery disappeared, although the thriving Southdown Enthusiasts Club was undoubtedly pleased that the company's registration was retained. Brighton Corporation's bus undertaking was acquired by its employees as Brighton Borough Transport Ltd (BT), still operating from the Lewes Road (Combe Terrace) depot.

In many parts of the country deregulation led to fierce competition, with 'bus wars' and over-bussing. However, in Brighton and Hove, although there was competition, particularly over fares, the worst excesses were avoided; in fact, the towns were recognised nationally as having one of the best examples of post-deregulation bussing. This was evidenced by the fact that at a time of national decline in bus travel the two main local companies (B & H and BT) reported one and a quarter million more passenger journeys in 1996, an increase of five per cent over 1995. Much of the credit was due to the co-operation of the respective managing directors, Roger French and Richard Clark.

The two companies invested over £6 million in new buses in the mid-1990s, with BT buying mostly single-decker 39-seat Plaxton-bodied Dennis Darts with low-pollution engines, low floors, no entrance steps and the ability to take on buggies, prams and wheelchairs. These 'midibuses', which replaced ageing double-decker Atlanteans on the busy 'early to late' cross-town No.49 route from Portslade to Moulsecombe, proved to be very successful, being versatile, economic and much more manoeuverable in the congested central areas; their introduction also meant that upper-deck vandalism on this route was eliminated.

This is far from being the end of the history of local buses, though, for in May 1997, by mutual agreement, the parent company of B & H (Go-Ahead Group plc) acquired the share capital of BT. These two companies duly merged as one undertaking with the name and livery of the former. As Roger French, the managing director of the new undertaking, stated:

> The deal represents a major boost for public transport in the area and formalises the very successful working relationship that we have enjoyed with Brighton Transport over a number of years ... the aim of the merger was to provide a quality service, continuing with a commitment to good value fares, investment in new vehicles and improvements to the frequencies of key bus routes.

Experience in the comparatively short period since the merger has shown that this statement of intent was certainly not simply 'spin', but is being fulfilled earnestly in every respect—despite the continuing problem of traffic congestion and illegal parking. The number of awards that the company has earned since the merger is evidence of this. The main depot and offices are still at Conway Street, Hove, but there are also smaller depots in Brighton at Lewes Road (Combe Terrace) and Whitehawk and 'outstations' at Newhaven and Uckfield. B & H actively work in partnership with the council in promoting public transport: the council have been introducing bus lanes and other measures and are themselves funding a number of essential bus services called Network Links, which would not normally be commercially viable, such as school, evening, Sunday, and park-and-ride services (from Withdean Stadium). The city council also funds EasyLink, run by Community Transport, a novel door-to-door service for the disabled and others who find it difficult to use conventional buses. Another notable transport initiative is a bus service to the Devil's Dyke operated by Southcoast Motor Services Ltd on behalf of a partnership between the National Trust (who now own the Dyke Estate), the City Council, the Countryside Agency, Mid-Sussex District Council, South Coast Power and the Sussex Downs Conservation Board. The service uses an open-top 1964 Leyland bus similar to the Southdown service that ran 30 years ago; there is even a conductor aboard! In 2000 the service carried 12,000 passengers, 42 per cent of whom would otherwise have travelled by car, and was highly commended in the Bus Industry Awards of that year.

Taxis and hire cars are an important complement to the buses. Starting from a lower base in popularity, however, they did not suffer to the same extent from the growth of car ownership. Deregulation under the 1985 Transport Act brought the prospect of unbridled competition, with local authorities given the power to license as many taxicabs as they saw fit. In Brighton and Hove, however, the councils acted responsibly: as at June 1997 (about the time the two authorities were amalgamated) there were some 459 licensed hackney carriages (taxis) and 261 hire cars.

The greatest casualty of the motor vehicle explosion in the 1960s was the bicycle. Not only did thousands of cyclists become car owners but also road conditions were often judged to be too hazardous for a means of transport that was otherwise economical and environment-friendly. As a result, many cyclists also switched to the bus services. In addition, the increasing use of commercial vehicles, the reduction in the number of small shops and fewer home deliveries virtually brought an end to the familiar working bike. However, in more recent times there has been an encouraging revival in cycling as a leisure pursuit, especially with the development of the all-terrain mountain bike. With the advent of protective clothing and the provision of cycle lanes on some of the busiest roads, the bicycle is increasingly seen as a means of city transport capable—admittedly with some risk and stress—of achieving better journey times than the car. It has been estimated that, nationally, cycle ownership doubled in the period 1975-91.

Emergency Services: Police, Fire, Ambulance

In 1947 the wartime amalgamation of the police forces ended. A feature of the post-war period was the increasing use of motor transport, facilitated by the introduction in 1946 of the 999 emergency call service. Towards the end of the 1960s a Home Office study focused on the reduction in the number of policemen on the beat. This led to the introduction of small 'panda' cars (Morris Minors and, later, some Ford Escorts) to augment the beat patrols, these being seen as an efficient substitute for the bicycles still in use. The pandas, which covered two or three beats, had the back up of more powerful response cars. However, in the early 1970s it became clear that the public were making much more use of the 999 services, so the pandas were phased out in favour of the response cars.

The Brighton and Hove Police Forces both moved to new headquarters in the 1960s, at John Street and Holland Road respectively. On 1 January 1968 these local forces were again amalgamated into a Sussex Police Force, with its headquarters at Lewes; the Brighton

128 *Hove Town Hall after the fire of 9 January 1966.*

129 *An oil painting by the author, based on eyewitness reports, of the terrorist attack on the Cabinet at the* Grand Hotel *on 12 October 1984.*

130 *The* Grand Hotel *after the terrorist attack.*

and Hove stations became divisional offices. Today the use of patrol cars, motor cycles and a variety of vans is widespread, with Brighton having its own control room, which also covers Hove and Shoreham. However, community policing associated with neighbourhood watch schemes is being developed as an important feature of local police policy. A vital addition to police mobility is a helicopter service based at Shoreham Airport, providing a rapid response to many incidents, as well as a search and rescue facility. Until the 1980s the Brighton division still used horses, particularly for crowd control at football matches, but these invaluable allies of the police were apparently given up to help pay for the helicopter service. With mounting street crime and vandalism, particularly on certain estates, there is now a vociferous demand to 'bring back the Bobby on the beat', notwithstanding the increasing number of close-circuit television cameras (CCTV) being installed.

The local fire brigades were denationalised in 1948: the Hove brigade was taken over by East Sussex County Council, but the Brighton brigade returned to County Borough control until local government reorganisation in 1974, when it, too, became a part of the East Sussex Fire Brigade. However, on 1 April 1997, when Brighton and Hove became a unitary authority, a combined East Sussex Fire Authority was created consisting of the unitary authority and a smaller East Sussex County Council. The Brighton division retains its HQ at Preston Circus, with a second fire station in Roedean Road. The Hove division, which includes Portslade, has its fire station at English Close off the Old Shoreham Road (established in 1972).

The first regular public ambulance service came into existence as a result of the 1948 National Health Service Act, under which county and county borough councils were required to provide services. As a result, Brighton (County Borough) established its own ambulance service at the top of Elm Grove next to Brighton General Hospital, and Hove Borough Council provided a service on behalf of East Sussex County Council at the Leighton Road Depot in Old Shoreham Road. In the latter case, the small staff was augmented by Albion footballers in summer and Sussex cricketers (from Hove's County Ground in Eaton Road) in winter!

In 1973, the ambulance services came directly under the NHS, the local services being administered by East Sussex Area Health Authority. In 1995 the service in the whole of Sussex became a separate national health trust with its HQ in Lewes. The Brighton ambulance station in Elm Grove remains, but a new station was built at St Joseph's Close in Old Shoreham Road, Hove, with a facility to control the complicated system of traffic lights in that locality. The trust has a paramedic attached to the police helicopter unit. In addition the volunteers of the St John Ambulance Service and the Red Cross continue to provide invaluable local services.

Traffic Control and Management

By 1960 it was obvious to the local authorities and police that urgent measures were needed to deal with the unprecedented growth in traffic, particularly in the centre of Brighton. Uncontrolled on-street parking—a legacy of those days when motorists considered it their right to stop outside the premises they were visiting—presented a special problem. A controlled parking zone was established in Brighton, therefore, in which on-street parking was restricted, but with special provision for residents. In 1963 parking meters and traffic wardens were introduced, the intention being that the receipts would be used as a contribution towards off-street car parks. Until the 1960s there were only a comparatively small number of these provided in an *ad hoc* manner on vacant sites at ground level, although developers were required to make provision in their schemes for employee or resident parking. Then Brighton Council constructed its first multi-storey car park—underneath the central lawn of Regency Square! This comprised two levels with 520 spaces. The scheme was bold and highly controversial, but not as intrusive as it might have been. This was followed by the major redevelopment south of Western Road near the Clock Tower, which produced the Churchill Square shopping centre with 1,530 parking spaces in three multi-storey car parks. Another multi-storey car park with 530 spaces was built in York Hill to serve the London Road shopping centre. In 1972 there were 9,622 spaces in Brighton town centre, of which 4,357 were public off-street spaces, about 2,000 private off-street spaces, and 3,265 public on-street spaces.

The worsening problem of moving traffic in the 1960s was met with one-way streets, turning restrictions and some road widening, as in Edward Street (which only funnelled vehicles into the narrower Eastern Road). A controversial proposal in the mid-1960s to widen Hove's seafront Kingsway to six lanes by demolishing the famous Decimus Burton ramps at Adelaide Crescent was, fortunately, defeated. Town planning now sought to tackle the menace of mounting traffic congestion from the 1960s onwards—and a 40-year-old battle between the environment and the motor vehicle began.

Town Planning, Heritage and Conservation

One of the major pieces of legislation introduced by the post-war Attlee government was the Town and Country Planning Act, 1947, which came into effect on 1 July 1948. Pre-war legislation in this field was haphazard, to say the least, and did not convey a duty upon local authorities; but the new Act required all county councils and county borough councils to prepare development plans and to control development through a system of planning applications. The new legislation recognised the growing concern of the public that Britain's heritage of landscape and townscape was fast being eroded by uncontrolled development. The planning system has been modified over the past 50 years, but today its basic principles are generally accepted across the political spectrum. Public concern about Britain's heritage and environment has widened, and continues to do so, with the growth of road traffic and the hazards, noise and atmospheric pollution that it causes.

In 1961 the Ministry of Transport set up a group headed by Professor Colin Buchanan 'to study the long term development of roads and traffic in urban areas and their influence on the urban environment'. Their report 'Traffic in Towns' (better known as 'the Buchanan Report') was published in 1963. As the group stated in its conclusion:

The broad message of the report is that there are absolute limits to the amount of traffic that can be accepted in towns, depending upon their size and density, but up to these limits, provided a civilised environment is to be retained or created, the level of vehicular accessibility a town can have depends on its readiness to accept and pay for the physical changes required.

The study group accepted the beneficial advantages of the motor vehicle, but said that there was a need to recognise the distinction between essential uses and optional uses. An urban network of roads should be defined to carry longer-distance traffic, leaving certain areas accessible only to service traffic. They emphasised the inter-relationship between land uses (as traffic generators) and transportation. Significantly, the group considered that there was an urgent need for vastly improved public transport, almost certainly subsidised. The Buchanan Report was a landmark in planning: it became a best seller. But, as Sir Colin wrote in *The Times* 25 years later, '... the report had more influence overseas, especially in Germany, than in Britain'. In 1963 there was an all-powerful roads lobby active in British politics.

Following the Buchanan Report, the local planning authorities jointly agreed to undertake a land use/transportation study for the Greater Brighton coastal conurbation from Lancing to Seaford (the BATS Study). Accordingly, a team was set up in 1965 to carry out a comprehensive transport survey and to develop mathematical models to predict future traffic flows. A serious drawback, however, was that the individual development plans prepared under the 1947 Planning Act were by then in need of updating. In 1967 planning consultants were commissioned to produce a plan for the town centre of Brighton and to study certain aspects of shopping and leisure in the wider study area, working in co-operation with the BATS Team.

The consultants published a draft plan in 1968. They proposed what amounted to a high-investment 'road construction solution' to traffic problems. A high capacity east-west road through the urban area was envisaged, the preferred route running from the A27 at Shoreham along the south side of the railway to Preston Circus and Lewes Road, from where it would turn south across the Hanover area and then east on or near the line of Edward Street to connect with the coast road beyond the built-up area. This road would also form part of a 'box' of roads on three sides of the Brighton town centre, the coast road being closed to most traffic or, alternatively, put underground. From Preston Circus a 'spine road', partly elevated, would cross the area south-east of Brighton station, now known as North Laine, which had long been earmarked for industry, in order to provide access to new massive car parks and high density land uses. These draft proposals, which would have necessitated the demolition of residential and other properties on an unprecedented scale, caused widespread public consternation.

This was the situation when, in 1969, the three planning authorities, Brighton County Borough Council, East Sussex Council and West Sussex County Council agreed jointly to set up a team to prepare a structure plan for the Greater Brighton area extending from Lancing, through Brighton and Hove, to Seaford. This was a new type of strategic plan introduced by the Town and Country Planning Act, 1968. It was intended that the new team (known as the BUSP Team) was to work closely with the BATS Team, although on the death of the latter's director they subsumed his responsibilities. In their work the team (with the author as Director) followed a programme of public participation, publishing for comment, in succession, survey reports, objectives and alternative strategies, culminating with a draft Greater Brighton Structure Plan (GBSP) in 1973. This was based on a conservation-orientated strategy: in essence, urban expansion would be limited, with growth in quality rather than quantity; traffic restraint would be progressively imposed with concurrent improvements in public transport; and an east-west distributor road would be provided outside the built-up area.

The plan was generally well received by the public, including the amenity societies. Following the consultants' proposals there was actually a vociferous demand for the outer distributor road (usually referred to as the Brighton by-pass). The end of the consultation stage in 1974 coincided with local government reorganisation, under which a two-tier system was introduced, with the county councils responsible for structure plans and the district councils, including Brighton and Hove, which remained as separate authorities (although the latter absorbed the former Portslade-by-Sea Urban District), responsible for local plans and development control. The new East Sussex County Council decided not to continue with the GBSP as a separate plan, but to 'subsume' its provisions into a proposed county structure plan. However, the new Brighton Borough Council promptly accepted the draft GBSP as an interim basis for development control.

There can be little doubt that the BUSP (or GBSP) Team, working in liaison with the amenity and other local societies, did help significantly to shift attitudes away from large-scale urban renewal. From 1970 onwards there has been a gradual trend in Brighton (and Hove) towards measures to restrain the motor vehicle and to improve public transport. These include pedestrianisation (particularly in parts of the Old Town); park and ride (from

131 *A visit by the Queen on 17 July 1962 for the opening of the George Street Improvement Scheme.*

132 *Looking eastwards from Ditchling Beacon, the highest point of the Downs, part of the Sussex Downs Area of Outstanding Natural Beauty.*

133 *The Saturday market in Upper Gardner Street, North Laine, Brighton. Part of the bustling life that gives the North Laine Conservation Area its character.*

Withdean, Saltdean and Lewes Road); traffic calming; limited access streets; bus and cycle lanes; computerised traffic lights; and CCTV and radar/still camera surveillance. There has been no significant overall increase in the number of parking spaces in the town centre, despite the construction of a 600-space multi-storey car park in King Street-Bond Street, which offset a reduction of spaces on temporary sites. In the 1980s the on-street parking meters were replaced by a system of voucher parking, which may have acted as a form of traffic restraint. One of the most important schemes involved excluding cars from Western Road during shopping hours, widening the footpaths at the expense of the carriageway, and introducing traffic calming measures: and this 50 years after this road was widened to facilitate traffic flow! Inevitably, however, traffic diverted to other roads, such as Upper North Street in the Clifton Hill Conservation Area.

The Civic Amenities Act, 1967 introduced the principle of designated conservation areas in which there would be a presumption against development that adversely affected their character. This legislation effectively supplemented the listing of buildings of architectural and historic interest introduced by the 1947 Act, recognising that the character of an area was often derived from other factors, such as street pattern, local history, land use and even the activities of the inhabitants. Many conservation areas have since been designated in Brighton and Hove: not only the Old Town, the villages and the Regency masterpieces, but also extensive Victorian developments, including Brighton's North Laine, formerly earmarked for redevelopment as a run-down Victorian working-class area, but now advertised as Brighton's Bohemian Quarter! It was, in fact, one of the conservation areas later recognised by the Ministry as outstanding for grant purposes. The recognition and confidence given by conservation status led to thriving communities with their own active societies, and special arrangements were made for them to make representations on planning applications to the local authorities. To this end, Brighton Borough Council established the Conservation Areas Advisory Committee which, upon amalgamation in 1997, was re-titled the Conservation Areas Advisory Group and its remit extended to

include Hove. Selma Montford, founder and secretary of the Brighton Society, has served as chairman ever since 1974.

Until amalgamation, Hove Borough Council, advised by its planning officer, Michael Ray, worked in co-operation with Brighton. Traffic congestion was not as acute in Hove, mainly because of the exceptionally wide roads, but one multi-storey car park was constructed in Norton Road as part of the town hall development in the early 1970s. Proposals over the years to pedestrianise George Street, the main shopping thoroughfare, have met with opposition from traders, but a scheme that involved closing the street during core shopping hours, together with extensive environmental improvements, has been implemented since amalgamation.

In the early 1970s there was public pressure for a by-pass, and provision was duly made in the approved County Structure Plan, based upon the proposal in the GBSP. In 1980 the government published alternatives for a route from the A27 at Falmer to the new Shoreham By-pass (A27) at Kingston (East Shoreham). Detailed proposals were the subject of a protracted public inquiry in

134 *Lennox Road, Round Hill Conservation Area, Brighton. Intriguing features of the city's townscape are the narrow, usually walled, footpath links between streets known as 'twittens'. Because of Brighton's hilly terrain some of these links comprise flights of steps known as 'cat's creeps'. This is part of the longest link, which connects Roundhill Crescent with Wakefield Road and Richmond Road.*

[161]

1982, at which the local authorities gave their support, subject to certain reservations. By then there was a groundswell of opinion against road building but, despite some opposition, the government subsequently approved a detailed scheme. However, Brighton Borough Council opposed the necessary compulsory purchase orders as a principal landowner, leading to a second public inquiry in 1987.

The orders were, however, duly approved, and in 1989 the Highways Agency commenced work on the first section from the A23 at Patcham to Dyke Road, intending to complete the whole scheme in four years. In 1992 a 'three quarter by-pass' was opened from Falmer to Hangleton, from where a link road down the Benfield Valley connected with the Old Shoreham Road at Portslade. Some members of an organisation that had originally pressed for a by-pass actually disrupted the opening ceremony, displaying a 'carmageddon' banner! However, it was a mild protest compared with the subsequent confrontations at Twyford Down and Newbury. The final stage of the by-pass from Hangleton to Kingston was the most intractable. It necessitated a tunnel under National Trust land at Southwick Hill, which presented engineering difficulties. As a result, the completed by-pass was not opened until 1996; Sir Herbert Carden might have judged it to be not just three, but 70 years late!

The following Highways Agency figures show the traffic flows on each section (between junctions) of the 'three quarter by-pass' after it opened in 1992:

Section	12-hour flow	24-hour flow
Falmer – Hollingbury	23,700	28,400
Hollingbury – Patcham	24,400	29,700
Patcham – Dyke Road	30,800	37,500
Dyke Road – Hangleton	19,700	24,100

In 1992 the Highways Agency also carried out a 'before and after' study on screen-lines and cordons intersecting many of the roads within the urban area, from which they were able to compare traffic counts taken then with those recorded in 1989. In general, the changes in total flows were similar to those that had been forecast using a mathematical model, although there were variations on individual roads. It had long been predicted that only a small proportion of the traffic on the new road would by-pass Brighton and Hove altogether, as the urban area—and the town centre in particular—serves as a powerful magnet for regional traffic. It was for this reason that the 1973 Greater Brighton Structure Plan referred to it as an 'outer distributor road' and not a by-pass. The Highways Agency's traffic counts on roads crossing a cordon around the Brighton town centre confirms this primary function: the total 12-hour traffic flow across the cordon in 1989 was 238,629 compared with 223,328 in 1992, a reduction of just 6.4 per cent.

The scale of the problem facing the town centre and the wider urban area can be appreciated from the forecast of a 50 per cent increase in car ownership by 2025. In the early 1980s East Sussex County Council, the then highway authority, proposed a Western Relief Road for the congested London Road (A23), which serves as a main shopping centre as well as a trunk road. This would have run from Preston Park to York Place across the railway land that has remained semi-derelict since the closure of the locomotive works and the goods yard. This scheme was later abandoned, however, and replaced by the present one-way system, which diverts southbound A23 traffic around Viaduct Road, Ditchling Road (south end), and Lewes Road. The Vogue Gyratory one-way system was constructed on the Lewes Road (then A27) at the congested junction with Hollingdean Road, Bear Road and Upper Lewes Road in the early 1980s.

These schemes are really little more than palliatives as traffic increases. Already, a major traffic accident, road works, building construction, a burst main, or even one of Brighton's famous road events, can bring gridlock. There are complaints from visitors that even on a fine summer's day it takes an interminable time to drive out of the resort. Radical measures to restrain traffic in the urban area seem long overdue. It is salutary to note that the dire warnings in the Buchanan Report and the somewhat radical proposals in the draft Greater Brighton Structure Plan were made nearly thirty years ago.

The Decline of the Railways

The post-war Attlee government nationalised the entire transport system, setting up a British Transport Commission (BTC) charged with integrating and rationalising all inland transport. Accordingly, the railways came under state control on 31 December 1947, and Southern Railways changed to Southern Region. However, the railway system was in a state of stagnation, not only as a result of the war, but inertia on the part of management in advance of the upheaval of nationalisation. The necessary long-term investment could not be sustained because of a near-bankrupt economy and the compensation due to share-holders. Consequently, the railways were not in the best position to meet the growing challenge of road transport—and an all-powerful roads lobby.

In 1960 the Macmillan government set up the Stedeford Committee to solve the 'railway problem'. In the following year one of its members, Dr Richard Beeching of ICI, was appointed chairman of BTC. In 1962 this body was dissolved and the nationalised railways were transferred to a British Railways Board. The outcome of these political events was the controversial 1962 Beeching Report, 'The Reshaping of British Railways', which proposed the closure of many uneconomic branch lines. A programme of closures was duly initiated. In 1964, the government of Harold Wilson was elected but, despite expectations to the contrary, the programme, with certain modifications, went ahead. It has been claimed that a 'roads conspiracy' was in place. A consequence for Brighton and Hove was that the services by steam train to Horsham, East Grinstead, Uckfield and Tunbridge Wells were lost as branch lines closed. But the most serious effect of the decline of the railways was the run-down of freight services over the next decade to the great advantage of road haulage (it is said that Dr Beeching was opposed and ended up as a scapegoat). All the local goods yards (at Brighton station, Sackville Road, Holland Road and Kemp Town) eventually closed.

Despite the downsizing of the rail network in the 1960s, there continued to be under-investment, resulting in the retention of obsolete rolling stock and the disrepair and under-manning of stations. Together with the modern scourges of trespass, vandalism and trackside graffiti, this neglect has tarnished the image of a once-proud service. On the positive side, however, there was an improvement in through services from Brighton to the Midlands and the West Country and the opening of a new station at Moulsecombe. It is probably too early to assess the full effect of the Channel Tunnel, but it will inevitably benefit the local economy, particularly in its relationship with the European Union.

Following the privatisation of British Rail, the infrastructure of track and stations was owned and controlled by a single company (Railtrack) and the southern region of British Rail was split up into smaller areas, Brighton and Hove being served by Network South Central. Railtrack promised massive, long-overdue investment in repairs and improvements to the rail infrastructure, including £14 million for the renovation of Brighton Central station. This work, which includes the renewal of the famous glazed roof, has now been completed to the great advantage of Brighton as an international tourist resort. It should be noted that some thirty years ago there were proposals to redevelop the building altogether, and even to incorporate office blocks above a new station complex.

The Brighton Locomotive Works continued in production after the war and in 1949 built the first of an intended 'Leader' class of steam locomotives with an unusual design: an 0-6-6-0 configuration, with one boiler driving through two sets of bogies, although the wheels were larger than normal size. It was controlled from cabs at each end and had the appearance of a diesel or electric locomotive. However, after trials in 1949 and 1950 the prototype was abandoned, as were three others that never ran under their own steam. For a few years the works concentrated on building orthodox steam locomotives while looking ahead to diesel and electric, but in 1954 the works closed altogether. Brighton had been responsible for some of the last development work of the steam era.

The closing of the works and goods yard at Brighton station left a large semi-derelict brown-field site in the heart of the town, thereby creating a planning problem which has still not been finally resolved after the best part of half-a-century. Not for the first time, plans have been formulated for a major commercial development comprising a superstore, two hotels, housing, offices, workshops and some 350 parking spaces. This has attracted strong opposition on the grounds that the superstore would compete with the London Road shopping centre and that the development generally would be a major traffic generator.

It is regrettable that the opportunity was not taken to retain a part of the Brighton Locomotive Works as a museum of steam like that at the former Great Western Railway Works in Swindon. It could have been a great asset to the city. Attempts to create such a museum at the old Pullman Works in the 1970s proved to be abortive.

Maritime Brighton, Hove and Portslade—a Harbour at last!

The post-war period saw the gradual restoration of the Brighton and Hove seafront: the debris of war was cleared away; the fishermen returned, many from service in the Royal Navy or Merchant Navy; the fish market came back to the beach; the sailing, cruising and deep-sea angling clubs reappeared; and the piers reopened. Even the paddle-steamers plied along the coast until 1954, the last of the breed being P. & A. Campbell's *Glen Gower*, but the vast crowds of trippers and holiday-makers that once thronged to that famous man-made bay formed by the two piers were missing. Over time parts of Brighton's lower promenade and arches became run-down and in 1975, after years of wrangling, changes of ownership and attempts to update its image, the newly grade 1 listed West Pier was closed and abandoned to the sea. This came not long after it established a lasting claim to fame when, in 1968, it was the prime location for the satirical film, *Oh! What a Lovely War*, directed by Richard Attenborough with a host of stars, including Dirk Bogarde, Phyllis Calvert, John Gielgud, Jack Hawkins, John Mills and Ralph Richardson. (The Devil's Dyke and Brighton's Sheepcote Valley were used as locations for action on the Western Front.) However, thanks to the determination of the former West Pier Society and, subsequently, the West Pier Trust, who now own the structure, there is still hope

135 *Crowds at the post-war re-opening of the West Pier.*

that, with the aid of grants from the national lottery fund and private investment, it can be restored to its former glory.

Meanwhile, the focus of attention had switched again to fashionable Kemp Town—as it had when the old Chain Pier was built. Once more the idea of a harbour came alive. This time it was the brainchild of a local garage proprietor and yachtsman, Henry Cohen. In 1963 he and his associates put forward a colossal and revolutionary scheme to be known as Brighton Marina, comprising not just a harbour but an entertainment, residential and conference complex such as not even Brighton had seen before. At first, the idea was that it should be located on the shore and over the sea between the Madeira lift and Duke's Mound east of Black Rock; then, after being approved in principle by Brighton County Borough Council, the scheme was greatly enlarged and a new site proposed between the Palace Pier and the Madeira lift.

The proposals initiated an unprecedented controversy, locally and nationally. One of the leading protestors was Sir William (later Lord) Holford, a well-known architect/town planner, who lived in Kemp Town. In 1964 he urged that a site east of Black Rock should be considered, as this would be less damaging to amenities and allow better access. This suggestion was received favourably by the Brighton Marina Company and by the council. The next few years were spent in planning and parliamentary procedures, with interminable amendments, wrangling and accusations of intrigue. Eventually, all the necessary consents were obtained to allow the construction of a harbour below the cliffs on the east side of

136 *The paddle steamer* Glen Gower, *c.1954, which plied between the piers.*

Black Rock with access roads, including a tunnel and ramps, to begin in 1971. Lord Holford was undoubtedly right and one wonders what the outcome might have been had the Black Rock site been put forward in the first place.

The Queen formally opened Brighton Marina as a working harbour on 31 May 1979. Protected by two large breakwaters, comprising 100 huge caissons, it encloses an area of over 126 acres beneath the cliffs. The larger outer harbour, providing direct access to the sea, is separated from the smaller inner harbour by an east-west 'strand', the two harbours being connected by a lock at the eastern end. Two floating jetties extend into the outer harbour, from which a system of pontoons is connected, providing berths (as at 1997) for 1,357 8-18 metre and 18 35-70 metre boats. There are also visitor reception, waiting and fuelling pontoons.

Detailed plans for the related development (a so-called 'city-in-the-sea') were approved in principle by the Secretary of State after a public inquiry in 1974. However, because of financial set-backs and changes in ownership and management, the scheme, with significant changes, has taken many years to come to fruition; but now, at the beginning of the new millennium, it is nearing completion under a new ownership and management structure. Brighton Marina Co. Ltd, which is a wholly owned subsidiary of Brunswick Development Group Plc, holds the 125-year head lease from the freeholders, Brighton and Hove City Council. In turn, under leases have been granted to three principal operational companies: Premier Marinas Ltd, who are responsible for the 'wet side' of the marina, including berths, the boatyard and the West Quay; Parkridge Developments Ltd, who are responsible for the commercial side; and Brighton Marina Residential Management Co. Ltd. The marina now comprises—besides its harbour and boatyard—the Marina Village with quayside shops, restaurants and pubs; a multiplex cinema and bowling centre; a superstore; car parks; and extensive residential accommodation. The latter mainly takes the form of prestigious three- or four-storey apartment blocks attractively arranged on promontories in the inner harbour with private berths for motor yachts. A new feature is a casino that promises to enhance further Brighton's image (according to *The Argus*) of Las Vegas-on-Sea! Parkridge Developments Ltd is building a stylish waterfront building, comprising retail outlets and a long awaited 100-bed hotel: with the possible addition of a night club, this development, which should be completed in 2002, will see the final realisation of Henry Cohen's dream.

Brighton Marina—the largest in Britain—is undeniably a major traffic generator, although it is served by buses, taxis and even the Black Rock station of Volk's Electric Railway. On the other hand it does represent another facility that has helped keep Brighton firmly on the tourist map and diversify its economy. Casual visitors come not only for the on-shore facilities but for the marine activities, which include regular racing organised by the Brighton Marina Yacht Club (which also has cruising, diving and dinghy branches), motor boat cruises and a variety of visiting craft, such as naval patrol boats of the University Boat Squadron. In 1983-7 HMS *Cavalier*, the last surviving destroyer from the Second World War, provided a popular attraction. Since 1979 an RNLI lifeboat station has been fully operational at the Marina, equipped with a 22ft. by 8ft. Atlantic 21 with twin engines: this is a rigid inflatable, having a hull of glass-reinforced plastic, but, also, a gas-activated bag for emergencies.

The opening of the harbour in 1979 coincided with the inauguration of a 100-minute service to Dieppe by Seajet, a version of Boeing's Jetfoil. The 'ship that flies' with its water jet propulsion could cruise at 43 knots (50 m.p.h.) when 'foilborne'. Alas, the service did not come up to expectations in adverse weather conditions and was later withdrawn. In more

137 *The Queen escorted by the mayor, Dennis Hobden, visits the Royal Pavilion on the official opening of Brighton Marina, 31 May 1979. After Queen Victoria visited the Pavilion for the last time in 1845 the building was gutted and about to be demolished but was saved by the action of the Town Commissioners, who acquired the property. Period furniture has been loaned to the council in more recent times.*

138 *Aerial view of Brighton Marina from the east. Photograph courtesy of Premier Marinas Ltd.*

recent times catamaran services have been tried, but these, too, were unsuccessful. It is, perhaps, too much to hope that further cross-Channel services will be inaugurated—although it should be noted that the last surviving paddle-steamer, *Waverley*, has visited the Marina. In any event, after various set-backs, the fortunes of Newhaven have been restored by the reintroduction of fast ferry services to Dieppe. With improved road connections via the Brighton and Lewes by-passes, as well as the rail service, this is to the advantage of the city. Newhaven is a part of the Greater Brighton conurbation, and could well have been included, along with Peacehaven and Telscombe Cliffs, in the unitary authority area in 1997.

One significant feature of the Marina development has been the transfer of the Brighton fishing fleet (now mainly trawlers) to moorings in the outer harbour. Although an advantage operationally, the removal of the fleet from its traditional site, and the consequent transfer of the fish market to the wholesale market in Circus Street, Brighton, was regretted from an historical point of view. However, an excellent Brighton Fishing Museum, run by a private trust, now occupies arches on the old site between the piers. This complements the restoration of the lower promenade and arches, which includes an artists' quarter in keeping with the traditional character.

In recent years the Palace Pier (regrettably renamed Brighton Pier) has had a new lease of life and is now one of Britain's leading tourist attractions. There is every hope that a restored West Pier would complement, rather than rival its neighbour to the east, the two perhaps echoing the dual sides of Brighton's character—the raffish and the refined. There may not be the huge crowds of old on the beaches, but there are so many water sports, such as sailing, power-boating, water-skiing, parascending, windsurfing, surf-riding and jet-skiing, that offshore traffic regulations have had to be introduced!

The fortunes of the port of Shoreham, and the canal in particular, have fluctuated considerably since the war. Much of its prosperity had been due to the patronage of the electric and gas utilities, which in 1952 was boosted by the commissioning of the second (Brighton B) coal-fired power station. This was followed by the construction of the larger Prince Philip lock, which allowed vessels up to 105 metres in length and 16.4 beam to use the canal. However, in the early 1970s, with the advent of natural gas, the gas works at Portslade was closed; then, in the next decade, both the Brighton 'A' and 'B' power stations were decommissioned in turn by the former Central Electricity Generating Board, electricity being supplied from the national grid.

The sites of the gas works and the adjoining 'A' power station were subsequently redeveloped for cargo handling, but the 25-acre site of the 'B' station became a bone of contention after demolition began in 1988, following its acquisition by the Shoreham Port Authority, which included representatives from Brighton and Hove. Their intention was to use the land for operational purposes, but planning permission was refused because of inadequate road access to the south side of the canal, this decision being upheld by the Secretary of State in 1990 after a public inquiry. As a consequence, a new gas-fired power station has since been built on part of the site by South Coast Power, a private company who lease the site from the port authority, natural gas being supplied by trunk main.

The port was disadvantaged further by recession, but has since revived: in 1994, 715 commercial vessels with nearly 1.4 million tonnes of cargo used the canal, an increase of 22.9 per cent and 8.8 per cent respectively on 1992, but still below pre-recession figures. In 1994 the canal carried over 60 per cent of all the traffic in the Port of Shoreham, which

139 *The inner harbour at Brighton Marina, 1997.*

also comprises the Western Arm (the River Adur at Shoreham) and the Eastern Arm (from the entrance at Kingston to the locks which give access to the canal). The principal cargoes now handled are sand, shingle and other aggregates, timber, oil, wine, fish, fruit and vegetables, grain, steel, cement and a wide range of other building materials. The export of live animals caused considerable controversy in 1995, but was subsequently greatly reduced.

The canal has also developed as a centre for small boats, with facilities at the Lady Bee Marina at Southwick and the smaller Aldrington Marina at Hove. The pre-war Prince George lock was converted in 1994 to provide access for such boats. Unbeknown to many Hove residents, a small fishing fleet has been based in Aldrington basin at the eastern end of the canal.

The Port of Shoreham, which has operated as a statutory undertaking since 1760, has good prospects, being well placed in relation to the South, London and the Midlands, particularly since the construction of the M25 and M23, the improvement of the A23 and the opening of the Brighton by-pass. However, the absence of a satisfactory connection between the by-pass, via the Hangleton link road, and the A259 coast road remains a serious problem. This inhibits the potential development of the port as a roll-on/roll-off facility for container traffic and provision of a cross-Channel service. Post-war development plans made provision for the widening of Trafalgar Road/Church Road, Portslade, but this was later abandoned because of the demolition involved. One suggestion put forward by consultants has been the construction of a tunnel underneath Portslade from the southern end of the link road near its junction with Old Shoreham Road to the coast road, but cost and disruption may well be prohibitive.

140 *The Seajet,* Normandy Princess, *on trials off the Palace Pier in 1979. This Boeing Jetfoil of Jetlink Ferries Ltd, 'the ship that flies', had turbine-driven, waterjet propulsion. Its terminal was in the new Marina and it could carry up to 365 passengers to Dieppe in 100 minutes.*

141 *An aerial photograph looking east across Shoreham Harbour entrance to the canal, 1949. The Brighton 'A' Power Station and the gas works beyond (in Southwick and Portslade respectively) have since been demolished. The Brighton 'B' Power Station had yet to be built on the site beyond the harbour entrance; this too has now been demolished and replaced by a gas-powered power station!*

Development and Demographic Change

The serious post-war housing shortage was tackled with vigour. Prefabricated single-storey dwellings were the government's immediate response. These 'pre-fabs' were erected on vacant sites locally: in fact, they were so successful that many outlived their projected five- to ten-year life. Materials for permanent building were in short supply for several years, so priority was given to municipal development (at the, then, high 'Parker Morris' standards) to meet local needs; private houses required a council building licence well into the 1950s.

In Brighton, council development took place mainly at Bevendean, Coldean, Hollingbury, Hollingdean and Woodingdean; in Hove, at West Blatchington (Sunninghill Estate) and Hangleton (St Helen's Estate); and in Portslade, at Mile Oak. Private development took place in the same suburbs; also in new suburban estates at Westdene, and Saltdean in Brighton. As in pre-war times, much housing related to the local area was outside the administrative boundaries, particularly at Peacehaven and Telscombe Cliffs, Southwick, Shoreham and the expanding settlements of mid-Sussex. In more recent years, with a diminishing supply of building land, development has taken place mainly by consolidation and infilling: new housing on the steep hillside east of Sutherland Road has unfortunately encroached upon the skyline of Whitehawk Hill, in one place almost to the outer ramparts of the neolithic camp.

Despite these housing developments taking the form of low-density suburbs influenced by the motor vehicle, there was still little anticipation of the pending upsurge in car ownership. This has resulted in some comparatively narrow suburban streets, as well as older urban

142 *The view from Sussex Heights tower block behind the* Metropole Hotel, c.1980. *Suburban development can be seen on the slopes of Hollingbury Hill in the distance.*

streets, becoming choked by on-street parking. Even where garages were provided, second and visitor cars often constitute a hazard, to say nothing of vehicles left out during the daytime, and also 'old bangers' abandoned by the roadside. The garden environment of suburbia is sometimes spoilt by the provision of hard-standings in front gardens for cars and caravans, and by parking on verges. The latter is particularly prevalent near schools, and is increasingly being challenged by neighbouring residents, who line verges with lumps of concrete and suchlike. In some areas leafy suburbia is gradually being turned into what Ian Nairn in his 1950s book *Outrage* called 'subtopia'.

Redevelopment at high densities was also a feature of the 1950s and '60s. This was positively urged by the government in the early 1960s in order to safeguard agricultural land (this was before food mountains and set-aside!). The designation of the South Downs as an Area of Outstanding Natural Beauty in 1965 also put a break on outward growth—although not an absolute prohibition. In Brighton, the County Borough Council demolished more working-class Victorian housing under slum clearance powers, particularly in the eastern part of the town around Albion Hill, Carlton Hill and Eastern Road; the replacement housing was mainly flats in slab and tower blocks, made possible, of course, by 'vertical transport'.

Similar demolition also took place in the old 'railwaymen's quarter' between the Central station and London Road following the closure of the locomotive works, although here the new development was something of a hotchpotch of high-density housing and commercial uses, including a 'flatted' factory slab block and a dominant residential tower block—perhaps an indication of the redevelopment then destined for North Laine and the vacant railway land in the 1960s. High-rise council flats also made an incongruous appearance at Hollingdean, Bristol Gate and Whitehawk, which were outside the inner urban area.

Private enterprise also contributed to Brighton's changing skyline, particularly with the erection of the soaring Sussex Heights, part of the rebuilding behind the *Metropole Hotel*, which involved the demolition of the historic St Margaret's chapel-of-ease built in 1824 to serve the Regency Square area, and also Chartwell Court, part of the Churchill Square development. Fortunately, proposals to demolish the *Metropole* and *Grand Hotels* in the 1960s were thwarted. The skyline of the original Kemp Town was changed by the erection of a tower block addition to the Royal Sussex County Hospital.

Council redevelopment in Hove in the 1960s was limited to the Conway Street area near the station, where slab blocks of flats were erected, although some private blocks—generally limited to ten storeys—were permitted, particularly in parts of Kingsway, Grand Avenue and the Drive. In both Hove and Brighton, the change in the social character of the fashionable Regency and Victorian areas continued apace after the war, with conversions of large houses into self-contained flats, multiple occupation units or bed-sits, so that there are now even pockets of deprivation. The increase in the number of households has also added greatly to traffic congestion, on-street parking problems and pollution, as the number of cars greatly exceeds the availability of garages in the old mews. During the last decade of the 20th century double-parking in breach of traffic regulations became a serious problem in many of the older parts of Brighton and Hove, causing obstruction, particularly to fire appliances and other emergency services, as well as to refuse collection and other public service vehicles, including buses. In fact, the enforcement of parking regulations progressively went beyond the resources of the police, with the result that many motorists were no longer deterred by the prospect of conviction.

In the post-war years Brighton County Borough Council wisely promoted light industrial estates adjoining the suburbs of Hollingbury, Moulsecombe, Bevendean and Woodingdean, thus reducing the incidence of commuting by road. In addition, the Freshfield industrial estate was developed on the site of the former Kemp Town station and goods yard after closure in the early 1970s. Substantial office development also took place in the post-war years, not only in the Brighton town centre, but also in Preston Road (A23) opposite Preston Park, involving the demolition of the former Victorian villas. In the early 1970s the large European headquarters of American Express was established in Edward Street. However, office development was subsequently restricted because of pressure on scarce housing land.

In Hove, light industry formed part of the Conway Street redevelopment in the 1960s; while in Portslade, working-class housing in the North Street area was similarly redeveloped when the gas works closed. A number of large office concerns were established in Hove: the former *Princes Hotel* (which became the headquarters of the new Brighton and Hove Unitary Authority in 1997) was taken over by the South Eastern Electricity Board as their regional headquarters; the Alliance Building Society built an office block in Orchard Road; and the Legal and General Assurance Society converted a former furniture depository in Montefiore Road into a head office. The latter was commendably well-designed, securing the restoration of a fine Victorian Gothic building; but, as with other offices in the vicinity, the original parking requirement was greatly exceeded by subsequent demand, thus causing congestion and parking problems in nearby residential streets.

143 *Old Albion players at the Goldstone Ground, Hove, 1932. The ground was sold for development as a retail park and the last game was played here on 26 April 1997 after 96 years. After playing at Gillingham for two years, the Albion now has a temporary home at Brighton's Withdean Stadium, but has applied for planning permission for a stadium at Falmer, a proposal that is highly controversial.*

One of the most significant changes since the war has been in the pattern of shopping. At first, town centre supermarkets brought about the demise of many small local shops; but more recent times have seen the development of edge-of-town superstores and retail warehouses at Hollingbury, Lewes Road (the former Preston Barracks site), Brighton Marina, West Hove (Hangleton link road), Hove Greyhound Stadium, Sackville Road, Old Shoreham Road (former site of St Joseph's Home), and the former Goldstone football ground. The superstores have also attracted trade away from the town centres: the speciality shops of the Old Town and North Laine have thrived, but some supermarkets and other retail establishments have been lost, particularly in Western Road, St James's Street and the town centre of Hove. In many cases, charity shops, offices and restaurants have occupied the vacated shop premises. Church Road and Western Road, Hove have now become fashionable

144 *Sir Harry Lauder being welcomed by the mayor at the Town Hall, 1922.*

145 *Sussex County Cricket Ground, Hove, c.1900. Until amalgamation in 1997, Hove was promoted as 'the Sports Centre of the South': it was home to both the Albion and the Cricket Club, and also the Greyhound Stadium in Nevill Road, the King Alfred Swimming Pool complex on the Kingsway and numerous public sports facilities along the seafront. With the Albion gone and the King Alfred due for redevelopment, the sobriquet has less truth today.*

restaurant streets in the manner of Brighton's Preston Street. In the mid-1990s the Church-ill Square shopping complex was redeveloped as a modern enclosed shopping mall, and this has acted as a counter-magnet. A proposed redevelopment of the redundant gasholder site and adjoining school west of George Street, Hove to provide a superstore or large supermarket is intended to have the same effect.

In terms of population, the effect of planning policies and development since the war has been a deceleration in the rate of growth, followed by an actual decline due mainly to smaller households. The population of Brighton, Hove and Portslade in 1969 was estimated to be 253,210, an increase of 5.1 per cent on 1951: the 1991 census figure was 228,946, a decline of 9.6 per cent. This was mainly due to natural change (the balance of deaths and births), which was no longer offset by net immigration. However, two factors should be noted: firstly, much locally-related growth takes place beyond the administrative boundaries but within the Greater Brighton sub-region; secondly, the actual number of households is increasing due to modern lifestyles. Both of these factors have a bearing on the incidence of car ownership and traffic generation.

Epilogue

A City in Crisis

At times throughout their history the settlements that merged to become the millennium city of Brighton and Hove experienced a crisis in their development, which transport in one form or another helped significantly to resolve. In the early years of Brighthelmston the development of the hog-boat or 'hoggy' enabled the settlement to survive, against the odds, as a fishing community when there was no longer a harbour at the mouth of the Wellesbourne. In the mid-18th century, when the town was seemingly on its last legs, it was the development of the sprung coach and the macadamised turnpike road that enabled Brighthelmston to emerge from its chrysalis and become a fashionable seaside resort under the patronage of Dr William Russell and George, Prince of Wales.

In the mid-19th century, when it appeared that Brighton, with its expansion into the parish of Hove, had over-reached itself with the ending of royal patronage, it was the steam train that brought the patronage of the so-called middle and working classes and gave an impetus for growth, not only as a popular seaside resort, but as a dormitory town for the retired and the London commuter; even, with the opening of the locomotive works, as an industrial centre. At the beginning of the 20th century when the popularity of Brighton was again flagging, it was the motor car that helped revive its fortunes. Then, after the devastating Second World War and the decline of the traditional seaside holiday, Brighton diversified its economy (to the advantage also of Hove), particularly as an international conference and exhibition centre: to a large extent, this was made possible by the development of the jet airliner and the accessibility of the new Gatwick Airport.

The new City of Brighton and Hove is faced with a crisis of a different kind in the new millennium. It is a crisis of space, or rather lack of it: space in terms of land upon which to build housing and related uses to meet the essential needs of its own people; and space to accommodate the ubiquitous motor car, which came to Brighton's aid early in the 20th century but now causes gridlock, atmospheric and noise pollution—and road rage.

Housing Space in Crisis

Brighton and Hove now presents the image of a dynamic city with a thriving economy and a cosmopolitan, highly tolerant character. The slogan of the successful campaign for city status led by Simon Fanshawe was 'The Place To Be'. This is not hollow rhetoric; in fact, so many people from London and other parts of the country would like to live here that house prices and rents have been rocketing, with the result that many local people are

146 *Balsdean Valley (east of Woodingdean) from the dewpond near the Juggs Road track. This priceless landscape, within the Sussex Downs Area of Outstanding Natural Beauty, actually lies inside the boundary of the city. Such superb scenery is typical of the Downs to the north and east of Brighton and Hove and fully deserves protection as a National Park.*

unable to compete in the housing market, and essential, but comparatively low-paid, public service workers are difficult to recruit.

Councillor Tehmtan Framroze reported in *The Argus* of 9 September 2001 that the city council faced a projected deficit of £2.2 million in their housing budget, almost entirely because of the cost of housing homeless families in special accommodation. In 2000, 3,700 homeless families sought help from the council, 50 per cent more than in 1998. A council survey has shown that some 25,000 residents are living in unsuitable accommodation, which amounts to 12 per cent of the population—twice the national average. In addition, because of its image and mild climate, the city is a lure for a migrant population of 'rough sleepers' and for 'new age travellers' who frequently set up camp with their fleets of cars, caravans and lorries on public and other open spaces on the outskirts: the council has already established one permanent site at Horsedean on the north side of the by-pass at Patcham. Furthermore, the city is faced with something of a crisis in the care of the elderly because of a reduction in the number of care homes due to prohibitive costs: one result is that urgently needed hospital beds are often 'blocked' by elderly patients with nowhere else to go.

Road Space in Crisis

It has been recognised since the Buchanan Report in the 1960s that land use and transportation are closely related. Housing and other uses generate predictable volumes of road traffic, with a consequent demand for parking and road space. Throughout the 20th century the motor car and the motor bus influenced the form that development was to take, enabling housing and other uses to be spread widely over the dip-slopes of the Downs in the form of suburban estates, in contrast to the more nucleated settlement around stations in the Victorian railway era. But even without taking into account the traffic generated locally by new development and population growth in the future, it is forecast that car ownership and usage is likely to continue to grow.

With a policy of traffic restraint a 'sticks and carrots' approach is essential. Here the big stick of enforcement has been matched by the marked improvement in the bus services, with an alliance between the bus operators and the council, as discussed in the last chapter. History has shown that integration and co-operation produces a better transport system—as with the horse-buses, the railways (1923-95), the taxis and the motor buses. It is salutary to recall that Brighton's own Magnus Volk produced a small electric vehicle over one hundred years ago, and that electro-buses were running locally early in the 20th century.

Cyberspace

It is too soon to write the history of the next decade, let alone the 21st century or the Millennium. However, we can draw certain inferences from the immediate past. In 1968 few could have imagined the concept of cyberspace, as we know it today. It has advanced exponentially since that date, so much so that it almost seems to verge on the paranormal. It is possible, at least, to imagine that if the same rate of progress is maintained in the future then more and more of our activities will be conducted in cyberspace, especially with the rise of a younger generation who have grown up with computer technology. This could have ramifications for land use and transportation as we know it.

At the beginning of the 21st century it is virtually impossible to predict the history of development and transport over the next 100 years. At the end of the century—God forbid—Brightonians may, like their prehistoric forbears, have sought refuge on the hilltops, descending to the coastal plain only to load their primitive carts with salvage; or they may be living (God also forbid) in a gleaming high-tech, high-rise city, and Roger French's successor at the re-named Brighton, Hove and District Space and Time Travel Co. may be running excursions to our Eden Centre colony on Mars—or even back to 1896 in their latest Easyrider Tardis to enjoy the leisurely 'Emancipation Run' down the Brighton Road! Citizens of Brighton and Hove, never forget Brighton's old motto *IN DEO FIDEMUS!*

Bibliography

Note: The books and other reference material below are listed under those chapter headings to which they are most relevant. The designatory letters of authors are not shown.

Preface
Fines, Kenneth D., *The Treasure of Herstmonceux: An Adventure in Genealogy*, Philip Marshall Correll, Stratford-upon-Avon, 1989 (available at Hove Reference Library, the British Library, the Bodleian Library and the Library of the Society of Genealogists)

Chapter One: The Prehistoric 'Brightonians'
Allcroft, A. Hadrian, *Downland Pathways*, Methuen & Co. Ltd, London, 1924
Allcroft, A. Hadrian, personal unpublished record book, *ex libris* Dr Curwen
Curwen, E. Cecil, *The Archaeology of Sussex*, Methuen & Co., Ltd, London, 1937
Williams, Guy R. and Deutsch, Andre, in association with Rainbird Reference Books, *The World of Model Ships*, London, 1971 (reprinted 1975)
Wooldridge, Dr S.W. and Goldring, Frederick, *The Weald*, Collins, London, 1953

Chapter Two: Roman, Saxon and Norman Invaders
Beckett, Arthur (founder and one-time editor), *The Sussex County Magazine*, vols. 1-30, T.R. Beckett Ltd, Eastbourne, 1927-56
Margary, Ivan D., *Roman Ways in the Weald*, Phoenix House, London, 1948
Morris, John (ed.), Domesday Book: *Sussex*, Phillimore, Chichester, 1976

Chapter Three: The Old Town of Brighthelmston
Aitchison, George, 'Early History of Brighton', in *Brighton 1934*, NUT Conference Souvenir, Brighton Herald Ltd, Brighton, 1934
Aitchinson, George, *Unknown Brighton*, John Lane The Bodley Head Ltd, 1926
Dale, Antony, *The History and Architecture of Brighton*, Bredon and Heginbothom Ltd, Brighton, 1950
Fiennes, Celia, *The Illustrated Journeys of Celia Fiennes (1685-c.1712)*, edited by Christopher Morris, MacDonald & Co., London and Sydney; Webb & Bower, Exeter, 1982
Gilbert, Edmund W., *Brighton—Old Ocean's Bauble*, Methuen & Co., Ltd, London, 1954
Holden, E.W., 'Excavations at the Deserted Medieval Village of Hangleton', *Sussex Archaeological Collections* Vol. 101, Sussex Archaeological Society, 1963
Martin, Alderman Henry, *The History of Brighton and Environs*, John Beal, 1854
Musgrave, Clifford, *Life in Brighton*, Faber and Faber, London, 1970

Waugh, Mary, *Smuggling in Kent and Sussex 1700-1840*, Countryside Books, Newbury, Berkshire, 1985

Yeakell, T. and Gardner, W. (Surveyors), *Plan of Brighthelmston 1779*, published by Richard Thomas, *c*.1780

Chapter Four: Royal Patronage and the Brighton Road

Bishop, John George, *A Peep into the Past: Brighton in the Olden Time*, published by the author, Brighton, 1892

Bishop, John George, *The Brighton Chain Pier—in Memoriam*, Brighton Herald Office, 1896

Bishop, John George, *The Brighton Pavilion and its Royal Associations*, by authority of Brighton Town Council, 11th edition, 1903

Cheal, Henry, *The Story of Shoreham*, Combridges, Hove, 1921

Cobbett, William, *Rural Rides* (1830), vols. 1 and 2, Everyman Library, J.M. Dent and Sons Ltd, London, 1912

Dale, Antony, 'Fashionable Brighton 1820-1860', *Country Life*, London, 1947

Dale, Antony, *The History of the Kemp Town Gardens, Brighton*, published by the author, 1964

Dale, Antony, *Brighton Town and Brighton People*, Phillimore and Co. Ltd, London and Chichester, 1976

Erredge, John Ackerson, *History of Brighthelmston*, Observer Office, Brighton, 1862

Jones, Lavender and Pollard, Jacqueline, *Hilly Laine to Hanover—a Brighton Neighbourhood*, Brighton Books Publishing, 1999

Lucas, E.V., *Highways and Byways in Sussex*, MacMillan and Co. Ltd, London, 1912

Morley, John, *The Making of the Royal Pavilion Brighton*, Sotheby Publications, 1984

Odell, Mary Theresa (compiler), *The Brighton Theatre 1814-1819*, Aldridge Bros., Worthing, 1944

Registrar-General, *Censuses (Brighton, Hove and District) 1831* and *1841*

Stanford, Charles Thomas, *Wick: a Contribution to the History of Hove*, Combridges, Hove, 1923

Swinson, Arthur (ed.), *A Register of the Regiments and Corps of the British Army*, The Archive Press, London, 1972

Walpole, Horace, *Letters of Horace Walpole (1717-1797)*, selected and edited by C.B. Lucas, Simkin, Marshall Hamilton, Kent & Co. Ltd, London, 1904

Chapter Five: Queen Victoria and the Brighton Line

Ainsworth, William Harrison, *Ovingdean Grange* (which contains 'The Legend of the Devil's Dyke as related by Master Cisbury Oldfirle, Schoolmaster of Poynings'), George Routledge & Sons Ltd, London, *ante* 1876

Baines, Inspector James W., *History of the Brighton Police 1830-1967*, Brighton Watch Committee, *c*.1968

Betjeman, Sir John and Gray, James, *Victorian and Edwardian Brighton from Old Photographs*, B.T. Batsford, Ltd, London, 1972

Blaker, Nathaniel Paine, *Sussex in Bygone Days*, Combridges, Hove, 1919

Blyth, Henry, *Smugglers' Village—The Story of Rottingdean*, H.E. Blyth Ltd, no date

Brighton Public Libraries, *Bygone Brighton—a Portfolio of Prints*, Brighton Council, *c*.1970

Clark, Paul, *The Railways of the Devil's Dyke*, Turntable Publications, Sheffield, 1976

Clarke, John L., *Outlines of Local Government of the United Kingdom*, 14th edn., Sir Isaac Pitman and Sons Ltd, 1939

Dale, Antony, *Brighton Cemeteries*, Brighton Borough Council, 1991

Gray, Adrian, *The London to Brighton Line 1841-1977*, Oakwood Press, Blandford Forum, 1977

Harris, Melvin, ITN *Book of Firsts*, Michael O'Mara Books Ltd, London, 1994

Hollingdale, E.A. and Drummond, H., *Brighton in Retrospect*, East Sussex County Library Local History Series, 1974

Hollingdale, Eileen, *Old Brighton—a collection of Prints, Paintings and Drawings* (from the Local History Collection in Brighton Reference Library), George Nibbs Publishing, Norwich, 1979

Kebbell, William, *The Climate of Brighton*, Longman, Green and Roberts, London, 1859

Martin, Ron, *Brighton General Hospital* (courtesy of Sue Trimingham, South Downs Health NHS Trust), 2000.

Middleton, Judy, *A History of Hove*, Phillimore & Co., Ltd, Chichester, 1979

Montford, Selma, Pollard, Jacqueline and Sanderson, Robert (compilers), *The Vanishing Villas of Preston and Withdean*, Brighton Books Publishing, 1996

Nairn, Ian and Pevsner, Nikolaus, *The Buildings of England—Sussex*, Penguin Books, Harmondsworth, Middlesex, 1965

Oakensen, Supt. Derek, 'The Origins and Development of Policing in Brighton and Hove, 1830-1900, with special reference to Local Political Control', unpublished Ph.D thesis (University of Brighton), 1994

Ordnance Survey plans 1: 2500 scale: *LXV 12* (*c*.1870—Old Hove and Cliftonville), *LXVI 9* (1877, surveyed 1875—Brighton and Brunswick Town), *LXVI 10* (1877, surveyed 1873-5—Brighton Kemp Town North), *LXVI 14* (1877, surveyed 1875—Brighton Kemp Town South)

Page's Directory—Brighton, Hove and District, annual vols. 1865-98

Rapkin, J., 'Plan of Brighton 1852' (originally published by John Tallis), in Baynton-Williams, Ashley, *Town and City Maps of the British Isles 1800-1855*, Studio Editions Ltd, London, 1992

Patching & Son (Builders), 'We arrived before Brighton', *The House Builder*, April 1975

Peasgood, Adrian, *The Horse Buses of Brighton and Hove*, Centre for Continuing Education, University of Sussex, 1985

Porter, Henry C., *The History of Hove Ancient and Modern*, printed by Elmutt Clifton, Hove, 1897

Registrar-General, *Decennial Censuses 1841-1891*

Sitwell, Osbert and Barton, Margaret, *Brighton*, Faber and Faber, London, 1935

Smith, Michael, *Rudyard Kipling—The Rottingdean Years*, Brownleaf, 1989

Sussex Police (Brighton Division), Hove Police File, including Watch Committee Minutes

Towner's Directory, 1899

Treacher's New Plan of Brighton and Hove 1898 (based on the Ordnance Survey), H. and C. Treachers, Brighton

Volk, Conrad, *Magnus Volk of Brighton*, Phillimore & Co. Ltd, Chichester, 1972

Wagner, Sir Anthony and Dale, Antony, *The Wagners of Brighton*, Phillimore & Co., Ltd, 1983

Chapter Six: Motor Cars, Aeroplanes and the Suburban 'Woodby-Happeys'

Brighton General Purposes Committee (Estates and Town Planning Sub-Committee), Minutes 1928-1930 (ref: The Dyke Estate)

Brighton's Motor Jubilee 3-7 September 1946, Souvenir Programme, *50 years in the Motor Industry, 1896-1946*

Church of England, *Hove Parish Magazine* Jan. 1897 and Sept. 1897

Collins, Joyce, *Dr Brighton's Indian Patients December 1914–January 1916*, Brighton Books Publishing, 1997

Cornell, A., 'Famous Run to Brighton' (in *A History of the First Ten Years of Automobiles 1896-1906*), The Car Illustrated Ltd, London, 1906

Dunstall, David M., Archive and Research, The Shoreham Airport Collection (to 1997)

Elliott, A.G., A *Portrait of the Brighton Trams 1901-1939*, published by the author, 1979

Gibson, J. Eason, 'London-Brighton Veteran Car Run', *Country Life*, London, 1946

Gray, James S., *Brighton between the Wars*, B.T. Batsford Ltd, London, 1976

Hobden, Arthur, *Streamline 1936-1986*, Brighton Streamline Taxis, Brighton, 1987

Hodges, David, Burgess-Wise, David, Davenport, John and Harding, Anthony, *The Guinness Book of Car Facts and Feats* (4th edn.), Guinness Publishing, London, 1994

Hollingdale, E.A. and Thomas, J.P., *Brighton Fire Brigade: a History*, compiled at the instigation of Chief Officer F. Furlong, Brighton, 1974

Hudson, R.A. and others, 'Report on the Regional Planning Scheme 1932', Brighton, Hove and District Joint Town Planning Advisory Committee (Chairman: Alderman Sir Herbert Carden)

Kelly's Directories, 1971-9

Middleton, Judy, *Britain in Old Photographs—Hove*, Sutton Publishing Ltd, Stroud, 1996

Middleton, Judy, *Britain in Old Photographs—Portslade*, Sutton Publishing Ltd, Stroud, 1997

Montagu of Beaulieu, Lord, 'Seaside Outing', *Autocar*, 31 October 1981

Morris, Colin, *Southdown, vol. 1 - The History, vol. 2 - The Details*, Venture Publications, Glossop, 1994

Motor Car Club (First Meeting), Instruction Leaflet, *Motor Car Tour to Brighton*, 14 November 1896

Ordnance Survey maps 1:10,560 scale, all 1912 edns. (revised in 1909) except where otherwise stated: *LII NE, LII SW, LII SE* (1932 edn., revised 1930); *LIII NW, LIII NE, LIII SW, LIII SE, LXV NW, LXV NE, LXV SW, LXV SE, LXVI NW, LXVI NE, LXVI SW, LXVI SE, LXVII NW* (1911 edn., revised 1908), *LXVII SW* (1911 edition, revised 1908)

Ordnance Survey maps 1:10,560 scale, all wartime provisional editions based on revisions variously 1929-1940, but with additions variously 1938-50: *LII SW, LXV NW, LXV NE, LXV SE, LXVI NW, LXVI SW*

Page's, Pike's, Towner's Directories—Brighton, Hove and District, annual vols. 1900-30

P.S.V. Circle and the Omnibus Society, *Fleet History—Thomas Tilling Limited*, at Brighton Reference Library—seen 1997

QueenSpark (community writing and publishing group) and the Lewis Cohen Urban Studies Centre at Brighton Polytechnic, *Backyard Brighton—photographs and memories of Brighton in the thirties* (Books Nos. 20, 22)

Robinson Printing Company Limited, *Who's Who and Where, the Illustrated Year Book of Hove*, 1907

Stitch, Wilhelmina, Lister, L.W. and Browne C.G., *Hove* (Guidebook 1934-5), Hove Corporation Publicity Committee

Walbrook, H.M., *Hove and the Great War*, Hove War Memorial Committee, The Cliftonville Press, 1920

Ward, Lock & Co. Ltd, A *Pictorial and Descriptive Guide to Brighton and Hove* (9th edn.), Ward, Lock, London and Melbourne, 1919

Webb, T.M.A. and Bird, Dennis L., *Shoreham Airport, Sussex: Story of Britain's Oldest Licensed Airfield*, Cirrus & Associates, Gillingham (Dorset),1996

Chapter Seven: The Road to the Millennium—and Gridlock

Beckett, Arthur, *The Spirit of the Downs* (8th edn.), Methuen & Co. Ltd, London, 1949

Brighton and Hove Bus and Coach Company Limited (Managing Director Roger French), *On Route—Summer Issue* (Issue 9) *2001; City Bus Times—Summer Edition*, 29 April–29 September 2001

Brighton Library, cuttings index 1982-1996 re Brighton Bypass

Brighton Marina Company Limited, *Fifty North—Harbour Guide*, 1997

Buchanan, Colin (Head of the Working Group) and Crowther, Sir Geoffrey (Chairman of the Steering Group), 'Traffic in Towns—a study of the long term problems of traffic in urban areas', Ministry of Transport, H.M.S.O., 1963

Buchanan, Colin, 'The Outlook for Traffic in Towns', Annual Conference of the Society of Town Clerks, Folkestone, 1965

Buchanan, Colin, 'Jam Today and Tomorrow', *The Times*, 22 November 1988

Ellis & Clayton (architects) for Mr Alan Hawes of Metrim Precision Engineering Ltd, 'The New West Pier', July 1980. Also, Morgan, R.E. (Chief Executive) and Fines, K.D. (Borough Planning Officer), 'Report on Planning Application to restore the West Pier submitted by Metrim Precision Engineering Ltd', Brighton Borough Council agendas May 1980–April 1981

Fines, K.D., 'Landscape Evaluation: a Research Project in East Sussex', in *Regional Studies* (vol. 2, no. 1), Pergamon Press Ltd, Oxford and New York, September 1968

Fines, K.D. (Director) and Brighton Urban Structure Plan Team, *Greater Brighton Structure Plan— Survey Reports 1-12 and Draft Written Statement*, Brighton County Borough Council, East Sussex County Council and West Sussex County Council, 1970-3

Kelly's Directory—Brighton, Hove and District, annual vols. 1945-74

Meynell, Esther, *Sussex*, the County Book Series, Robert Hale Ltd, London, 1945

Newspapers: *The Argus* (formerly *The Evening Argus*), *The Times*, *The Brighton and Hove Leader*, *The Brighton and Hove Gazette*, *The Brighton and Hove Herald*

Ordnance Survey, *East Sussex Street Atlas* (3½ inches to one mile), Ordnance Survey, Southampton and George Philip and Son Ltd, London, 1988

Ray, M.G.I., *Hove—Planning Handbook* (3rd edn.), Hove Borough Council, 1989

Wilson, Hugh and Womersley, Lewis, with Drivers, Jonas & Co., 'Brighton Town Centre Interim Report' (April 1968) and 'Brighton Central Area Study' (October 1972)

Wright, Sarah, *North Laine Life Lines*, Sussex Publishing Ltd, Brighton, 1997

Epilogue

Government Office for the South East, *Draft Revised Regional Planning Guidance for the South East* (RPG 9), Secretary of State for the Environment, Transport and the Regions, December 2000

Marsh, Burton W., 'Getting Us Out of the Traffic Jam', reprint from the *Daily Telegraph*, 1959

McCarthy, Alan (Strategic Director), 'Environment and Housing, Brighton and Hove Council', 'Brighton and Hove Local Plan, First Deposit Draft', Brighton and Hove Council, 2000

Newspapers: *City News* (Brighton and Hove City Council)

Wilkins, Bob (Director of Transport and Environment, East Sussex County Council) and McCarthy, Alan (Director of Environmental Services, Brighton and Hove Council) *East Sussex and Brighton & Hove Structure Plan 1991-2011*, November 1999

Index

compiled by Auriol Griffith-Jones

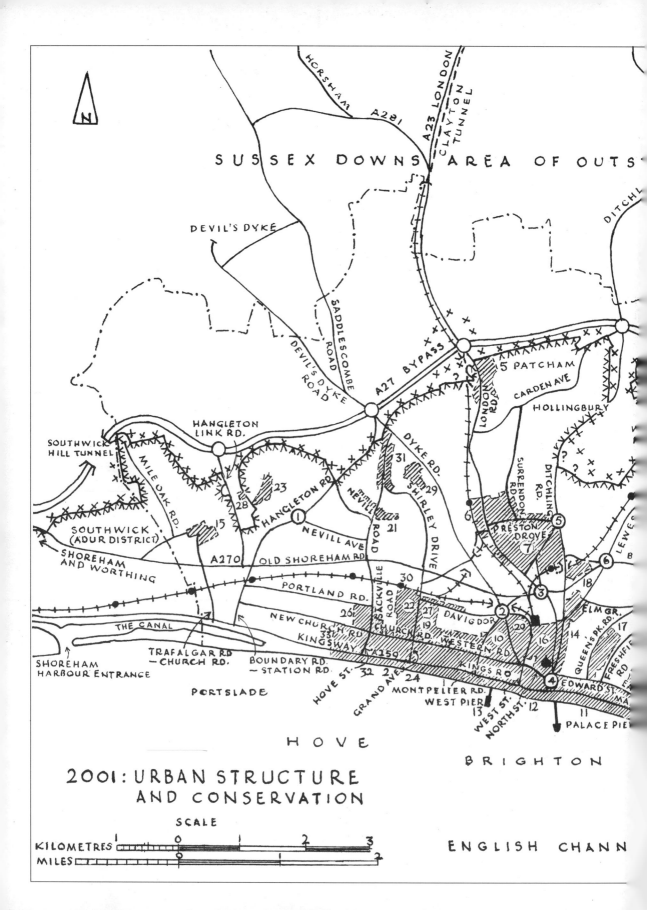